Don't Worry About Micro

Dominik Heckner · Tobias Kretschmer

Don't Worry About Micro

An Easy Guide to Understanding the Principles of Microeconomics

With 76 Figures and 19 Tables

Springer

Dominik Heckner
Standard Bank plc
Cannon Bridge House
25 Dowgate Hill
London EC4R 2SB
United Kingdom
dominikheckner@gmail.com

Professor Tobias Kretschmer
Institute for Communication Economics
Munich School of Management
University of Munich
Schackstraße 4/III
80539 München
Germany
t.kretschmer@lmu.de

Library of Congress Control Number: 2007934933

ISBN 978-3-540-46470-9   Springer Berlin Heidelberg New York

Springer is a part of Springer Science+Business Media

springer.com

© Springer-Verlag Berlin Heidelberg 2008

Production: LE-TEX Jelonek, Schmidt & Vöckler GbR, Leipzig
Cover-design: WMX Design GmbH, Heidelberg

SPIN 11892762   88/3180YL - 5 4 3 2 1   Printed on acid-free paper

Preface I

You know what they say…
…there is always a first. And when I was about to start teaching my second-year undergraduate economics course at the London School of Economics for the umpteenth time, I had no idea that this would be the start of a first. I had been teaching the course for a while now, and I knew more or less what to expect from my students. I was pretty confident by then that I had developed a style of teaching that was intuitive and rigorous at the same time, and that my students would leave the course having learnt about some basic (and some not so basic) concepts of applied microeconomics. But somewhere, sometime, somehow, teaching microeconomics in that particular year led to the writing of this book. My first.

The Conundrum
After a few weeks of teaching, the course had settled in. Students got used to my style, I got used to their style. As the term wore on, the usual student visits to my office became more frequent as the end-of-term exam was drawing nearer, and the questions ranged from the very technical ("can you tell me why you took the square root of this expression to get the elasticity of demand with respect to the price of the substitute good?") to the very basic ("what was monopoly pricing all about?"). In many cases, it seemed that some of my notes and transparencies left out a number of steps that students found useful once I explained them in more detail. Of course, with time constraints and a list of topics to get through, it was not always possible to work through everything in detail, but I was convinced that students really did find the bigger picture easier to grasp if they knew how to get from a set of basic assumptions to an end result.

But that is what theory would have told you anyway. In practice, however, teaching a course in microeconomics often means relying on an existing textbook and filling in the blanks and missing derivations as you go along. As the student visits I received towards the end of term demonstrated, some of the things I explained in class got lost on the way from lecturer to student, and students found it difficult to retrace the steps by themselves. So the question I was faced with that year (as every year) was how to deliver the material accessibly and efficiently while leaving some kind of "paper trail" for the students to go back to when revising for their exam.

The Proposal
One of the students I spoke to on a regular basis was Dominik, who usually came with a set of questions on the material and an impressive set of classnotes. The problems he was having with the course were similar to many of his fellow students, and I think (I hope!) he found my answers helpful in building a more coherent picture of the principles of microeconomics, drawing connections where an incomplete understanding would mean compartmentalising knowledge into "topics" or "lectures". So, as Dominik's classnotes grew, he remarked somewhat offhand that these might look good in a book. At first, this seemed like an odd idea. Any book based on a student's lecture notes would necessarily look very different to the leading titles in the field, and I found it difficult to see what a book like this could add to an already crowded market. As I am writing these lines, a well-known e-commerce website throws up 2,200 books with "microeconomics" in the title! However, the idea grew on me.

After all, looking different can be an advantage as well as a disadvantage. While an alternative approach may not appeal to everybody, we thought that it might just be the missing piece for some students and lecturers who are searching for a new way of looking at things. So, in short, the plan was hatched by the two of us to develop a concept for a different type of microeconomics textbook, one that uses first-hand experience not just by a lecturer familiar with explaining microeconomics to students, but also using the experience of a student who has gone through the process of studying microeconomics only recently, and could thus relate to many of the problems his successors might have.

From an Idea to this Book
At that point, we marketed the idea to our friends and colleagues. Speaking to a number of people, we found that the world neatly divided into two camps: the people who thought that this was a completely pointless idea and that we should be spending our time more productively, and the people who encouraged us in our plans and thought that such a book could fill a niche in the market for microeconomics textbooks. Moreover, we were especially encouraged by a number of students who, when hearing about the idea and reading the first chapters, said that they would actually enjoy reading such a book. Suddenly it looked like we had found a market! And the rest, as they say, is history, and the book that you have in your hands is the result of a quite unusual collaboration between a fresh graduate and a

veteran lecturer. We think it works quite well, and of course we hope that you agree with us. Still, if you have any comments about how to make this book better, we are all ears. E-mail me at *t.kretschmer@lmu.de*, or leave a comment on the book's homepage, *www.dontworryaboutmicro.eu*. This is also where we will regularly publish updates on the book.

For now, however, sit back, relax and get started, and most of all, *Don't Worry About Micro*!

Tobias,   Munich, Summer 2007

Preface II

The Very Beginning
I was 18 years old when I was first introduced to economics. At the time, economics was synonymous to business for me and because I always wanted to pursue a career as an entrepreneur, taking economics in high school was an obvious choice for me. I was fortunate enough to have had a great economics teacher in Drew Allen at Trinity College School in Ontario, Canada. He communicated his enthusiasm for economics by showing us its significance in the real world.

At University
After high school, I started my BSc in Management at the London School of Economics. Renowned economist Prof. Danny Quah taught EC102 (Economics B), and from his very first lecture I learned that the academic field of economics entails an abundance of mathematical models, formulae and all sorts of things that were very un-business like — not at all what I was used to in high school. The mathematical intensity of the models meant that some of us had a hard time understanding the logic, and worse, failed to understand why the models were relevant. Professor Quah's lectures were stimulating and interesting, but I, and many of my peers, found it difficult to relate some of the very technical material in the course textbooks to the content and style of the lectures. Although we enjoyed the lectures, preparing and recapping the lecture content was hard, especially since many of the technical details were skipped in the books we used.

A Grey Blob
Not surprisingly then, many of us had a hard time preparing for exams, but somehow most of us managed to pull through. Every time when I conquered a certain area, however, I used to think to myself: "why could the author not have said this early on, it would have helped me so much!" In particular, what was almost completely missing was some sort of willingness to look at the book from a student's perspective. There was no guidance on what was central to a topic or what was peripheral, and in particular the difficult technical bits were skipped all too often. Everything was equally important and the subject became a big grey blob.

Economics Another Way

In my second year, I took another economics course that was especially designed for management students. One of the lecturers for this course was Tobias. All of a sudden, I felt that the relevance was put back into economics. The fun that I had during high school learning about the subject was back!

This was when I knew that long nights sweating over textbooks that I didn't understand was nothing that needed to be or even should be part of studying economics. I felt that there should be a different way to let students know why what they are learning is important. Why couldn't there be a text that was fun and engaging, taking students through the thought process step by step without discouraging them with tangential information and sentences like "one can see quite easily from the diagram" when there was nothing easy about it?

Making Reality of a Pipe Dream

One evening I was on the phone to my good friend Dr Farrah Jarral, and I told her about my dissatisfaction of the teaching materials in my first year now that I had seen that challenge and fun were not mutually exclusive. She listened to what I had to say and replied: "why don't you write a text yourself?" At first I thought that she was kidding and so I dismissed her idea, but as a medical student at the time, she told me that many of the texts she found most compelling were indeed co-written by students. And so my idea for *Don't Worry about Micro* was born, thanks to her impetus. For this reason this book is dedicated to Farrah!

Teaming up with Tobias

Of course, I was not able to write a textbook all by myself about a subject as complex as microeconomics, given I had just about understood it myself. There was only one person I could think of who would take my idea seriously and support me: Tobias Kretschmer. To be perfectly frank, I was surprised when I got such positive feedback on my idea and my sample chapter, but it seemed that I was not alone with my opinion. I would like to thank Tobias at this point for being such a good friend, for never doubting our project and for generally being extremely encouraging towards all of my endeavours, both academic and otherwise. Thank you!

The result of working with Tobias is this text. While I wrote the first draft, he gave me his feedback regarding improvements and corrections. On certain occasions, I have to admit, he also had to take over the steering wheel for a while in order to keep the focus sharp. After all, he has many years of experience in teaching, writing and publishing, whereas I am a mere novice!

Well, this is it! I sincerely hope that this text will help you to derive a sense of academic satisfaction from understanding the principles that microeconomics has to offer. There is a certain sense of pride to be gained from mastering a subject as complex as this. I do not kid myself (or you) into thinking that it will always be fun. I am not going to lie to you. Some concepts really *are* quite hard, and require dedication on your part. Still, I hope that this text will help you along the way, and I wish you all the best in your studies. Should you have any ideas, criticisms or questions about this text, simply drop me a line at *dheckner@gmail.com* or leave a comment on the book's website, *www.dontworryaboutmicro.eu*. Let my final words be: "nothing can take the place of persistence, so never give up in the face of great challenge!"

Dominik,   London, Summer 2007

Acknowledgments

In turning the idea for this text into reality, we are extremely grateful to those who have continued to support us. First of all, we have to thank Katharina Wetzel-Vandai at Springer publishing for believing in our project and providing us with the means to propel it further. Dr Charles Marshall helped in the concept development of the text. Dr Arunish Chawla of the London School of Economics and Dr Ken Le Meunier-FitzHugh of Birkbeck, University of London were helpful in the polishing of our ideas for Chapters 4 and 8.

After the first draft was created, Caroline Dotter was our test student for this text. She read the vast majority of it during her studies and has given us invaluable suggestions for improvements regarding the book's user friendliness. Dominik's flat mate and professional copy editor for *Nature Reviews* journals, Tom Frost, looked after the correctness of the language. Art student Carli Vallance took all photos for the text. Sebastian Meitz created the index.

Especially in the later phases the project was aided immensely by Tobias' PhD students in Munich. Mariana Rösner read the text in its entirety. Her eye for detail and consistency was enormously helpful and all of her work was extremely diligent and her comments unfailingly constructive. Thorsten Grohsjean and Ferdinand Mahr read the whole text, and ensured that all of the small wrinkles were ironed out at the very end.

Moreover, during all stages of development, many of our friends, family and colleagues volunteered to read sections of the text and to give their suggestions. Starting from the most industrious helper, they were: Dr Johnann Custodis, Markus Heckner, Wolfgang Funke, government economists Nilum Patel and David Stallibrass, Paul Gaggl, Wendy Billingslea, Rhona Munck, William Davidson, Rainer Martl and Neil Baxter.

Thank you everybody!

Dominik and Tobias

Contents

List of Abbreviations

AFC	average fixed cost
AP	average product
ATC	average total cost
AVC	average variable cost
CS	consumer surplus
FC	fixed cost
ICC	income consumption curve
LAC	long-run average cost
LMC	long-run marginal cost
LTC	long-run total cost
MC	marginal cost
MES	minimum efficient scale
MP	marginal product
MR	marginal revenue
MRP	marginal revenue product
MRS	marginal rate of substitution
MRTS	marginal rate of technical substitution
MU	marginal utility
PS	producer surplus
TC	total cost
TR	total revenue
VC	variable cost
VAP	value of average product
VMP	value of marginal product
WACC	weighted average cost of capital

1. An Introduction to Economics and this Book

Introduction
In this chapter we will tell you in an informal way what economics and this text are all about. Many of the things that you might expect from an introduction are included here, such as definitions and a brief history of the subject. Moreover, this introduction provides the building blocks for an appreciation of the study of economics, showing you that it can be as exciting and fun as it is challenging and demanding. Here, we also introduce the most critical concepts, which serve as basic knowledge for later chapters.

Required Background Knowledge
At this point we merely require a very basic understanding of mathematics.

Key Terms/Names
Adam Smith, laissez faire, invisible hand, David Ricardo, comparative advantage, mercantilism, protectionism, free trade, Karl Marx, exploitation, John Maynard Keynes, monetary and fiscal policies, Great Depression, Joseph Schumpeter, business cycle, creative destruction, Milton Friedman, Chicago school, agent, microeconomics, macroeconomics, positive questions, normative questions, consumer, firm, good, bad, intermediate good, profit, opportunity cost, market, utility, disutility, marginality, *ceteris paribus*, function, algorithm, slope, "rise over run", derivative, asterisk.

1.1 About this Book

Introducing Our Text
The core idea of this book is to create a new genre of microeconomics text rather than to write yet another book adding to an already long list. We combine the strengths of traditional textbooks, study guides and "popular" publications. Attributes that we retain from standard textbooks are clarity, insight and academic rigour. Furthermore, we bring elements from study guides to our publication, a positive attribute of which is their application

of concepts in exercises. Standard textbooks do not offer this feature. In our publication we teach a concept and then show its application.

As the third category which we considered, popular publications also have positive aspects that we borrowed. These publications come in well-known series serving as introductions to laymen or fall in the category of if-you-buy-this-you-will-do-great-in-your-exams-without-exerting-any-effort book. Although they are not up to university standard, these texts still manage to present topics in an entertaining way, focusing on *you*, the reader.

Improving on Standard Textbooks

While this text adopts positive aspects of study guides and popular publications, it competes most closely with standard textbooks. We see considerable room for improvement in the standard way that students are taught, and so we want to do a better job. Each chapter in this book begins with a rather light introduction to the subject matter. Since we find it important that you know why you learn what you learn, we will explain the relevance of each topic before going into the intricacies straight away. This is important in developing students' intuition and it is also likely to help you stay motivated as the relevance of what you learn is made explicit.

We also accentuate different types of content. Not everything you will learn is equally important, although many authors will have you believe that by the way their texts are structured. Often, there is no way of telling whether something is simply a remark or a vital concept instead. We, however, are realistic in our approach because we know that sometimes you simply will not have the time to read everything there is to know about a certain topic. The usage of "heavy" economics textbooks often constitutes the reading (and re-reading) of a few key passages scattered across the entire text as well as the lingering feeling of not exactly knowing what to do next. This is because some of the texts that you would ordinarily be given in your first year are written by economists for economists. No wonder students are having a hard time.

A New Paradigm to Teaching

While independent thought should at the very latest begin when you set foot in the lecture theatre for the first time, there is still a big difference between independence and responsibility on the one side and simple frustration and waste of time on the other.

This is how we see it: first of all, it is okay not to understand. Guess what, economics *is* difficult. If you internalise this statement, you are ahead of 90% of your peers who let themselves be intimidated by the bright minds who teach them. Once you understand that at your level of experience, it is impossible to know everything regardless of how intelligent you are, the logical continuation is to find out what it is that you *can* know. In the absence of infinite time we hope that you agree with us that the most important things should be considered first. This text tells you what these are, and only once they are properly explained will we move on to the details.

Focusing on the Reader
This text is unique in that it is co-written by a recent graduate and his former lecturer. What this means is that we understand the problems that students tend to have in their studies. In fact Dominik, one of the authors, is likely to have had the same problems only a few years ago that might bug you and your peers now. This first-hand insight into the learning process of the student is combined with the expertise of Toby who has had years of experience in teaching at elite institutions. What is more, Tobias dedicates his time to his students rather than solely focusing on his research. In short: we understand you, at least with regards to your requirements in economics! From this understanding, we have crafted a student-friendly approach to learning that we hope will make your studies an enjoyable experience.

1.2 A Brief History of Economic Thought

Now that you have an understanding of the approach used in this book, let us get started properly! A logical starting point is the history of economic thought, and so we will have a look at the most influential minds in economics over the last 250 years. Rather than discussing models just yet, the way we will introduce these economists is by emphasising the political and social implications that their ideas brought about. We hope that by doing so we can increase the relevance of economics, showing you how it affects the lives of everybody in a profound way. Also note that the following discussion is merely an overview rather than an exhaustive analysis and so the subject matter has been simplified.

1.2.1 Adam Smith, 1723–1790

Often accredited with the title of "Father of Economics", Adam Smith was among the first to discuss modern theories of capitalism. He helped put the essential building blocks in place for what was to become the study of neo-classical economics (i.e. the way economics is taught at most universities today), and indeed the corner stones of modern capitalism.

Moreover, Smith was a proponent of **laissez-faire** economics, which is a doctrine opposing intervention by the government such as taxation or trade restrictions. "Laissez-faire" is French for "let them do", which is precisely the attitude Smith had towards the economic policy of the government. As the new £20 note communicates, Smith also advocated the division of labour, stating that the efficiency of production processes can be enhanced when workers specialise in individual tasks — a principle utilised in virtually every production process today.

Perhaps the most well-known piece of work by Smith was his 1776 book *Inquiry into the Nature and Causes of the Wealth of Nations* (or simply *The Wealth of Nations*). Many of his ideas appear common sense today but they constituted a big leap in thinking at the time. The most commonly cited quotation from his book is the following:

It is not from the benevolence of the butcher, the brewer, or the baker that we expect our dinner, but from their regard to their own interest. We address ourselves, not to their humanity but to their self-love, and never talk to them of our own necessities but of their advantages.

Smith meant that when people act in a self-interested way, this will have positive implications for everyone. Say the butcher works very hard and sells a lot of high quality meat, he is likely to spend the money that he earns from doing so on other things such as bread and beer, and by doing so giving part of his wealth to the baker and the brewer. Today, the pursuit of self-interest makes producers very creative in finding not only what consumers want today but also what they *might* want in the future. Thus, self-interest is a major driver of economic growth and economic growth is synonymous with higher quality of life[1].

However, Smith's reasoning goes one step further. He states that self-interest not only aids but is also necessary for social welfare. This view is largely undisputed today and seems particularly plausible when looking at nations such as the Soviet Union, during the existence of which public ownership (and not self-interest) was emphasised. In the absence of self-interest everybody lost. The majority of people did not work efficiently in the absence of the motivation that the fruits of their labour could be retained by them. In short, a successful economy not based on the pursuit of self-interest has yet to emerge.

What Smith is perhaps best known for is the concept of the **invisible hand**. Without revealing too much of the contents of Chapter 2, the concept of the invisible hand states that a seemingly chaotic market system regulates itself through the vehicle of price. Shortages and excess in supply and demand are regulated in this manner. If, for example, there are 20,000 tickets for a David Hasselhoff concert and 100,000 people would like to go if the tickets were free, the price of the ticket would, at least in theory, be raised to a point at which the number of people willing and able to purchase a ticket is equal to the number of tickets available. This process is one that almost happens automatically and hence the markets are "guided" to an efficient solution with the help of the invisible hand. The principle of the in-

---

[1] Critics would point to negative externalities such as pollution and global warming which are unwanted side-effects of economic growth.

visible hand holds true whether or not the talent of Mr. Hasselhoff warrants the attendance of scores of people.

1.2.2 David Ricardo, 1772–1823

What David Ricardo had in common with Smith is the fact that he too was an advocate of free markets and an opponent of regulation. However, Ricardo specialised in international economics.

The concept for which Ricardo is perhaps most famous is that of **comparative advantage**, which he included in his 1817 book *Principles of the Political Economy and Taxation*. Through this concept Ricardo showed that nations should engage in trade with each other even if one of them is not better at producing *anything*. Let us take the example of a two-good economy. If the UK was able to produce both cloth and wine more efficiently than Portugal, the UK should still engage in trade with Portugal. Why? Because Britain can then specialise in the type of production it is best at and trade accordingly. Portugal should also specialise in the production of the good it can produce most efficiently and trade with Britain. It is therefore likely that Portugal will produce wine and trade it for the cloth produced in Britain.

In a way, comparative advantage is similar to the division of labour. An experienced manager for example, who has spent many years as an analyst, would be able to do the analyst's work better than he can. But this does of course not mean the manager should do the analyst's work. The manager's time is more efficiently spent at jobs that the analyst would be bad at, such as strategic planning. Similar to our example with the two countries, simply being better at producing things than somebody else is no reason why one should not engage in trade.

So how does the theory of comparative advantage fit into the time of Ricardo's life? Prior to Ricardo's time, it was often assumed that someone's wealth was necessarily derived from the plight of others essentially viewing the international economy as a zero-sum game (i.e. a situation in which somebody's gain implies somebody else's loss). In international trade, this was known as **mercantilism**, and it was assumed that the most successful route to prosperity was to export as much as possible and to import as little as possible. Today we know that this is not optimal, as through international trade everybody can gain.

Comparative Advantage Today
Ricardo's idea of comparative advantage is as simple (in its basic form) as it is influential — and it still receives much attention today. If you keep up with the news, you will be aware that trade talks involving a number of countries are taking place on a regular basis. These talks often fail because richer countries protect their inefficient industries. One prominent example is cotton production in the US. Although Ricardo's theory is extremely simple and powerful, political interests sometimes override economic intuition. From a strictly economic perspective, all labour that is currently employed in the US to produce cotton would be able to create much more wealth in industries in which the US is simply much better — such as the semiconductor industry in Silicon Valley.

Not only do countries employing **protectionist measures** (i.e. imposing very high duties on products from other countries to protect their own industries) harm their own economy by not using resources most efficiently, it can also be extremely harmful for poorer countries. Cotton producers around the world suffer the consequences of artificially high prices due to the subsidies farmers in rich countries receive from their governments. If these farmers were no longer to receive subsidies they would eventually go out of business and move to industries in which prospects are better. The poor country would then be able to specialise in the production of cotton and export it to other countries around the world, become wealthy by doing so and import goods that it cannot produce efficiently relative to other goods.

For such a system to work, it is *not* necessary for the poor country to be more efficient at producing cotton. So long as everybody specialises at what *they* are best at, gains from trade can be realised on both sides compared to a situation when trade is not free[2].

Although this logic is perfectly sound, protectionism remains in place in many of the richest countries in the world. Part of the reason is that people who are employed in inefficient industries naturally do not want to lose their jobs. Hence these individuals and their associated trade unions campaign against the removal of protectionist measures.

Although trade has become much freer since WWII, we do not know whether true **free trade** will ever become reality. In any case, Ricardo's principle of comparative advantage is among the most powerful arguments in favour of free trade.

1.2.3 Karl Marx, 1818–1883

Often mentioned as the ideological opposite of Adam Smith, Karl Marx was an economist, philosopher and also a social revolutionary. Marx's writings mainly constituted a critique of the political economy. That is, he disagreed with the way the economic system was organised. Today, all of Marx's economic ideas have been discredited or at least weakened in their scope. Nonetheless, Marx was very influential during his time and beyond because the problems he was addressing were real and his writings compelling. He believed that he had found the solution to the suffering of the common man. Often associated with communism, Marxism finds fault with the existence of different social classes. Therefore, Marx called for an overthrowing of the bourgeoisie (the top class in a capitalist society) to attain a classless society.

---

[2] There are some arguments against free trade, some of which may be applicable in special situations (e.g. temporary infant industry protection to help countries develop competitive industries). However, it should be noted that free trade is in most cases beneficial for all participants.

How did Marx develop his thinking? 1867, the year he published *Das Kapital*, was a time when men, women and even children were slaving away long hours in truly terrible working conditions with few safety standards. Most countries' legal systems were simply not developed enough to protect the rights of workers. To Marx, this fact amounted to **exploitation**, which became the central tenet of his teachings. He found that the businessmen running the factories in which workers were employed were accumulating wealth, while workers were earning a pittance.

The view held by most people in developed countries today, however, differs greatly from what Marx had in mind. Few would, for example, state that the government exploits its civil servants, that a newspaper exploits its journalists, or that a consultancy exploits a managing director[3]. This is not to say that exploitation of workers is impossible today (and in particular, when looking at working standards in some developing countries one can see how it could be argued that exploitation of workers is still taking place), but the argument is that exploitation is not a necessary characteristic of the political economy — something that Marx thought to be true.

Rather than constituting exploitation, today we understand that the difference between the value workers create and what they get paid is a reward for the entrepreneur for the risk she is taking. If such rewards did not exist

---

[3] Despite the fact that the latter party may work extremely long hours.

(and implicit in Marx's complaint about the difference in value created by workers and the wages paid is that they should not), there would be little incentive for individuals to take the risk of running their own firms.

If Bill Gates had lived in an economy in which the realisation of an original idea with the help of others would have required him to pay them that precise sum of wealth they created, would he have invented Microsoft? This notion of the negative attributes of self-interest is why Marx's ideology can be regarded as the polar opposite to Smith's.

1.2.4 John Maynard Keynes, 1883–1946

John Maynard Keynes is often cited as the main founder of macroeconomic thought[4]. Keynes proposed interventionist government policies as a way to deal with negative effects of recessions, unemployment or excessive growth rates as he elaborates on in his 1936 book *The General Theory of Employment, Interest and Money*. Keynes's work was so important because, prior to his time, governments were not thought to have taken a significant role in the economic well-being of their citizens. In the classical

---

[4] As we will learn in Section 1.5, macroeconomics is the study of aggregated economic decision making. In other words, it is the analysis of how the economy of an entire country works.

sense of economic thinking along the lines of Smith, the only role that the government played was that of a provider of the most basic services such as security through the provision of the rule of law.

Of course, today we know that this is only the beginning of the story of what the government can do for the economic well-being of its citizens. A major way in which the government interacts in the economy is by means of the setting of the interest rates[5] thereby determining the amount of money in circulation (which is part of monetary policy) and regulating its spending, taxation and borrowing (which fiscal policy). Keynes was interested in both policies, but emphasised the impact of the latter.

Keynes achieved a shift in economic thought, as he communicated the profound impact of these measures in regulating the demand in the economy. Although it is intuitive to think of demand in purely positive terms, crucial problems with excessive economic growth are inflation, pollution and social divides; therefore a steady rate of growth is today accepted as desirable.

One major event in Keynes's lifetime was the **Great Depression** which started in 1929. Although most people when hearing the term picture bankers jumping off skyscrapers, the stock market crash (although being at least part of the cause of the problem, as it changed expectations for the future) was only one part of the crisis. In countries around the world but mostly in Western Europe and the US, unemployment was at record highs, businesses defaulted and misery was omnipresent. Arguably a vital factor in sustaining the negative situation throughout the 1930s was many countries' inability to deal with the crisis. As the money supply was cut in the US, businesses were not able to acquire or renew their loans and as a result went bankrupt.

Of course, the Great Depression was much more complex than the short synopsis above suggests, but what should be taken away from this passage is that the government holds vital powers for keeping the economy healthy. And it was through people like Keynes that the public became aware of this fact. While Keynes was a strong proponent of government intervention, today the decision-makers of Western economies take the view that "a little" intervention is just right.

---

[5] We take the simplified view here that it is the government that directly sets interest rates, although in many instances this will done by a body such as the central bank, which may have autonomous decision-making power.

1.2.5 Joseph Schumpeter, 1883–1950

Born in the same year as Keynes, Schumpeter's work focused on **business cycles** and innovation. The concept of the business cycle is familiar to most: while some periods of time are characterised by high growth rates, others exhibit low growth rates or even a contraction of economic activity. However, since economic growth has been persistent since the late 19th century, it is intuitive that periods of low growth or recession, are on average, less pronounced (both in duration and magnitude) than periods of high growth.

Interestingly, different economists have proposed widely differing periods of time these business cycles are said to last. While some theorists speak of a few years for one cycle, the Soviet economist Nokolai Kondratiev claimed that these cycles last for 45–60 years. Under this theory, the last big peak was around the year 2000 at the time when the technology bubble "burst". Under Kondratiev's theory, the next peak would perhaps materialise when fossil fuels run out and the energy production shifts to renewable energy sources.

In any case, the concept that Schumpeter might be best known for is likely to be that of **creative destruction**. Schumpeter did not view the market structure of perfect competition as the optimal market structure. Rather, some sort of dynamic competition was assumed to encourage innovation in the most effective way.

To give you some background, perfect competition is an economic model in which many firms produce homogenous products and no firm makes any economic profit[6]. Chapter 9 is dedicated to the market structure of perfect competition. Within the context of innovation, Schumpeter viewed dynamic competition in which firms could gain temporary monopoly power through innovation as ideal. Being lured into the market by the potential carrot of large profits for at least some period of time, these new entrants would constantly develop new products and services. The concept is referred to as "creative destruction" because the new creative ideas that competitors come up with often render older technologies obsolete. Examples of innovations superseding older goods are the colour TV, the DVD and broadband internet.

1.2.6 Milton Friedman, 1912–2006

Friedman was a strong proponent of the monetarist school of thought. As is the case for Keynes, the relevance of the work of Friedman is the insight it provides into how the government influences demand. Friedman conducted extensive research into the Great Depression and found himself agreeing with Keynes as to what one of the causes was: the failure of the governments in Western countries to supply enough money to businesses. Therefore, economies contracted even further and the Great Depression was prolonged throughout the 1930s.

However, Friedman disagreed with Keynes' view that ineffective fiscal policy was a major contributor to the Great Depression, and thus he has influenced public understanding that monetary policy is perhaps the most significant tool governments have at their disposal to ensure economic well-being.

As a Professor of the University of Chicago, Friedman's doctrines belong to the so-called **Chicago school** which is characterised by the promotion of free market capitalism and refutation of Keynesian ideas. Consequently, Friedman is — at least to some extent — to be credited for our modern understanding of "little intervention" that was mentioned earlier.

---

[6] View Section 1.6.2 for the definition of economic profit and how it is distinct from accounting profit.

1.3 The Modern Study of Economics

Having surveyed some of the most important economic ideas and how they have developed over the last two and a half centuries, let us now focus on how economics functions as an academic discipline today.

1.3.1 How Economics Differs from Other Social Sciences

Economics differs from all the other social sciences in a major way. It is the subject that arguably entails the highest degree of internal validity. Although the real world always looks different from the theory, in economics we can always say that "if person A performs action X, that action will be the best choice A can make". Provided there really is at least one optimal decision, such a statement will be objective and true. Whether person A will really do X is a different question, but it is not one that we would be interested in answering when we study economics. Questions of this kind are likely to be covered by sociology or psychology.

A distinguishing feature of economics is that some models are quite remote from real life. This need not be a weakness, however. It is rather a difference in emphasis. Economists will often build a model that is internally consistent and designed to highlight one particular economic mechanism[7]. Events in the real world are functions of many more variables than a model contains, but in economics, the beauty is often that a single mechanism is isolated and tested while key assumptions of the model are changed. We will see much of this throughout the remainder of the book.

In other social sciences such as sociology or anthropology the internal validity (i.e. the ability to demonstrate a causal relationship between variables) of models is much more difficult to achieve. It would be outright absurd to specify a set of rules that, if followed, would lead to social cohesion, personal happiness or peace.

Do not misunderstand this point, though. We do not suggest that economic models can solve all problems of an economic nature in the world. What we do say is that if you build a model using sound logic (i.e. you do not make any mistakes in your reasoning), then that model will be correct. This is less so the case in other social sciences because these subjects are not ordinarily quantifiable. In economics, by contrast, problems are formulated using the precise language of mathematics.

1.3.2 What Is Economics?

A Definition

Economics may be defined as *the study of how agents make decisions of resource allocation in conditions of scarcity*. Firstly, what is an **agent**? This has nothing to do with the FBI but is simply the word that we use to stand for "economic actors". It is necessary to use the term "agent" because some economic actors will be consumers while others will be firms. Secondly, what do we mean by "resources"? Resources could be anything, from machines or managerial skills needed for production to the amount of money an individual has in his wallet. Another important resource could be time, for example.

"Scarcity" means that these resources are available only to a limited extent. The people or firms possessing them may not have as much of them as they want. A good the scarcity of which can easily be observed is gold. This metal could be used as jewellery, tooth fillings, or high quality cables — but it cannot be used for all conceivable applications at the same time. Hence, decisions have to be made as to the usage of all resources.

---

[7] As you will see, this is interlinked with Section 1.6.6.

The term "resource allocation" means the way we allocate the (scarce) things we have among competing options. The money you have available for this month could be spent on almost anything so long as its price does not exceed your financial capabilities.

Imagine you are on vacation back home after you have moved to a foreign country some years ago. You are only home for a few days and there is so much to do. Your parents want to see you, your siblings want to get a glimpse of you and your grandparents always nag you that you do not spend enough time with them. Since it is also your holiday, you do want to relax as well. If you do so, you might not be able to see everyone. If you choose your siblings, you might not have time for your grandparents and so on. The analysis of trade-offs similar to this example are an important part of the study of microeconomics.

As can be seen with the above example it is indeed possible to apply economic reasoning to social situations in which money does not enter our analysis.

Micro and Macro
Coming back to how economics is studied, we can break down economics into two broad areas, **microeconomics** and **macroeconomics**. Microeconomics is the study of how consumers and firms (as well as the aggregation of firms otherwise known as industries) make decisions to optimise their well-being while macroeconomics studies the economy as a whole, including fiscal and monetary policy.

Microeconomics is the study of the behaviour of consumers, firms and industries.

The Focus of this Text — Parts I, II and III
This text focuses exclusively on the study of microeconomics, with the brief exception of the history of economic thought in Section 1.2. Within microeconomics we will look at how consumers (people like us and you) make decisions so that their utility is maximised. Part I of this book focuses on the consumer. The second big part of microeconomics is the theory of the firm, in which we will discuss how firms make decisions so as

to maximise their profit. This is covered in Part II. Finally, in Part III, we will see how a number of firms act together in different industries.

1.4 Why Should You Care About Economics?

Now that we have discussed the development of economic thinking, you may still ask yourself, why you should care? Why should you be learning about economics in the first place?

A Misconception
Most people who have not studied economics before tend to think of it as a subject that will teach one how to get rich. Unfortunately, we will have to disappoint. A lot of what we learn in economics does indeed revolve around money (such as cost analysis and production), but a large chunk of the discussion is also abstract. Economics is less applied than finance or business studies. Is this a bad thing? Not at all!

Economics — Learning for Life
While not everything that you will learn will find immediate applicability in your life, often understanding a particular *way of thinking* is very insightful. From personal experience, we know that almost any decision in real life can be approached wearing the economics "thinking hat". Therefore, understanding economics will help you to make smart decisions in general, whether these involve money or not. In many instances decisions are made in order to optimise (i.e. to maximise or to minimise) something, often money or costs but not always.

Optimisation is all about making optimal or "best" decisions. In a working environment you will have to make such decisions every day. And often these decisions will have to be made when information is scarce, i.e. when you do not know all the variables that influence the outcome of your decision. Economics uses a number of models that may not always be entirely realistic, but these abstractions from real life make you realise how the outcome of a situation changes (given certain assumptions) when variables within the system are changed. It is quite fascinating, and the thinking skills that you develop will almost certainly make you more effective in making decisions in life that require some deliberation.

Economics as a Foundation for Further Studies

You will also find economics to be a fantastic foundation for many further studies you may consider in the future. This might sound strange, but we know from our own experiences that one can often tell from somebody's approach to various types of problems whether or not they have studied economics at some point in their life.

Economics as a Door Opener

Along with engineering and mathematical degrees, economics is an excellent subject to have studied at university when applying for jobs. Although many employers will say that they consider students from any discipline, in practice a large proportion of the people working in the well-known professional firms have taken economics or economics-related degrees. The reason for this has less to do with what the recent graduate learned during their degree than with the fact that the economist's way of solving problems is regarded as very effective.

1.5 Positive vs. Normative Questions

There is one other point that we wanted to make: economics is different from other social sciences in the way that we seek to answer **positive questions**. This does not mean that the questions are good in one way or another; rather, it constitutes a type of question which is in contrast to **normative questions**.

Positive questions are something like: "what will happen to variable a under assumptions x, y and z if we change variable b?" As you will soon see, our text is full of questions like this and for the most part there is a definite answer. The beauty of economics is precisely this. You could question assumptions but you can never question the (correct) answer that is derived, as it is based on the assumptions that you made. This links back to Section 1.3.1.

In contrast to this are normative questions. These questions differ in the way they are asked. An example would be: "what should be done?" The answer therefore requires some sort of subjective norm. It is quite difficult to answer a question such as: "what should our economic policy be?" because the implications are wide-ranging and one would have to have perfect knowledge of what was going to happen as well as apply some sort of value judgement to different outcomes.

A positive question of the above problem would be: "if our economic policy was one of high interest rates, what would happen to foreign direct investment?" One may (provided one has the adequate training) quite easily give an answer to such a question after setting forth a set of assumptions.

You might have noticed that in this chapter we did actually ask: "what should be done?" However, what was meant by this was: "what should be done to derive the most benefit?" It is important to note that this was implicit in our way of asking the question.

1.6 Basic Economic Concepts

We realise that the following section might not be terribly exciting as there is no context surrounding the concepts as of yet. However, we ask you to make sure to familiarise yourself with the terms anyway, as you will need this basic tool kit to understand discussions in later chapters. It may well be that you are already familiar with some of these concepts from previous study.

1.6.1 Good, Bad and Intermediate Good

Consumer
Perhaps the most basic term in economics is the "consumer". As first discussed in Section 1.3.2, the consumer is one of the types of economic agent. The definition of the consumer in microeconomics comes relatively close to what we understand by "consumer" from everyday language. The assumption is that the only objective of consumers is to maximise their own utility (Section 1.6.4). This assumption is examined more closely in Chapter 3.

Firm
Another other economic agent is the firm. Firms produce goods for consumption by consumers. Similar to the consumer, the firm has only one objective and that is to maximise profits. The firm's behaviour is discussed from Chapter 5 onwards. A third economic agent is the government but it is not discussed in detail in this text.

Good

The term "good" is used in everyday language to mean a commodity, generally anything that may be acquired in exchange for money. In economics, *a good is anything from which consumers derive utility* (see 1.6.5) *upon consumption and that can be sold in a market* (see 1.6.4) *for a price*. Often, in a general discussion you will hear people talk about "goods and services" but in other instances the term "good" may include services as well. In this book we follow the latter convention.

Bad

A bad, as you can guess, is the opposite of a good. It is *anything from which a consumer derives disutility* (see 1.6.4), i.e. anything that would hurt the consumer. An often cited example of a bad is pollution. Other than goods, bads may have a negative market price. Things such as garbage are removed from households and firms while the agents pay the party for the removal. Hence the money and the bad flow in the same way.

Intermediate Good

Notice that above we were speaking about the consumer and the utility she derives from the consumption of goods. But are consumers the only agents to acquire goods? Of course not! In fact, more than two-thirds of all economic transactions in modern economies are done from business to business. When a good is acquired by a firm for the purpose of production it is called an **intermediate good**.

Unlike the consumer, businesses do not simply use up the good in question for their pleasure, but rather use it to produce something else, or in the economist's language, to put it into economic use. The term "intermediate good" seems intuitive when talking about a good such as lumber that is later transformed into furniture, for example. Yet there are other circumstances under which it is not perfectly obvious that something should be called an intermediate good. One such example is the cleaning fluid used to keep the windows of an office building clean or the fuel in the tank of the company car. These are goods that are part of the production of the firm, yet they are not transformed into the final product.

1.6.2 Profit and Opportunity Cost

Profit seems to be a very basic term, and we all use it in our everyday language. What many people are not aware of, however, is that there are two types of profit: **economic profit** and **accounting profit**. Accounting profit is what we take profit to mean in everyday language. It is the revenue of the firm minus all explicit costs such as materials, wages, rent etc.

Economic profit is a little different. It is revenue minus explicit *and* implicit costs. What are implicit costs? Let us take a simple example. Say you hire a machine for £1,000 per day. The machine can be operated in two modes. Mode *A* will result in the production of 1,200 widgets which can be sold for £1 each while mode *B* will produce 2,000 widgets. In both modes the firm incurs no cost beyond £1,000 daily rental cost.

If operated in mode *A*, assuming that we sell all of our output, we make an accounting profit of £200 (£1,200 − £1,000) while we make an economic loss of £800. This is so because the economic profit includes the revenue (£1,200) minus the explicit cost of the rental (£1,000) minus the implicit cost of not running the machine in the more efficient mode (£800). While our accounts would not show a loss, the lost opportunity of not switching the machine to function *B*, also known as the **opportunity cost**[8], constitutes £2,000 − £1,200 = −£800. This is equal to the number of units not produced due to the sub-optimal mode that the machine is run in. Unless otherwise stated in this text, the term "profit" will always mean economic profit. The discussion of explicit and implicit costs is taken up again in Chapter 3.

1.6.3 Market

The word "market" is one frequently used in the English language to mean a variety of things. One meaning of market is that of a physical market place. If somebody says: "I am going to the market" then they would usually mean that they are going to a place where they buy things like fruits and vegetables.

So how close does this description come to the economic term of market? Very close in fact. In economics, a ***market*** is defined as *a social arrangement in which buyers and sellers meet to take part in an economic exchange*. Notice that this definition does not include the word money. Theoretically, one could be a participant in a market in which no money changes hands. In fact, this is how the economy worked before money was invented. People simply bartered one good for another.

---

[8] The concept of opportunity cost is discussed in more detail in Chapter 3.

We use the word "social" as part of the definition because a market need not necessarily be a physical place, such as the vegetable market, but could possibly even be a virtual space on the Internet. eBay, for example, does not exist in any physical space[9] and is hence a virtual market place in which people meet online to buy, sell and trade almost anything.

Another important thing to recognise about any specific market is its definition. Above, we had one example of a particular market: a fruit and vegetable market. Generally, markets can be defined in various ways including variables such as size, geographical location, type of good sold, total revenue of all participants, price and much more. For now it shall suffice that you are aware that the term "market", as basic as it may seem, could in fact require some depth of analysis. In Chapter 8 we will discuss the topic in more detail.

1.6.4 Utility and Disutility

The term "utility" has already turned up in this chapter. The thesaurus on Microsoft Word offers "usefulness" or "value" as synonyms of utility. Another correct synonym in this context would be "pleasure". All of these words describe the same thing: that is something good. **Utility** therefore is *some amount of pleasure that a consumer receives from the consumption of a good*. A hamburger gives you utility. And so does your computer, your DVDs, and yes even your textbooks, washing machine and cleaning utensils. Any good (i.e. anything that fits the definition of a good) will give a consumer utility.

Disutility (or negative utility) is the exact opposite of utility and is something that a bad would give you. But it is not just bads that can give you disutility. Too much of a good may also give you disutility. The obvious example is food: too much makes you sick, which is equivalent to saying that you derive a disutility (or negative utility, as this is the same) from it. Do not worry about this fact too much, we will also discuss it in some detail in Chapter 3.

1.6.5 Marginality

One concept that might not be terribly easy to grasp at first is marginality. As you know by now, in economics we are often interested to see how

---

[9] Ignoring the existence of server installations, offices etc.

well-off people are and how much profit firms make. Not only do we want to know things like "would you be better off with a BMW rather than a Mercedes?", we also want to know how well-off you are *on the margin*.

Now what is that supposed to mean? In this context, we take the margin to mean a difference in something. For example, somebody may say: "Although I was not feeling bad, I still felt marginally worse than the day before." The person making the statement means that their overall well-being has decreased by some small margin. So as you see, "margin" means a *change* in something. So were we to quantify the person's well-being, their initial well-being would have been some value x while their new sense of well-being was $x - y$ where y was the change in their happiness. And this y is precisely what we are interested in.

So how does this tie into what we are doing? To take one example, in economics we are we are frequently interested in utility. And as was the case in the above example, we also examine utility on the margin. So, in this example, we are talking about *marginal* utility, i.e. the change in total utility. Let us say that you currently own 10 DVDs which give you a total utility of 100. If you were given an 11th DVD and your total utility increased to 110, the marginal utility would be 10 (which is simply the change in total utility resulting from the increase in the number of DVDs that you are holding). Marginality finds application in about every chapter in this text, in one shape or another.

1.6.6 *Ceteris Paribus*

In economics, the concept *"ceteris paribus"* is used in many models, although frequently it might not necessarily be stated explicitly. However, this does not diminish its importance. The Latin term *ceteris paribus* means "with other things [being] the same" or simply "other things being equal". So for example, we may ask a question such as: "by how much will a piece of metal expand when we increase the room temperature from 20 to 50 degrees Celsius *ceteris paribus*?"

Although we are no physicists, for the sake of argument we simply assume that there are many variables influencing the volume of a piece of metal other the temperature, such as the humidity perhaps. By stating *"ceteris paribus"* at the end of our question, we simply rule out the effect of all other independent variables that might affect our dependent variable. This dependent variable is what we are ultimately interested in: the volume. As we will learn in Section 1.7.1, an independent variable is simply an input whereas the dependent variable is an output.

In economics, there are many questions one can ask that imply some sort of causal relationship between two variables. As we will learn in Chapter 2, a common example is how quantity demanded reacts to a change in price. In such examples where one independent variable (the price) causes a change in one dependent variable (the quantity demanded), it would be very helpful to rule out any other factors which may influence the quantity demanded by attaching *"ceteris paribus"* to the end of the question.

While it is entirely correct to use *ceteris paribus* whenever discussing causal relationships between variables, we refrain from stating it separately every single time. Instead, in this text the reader is to assume that other things are held equal unless otherwise stated. Holding other things equal is an extremely powerful tool for many of our analyses. It helps us rule out the effects on the dependent variable of all other independent variables that we know, and even those we do not.

1.6.7 Reserved Letters and Symbols

Less a concept than a formality, we thought it might be useful to show the most important symbols that are used in microeconomics in one table. For a list of concepts and abbreviations please see the appendix of this text.

Table 1.1. A list of the most important symbols and letters used in microeconomics

Symbol	Explanation
$'$	"prime", a mathematical operator used in derivatives such as $f(x)$
∂	"partial differential", a mathematical operator used for partial derivatives such as $f'(x)$; not to be confused with δ
A	the coefficient in the Cobb-Douglas utility/production function
C	cost; rarely capital (as in Chapter 6)
d	used as a mathematical operator for derivatives
D	demand; degree of homogeneity in production
E	income (although we use M)
f	function
i	interest (although we use r); investment (in macroeconomics)
$\bar{K}$	"K bar", a constant level of capital; used for short run total product curves
K	constant; capital; not cost
L	labour; Lerner index

M	income (although other authors use Y or E); marginal, in the latter case not used by itself (e.g. MU for marginal utility)
N	number; number of time periods in capital growth
p	price; not profit
P	principal; present value; not profit
Q_X	quantity of good X
Q^D	quantity demanded
Q^S	quantity supplied
$\overline{Q}$	"Q bar", a constant level of output (used for isoquants)
r	rental rate (of capital); interest rate (although some authors use i here)
R	ray (used the measure the average of a curve); not revenue
S	supply
t	tax
U	utility
$\overline{U}$	"U bar", a constant level of utility (used for indifference curves)
w	wage rate
X or x	reserved as a variable for anything else unknown; often used in utility functions to denote the quantity of a good, e.g. X_1 (although we use Q_1 for quantity of good 1); the independent variable
Y or y	reserved as a variable for anything else unknown; income (although we use M); the dependent variable in a function
α	"alpha", the exponent on the quantity of capital K or a good Q_X in the Cobb–Douglas production and utility functions, respectively
β	"beta", the exponent on the quantity of labour L or a good Q_X in the Cobb–Douglas production and utility functions, respectively
δ	"delta", (lower case); discount factor, not to be confused with ∂
Δ	"delta", (upper case); used to show a change in a variable (e.g. ΔQ_X)
ε	"epsilon", price elasticity of demand (although we use η); income elasticity of demand
η	"eta", price elasticity of demand/supply; where confusion is possible, η_D and η_S should be used
Λ	"lambda", the amount of leisure consumed
Π	"pi", profit

1.7 Basic Mathematical Concepts

The one thing that can intimidate the most confident student of economics is their lack (or their perceived lack) of mathematical skills. Sometimes it seems that economists speak a language that is completely foreign to the untrained reader. What makes matters worse is that common mathematical steps in economics texts are not explained, as it is assumed that the reader already has some knowledge about the application of certain concepts.

However, it is often not stated exactly what knowledge the reader is supposed to have.

In this text we do our best never to skip steps in mathematical operations and to always explain what formulae mean rather than to "talk mathematics". The purpose of this section is to introduce the most basic mathematical concepts that the reader is required to understand for much of the discussion in this text.

1.7.1 Functions

A Machine
Let us start with a concept that we have all heard many times — the function. Although very familiar to most of us, there is no shame in not knowing exactly what it is. A function such as $f(x) = 2x$ is like a machine that converts one thing into something else. This "machine" is fed with an independent variable — here this is x — and spits out what we call the dependent variable which is $f(x)$ or simply y. An independent variable is a variable that we change, while the dependent variable is the one that is determined by the "machine", the function.

An Example
Let us look at an example of a function formalised in words: "The number of bacteria in a jar is a function of time." Here, the independent variable is time while the dependent variable is the number of bacteria. Note that a function, by definition, *can only give one output for each particular input*.

Conventions Used
The standard notation of a function is $f(x)$, which is pronounced "f of x". What you will also see quite often is that the $f(x)$ is replaced by a y, for example $y = 2x$ rather than $f(x) = 2x$. Such a notation is more specific (i.e. we name the dependent variable) but equally correct. Of course, your variables need not necessarily be x and y, they could be anything as long as they do not incorrectly use one of the reserved variables in Section 1.6.5.

The Algorithm
Let us talk more about the workings of the "function-machine" now. What the machine does to the independent variable is known as an **algorithm**. Generally, an algorithm is a procedure or a set of rules. In this case it is a set of instructions what to do with x. Examples of algorithms are: "multi-

ply x by itself" which would be $f(x) = x^2$, "multiply x by 3" which would be $f(x) = 3x$ or "take the square route of x" which would be $f(x) = x^{1/2}$.

If we come back to our initial example of $f(x) = 2x$, then y (which is the $f(x)$) will always be twice as large as x. If the machine is fed with 1, for example, it will produce 2, if it is fed with 3, it will produce 6. That is what the function does.

Multiple Independent Variables
So far we have looked at cases in which the dependent variable is only influenced by x, but there are also cases in which this is not true. Consider the following statement: "the vocabulary a person possesses is a function of the amount they read as well as their age". The principle of the function has not changed here; the only new thing is the fact that (at least according to the statement) the dependent variable is now influenced by *two* independent variables rather than one. In contrast to the above case where we wrote $f(x)$, we now state a new function $f(x, z)$, whereby x could be the amount the person reads and z is the age of that person.

Alternative Meaning of "Function"
Lastly, you should be aware that a function can also mean something else. It could be taken to mean the graphical representation of a relationship between two variables. In other words, a function can at the same time be what we described it to be above, as well as the graphical representation of that formula. For example, a straight line on a graph with axes x and y may also be called a function.

> A function is a "machine" transforming an input (independent variable) to an output (dependent variable) using a set of rules known as the algorithm. A function can also be the graphical representation of the above.

1.7.2 Slopes, Rise over Run

In economics, we are often interested in the slope of a line or a curve. The slope (mathematically known as "gradient") of the function tells us the rate of change. For example, we might want to find out by how much y (the dependent variable) increases or decreases when we change x by, say, 1 unit. This is interesting because it shows us the responsiveness of one variable with regards to the other.

As an easy example, let us assume a linear relationship between x and y such $y = 1.5x$. As you may recall from school, the slope of any line segment can be determined by its rise over run. But what does this exactly mean?

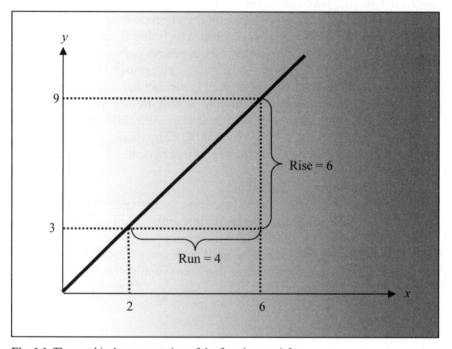

Fig. 1.1. The graphical representation of the function $y = 1.5x$

Fig. 1.1 is the depiction of $y = 1.5x$. If we want to know the slope of the line segment between $(2, 3)$ and $(6, 9)$[10] we need to divide the rise by the run. The rise is the vertical side of the triangle shown in Fig. 1.1 and constitutes the change in y. The run is the horizontal side of that triangle and is equal to the change in x. So we divide the rise by the run. The rise is $9 - 3 = 6$ while the run is $6 - 2 = 4$. Hence, the slope is $6/4 = 1.5$.

---

[10] This is the common notion for showing a point on a graph. Generally it is (x-coordinate, y-coordinate).

As the line in our example is straight and does not bend anywhere, the slope is the same on any point on this line. Let us now formalise our findings. The change of y divided by the change of x gives us the slope of a line segment. Rather than saying "the change" we can simply use Δs and so:

$$\text{slope} = \frac{\Delta y}{\Delta x} \tag{1.1}$$

1.7.3 Derivatives

A Need for More Precision
You may already have wondered what would happen if we did not have a straight-lined function but a curve instead. In such an instance one may still use the rise over run technique, but we have a problem there. The slope is not the same at any point of the graph, which would mean we would have to make many calculations if we wanted to know the slope on every point of the curve.

The Derivative in Principle
The solution to our problem is the derivative. It allows us to do in essence exactly what we did in the previous section, the only difference being that we can *compute the slope for a single point rather than a segment*. We will also be able to do this algebraically rather than graphically, which also adds to the convenience. Generally, the derivative measures the change in y for an infinitesimal change in x.

The Rules
Since this is not a mathematics text we will not go into detail about how one comes to the rules that govern the mechanics of the derivative. Instead, we merely present the method. Let us therefore take an example of a specific function $f(x) = x^2$. Taking the derivative of this function with respect to x means performing a mathematical operation so that we know what the slope of the original function is on any one particular point along the curve.

Mathematically, what we need to do is to multiply x by the exponent. Secondly, we need to subtract 1 from the exponent. So, the derivative of $f(x) = x^2$ with regards to x is $f'(x) = 2x^{2-1} = 2x$. If the function was $f(x) = x$ instead, the derivative would be 1, or if it was $f(x) = x^{1/2}$ then the derivative would be $f'(x) = 0.5x^{-1/2}$, for example.

You will also have noticed that the notation of the derivative is slightly different from that of the function in one respect: the convention is to include a prime symbol (') after the f. $f'(x)$ is pronounced "f prime of x". In general terms, the derivative of $f(x) = x^N$ is

$$f'(x) = N \cdot x^{N-1} \qquad (1.2)$$

Lastly, it should be noted that it is necessary to be specific with respect to what variable we want to use to differentiate a function, especially when there are multiple variables. So, for any of the above functions, we would say that we have taken the derivative of function y "with respect to x". The mathematical denotation of the derivative of function $f(x)$ with respect to x is:

$$f'(x) = \frac{dY}{dX} \qquad (1.3)$$

Of course, the function could be rearranged so that x is a function of y. In such an instance the variables in Equation 1.3 on the fraction would be switched around. It should also be noted that in an instance in which there are multiple independent variables, ∂ signs have to be used instead of the ds. This indicates the fact that we are dealing with a partial derivative. In such an instance we need to say that we are taking "the partial derivative with respect to x", for example. All other independent variables are then treated as constants.

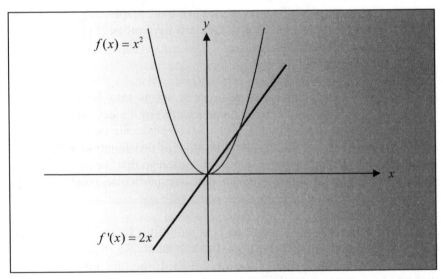

Fig. 1.2. The graphical representation of a function and its derivative

One Example

As we have seen in the above example, the original function ($f(x) = x^2$) will become $2x$ when differentiated with regards to x. So if $x = 1$, the gradient will be 2, if $x = 2$, the gradient will be 4 and so on. This makes sense if we look at the graphical representation of the original function and its derivative in Fig. 1.2.

For x values smaller than 0, the graphical representation of the derivative lies in the negative y-region of the graph. This means that the slope of the original function is negative, as the y-position of the derivative shows the gradient of the original function.

For example, the y-position of $f'(x)$ at $x = 0$ is also 0. This means that the gradient of $f(x)$ is zero. Looking at the graph, this is true. The original function is flat and therefore its gradient is nil.

1.7.4 Asterisk

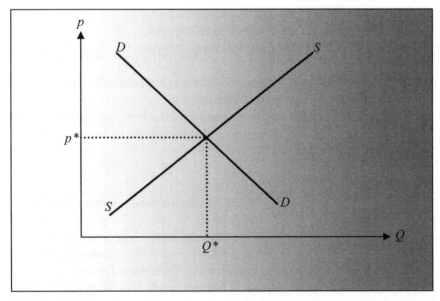

Fig. 1.3. A basic supply and demand graph showing optimum quantity and price Q^* and p^*, respectively

We find that, most of the time, it is simply assumed that the student knows what an asterisk sign means and that it is not commonly discussed explicitly. Fig. 1.3 above is perhaps the most basic graph of economics, showing us supply and demand. But at this point we are not interested in the meaning of the graph.

What we are interested in, however, is the asterisk sign to be found on the variables p and Q. All the asterisk sign says is that the particular value of a variable (in this case p and Q) is optimal. Since Q is a variable, it can take any value (at least in theory) but there will be only one Q which is optimal; this could be 10, 20 or 3.67. Whatever it is though, as long as it is optimal we have to write Q^*, pronounced "Q star", to indicate the optimality.

1.8 Chapter Summary

Adam Smith

- Adam Smith (1723–1790) is often accredited with the title of "Father of Economics" as he strongly influenced neo-classical economics and modern capitalism.
- Smith was an opponent of government intervention and advocated a "laissez-faire" approach to economic policy, as he was against any form of government intervention beyond the most basic services.
- In *The Wealth of Nations* he wrote that material self-interest is a prerequisite for economic success.
- The concept of the invisible hand explains how the vehicle of price regulates the market system so that there is no excess demand or supply.

David Ricardo

- David Ricardo (1772–1823), like Smith, was a proponent of free markets.
- His concept of comparative advantage, which he introduced in *Principles of the Political Economy and Taxation*, describes that nations should engage in trade even if one party has no absolute advantage (i.e. the ability of cheaper production of a good relative to the other country).
- Instead, each country specialises in the production in which it has a comparative advantage, i.e. it should produce that product which it can produce most efficiently, not relative to the other country, but relative to the production of other goods within itself.

- Ricardo's idea to promote free trade was an important advancement from the economic system of mercantilism which viewed trade as a zero-sum game in which the gains of one party must be derived from the loss of another.
- Today, the principle of comparative advantage is often overridden by political interests as countries impose protectionist measures.

Karl Marx

- Economist, philosopher and social revolutionary Karl Marx (1818–1883) is often cited as the ideological opposite of Smith as he was *against* capitalism.
- Marx observed horrific working conditions in his book *Das Kapital* and concluded that these were a result of the exploitation of the working class by the top class, the bourgeoisie.
- Although Marx's economic ideas are today regarded as false by most, they still appear to be an explanation for inequality in the world at first sight.

John Maynard Keynes

- John Maynard Keynes (1883–1946) is one of the most important founders of macroeconomic thought as he was a proponent of government intervention to counteract unemployment, among other things.
- Prior to the Great Depression of 1929, macroeconomic policies were almost non-existent.
- Thanks to Keynes, governments started using the tools of monetary policy (determining the amount of money in circulation) and fiscal policy (taxation and government spending).

Joseph Schumpeter

- Joseph Schumpeter (1883–1950) focused his work on business cycles and innovation.
- Business cycles are alternating periods of high and low economic activity within a country and/or region, while each cycle lasts for several years.
- Moreover, Schumpeter is well known for his concept of creative destruction. This concept explains that perfect competition is not the best market structure but rather some kind of dynamic competition in which firms gain temporary monopoly status.

Milton Friedman
- Milton Friedman (1912–2006) was part of the monetarist school of thought known as the "Chicago school".
- By studying the Great Depression, he came to the conclusion that monetary policy is a more important tool than fiscal policy for governments to control economic growth and prosperity.

What Is Economics?
- Economics may be defined as the study of how agents make decisions of resource allocation in conditions of scarcity.
- An agent is an economic actor.
- It is possible to apply economic reasoning to social situations in which money does not enter our analysis.
- Microeconomics is the study of the behaviour of consumers, firms and industries.
- Macroeconomics studies the economy as a whole, including fiscal and monetary policy.

Positive vs. Normative Questions
- Economics attempts to answer positive rather than normative questions.
- Positive questions are questions about the specific consequences of changing a variable.
- Normative questions are questions regarding which actions should be taken. Such questions take into account value judgments.

Basic Economic Concepts
- A consumer is an economic agent with the aim of maximising utility.
- A firm in an economic agent with the aim of maximising profit.
- A good is anything from which consumers derive utility upon consumption and that can be sold in a market for a price. In economics, the term "good" is often understood to encompass both goods and services.
- A bad is the opposite of a good. Consumers derive a disutility (or negative utility) from it.
- When a good is acquired by a firm for the purpose of production, this is known as an "intermediate good".
- Accounting profit is the revenue of the firm minus all explicit cost.

- Economic profit, on the other hand, is the revenue of the firm minus all explicit *and* implicit costs. Frequently, opportunity cost is part of implicit cost.
- An opportunity cost is a type of cost accounting for a lost opportunity (e.g. the amount of money that could have been made in an alternative activity).
- A market is defined as a social arrangement in which buyers and sellers meet to take part in an economic exchange.
- Utility is some amount of pleasure that a consumer receives from the consumption of a good.
- Disutility is the opposite of utility and it is what the consumer derives when she "consumes" bads.
- In economics, the term "marginality" entails the analysis of a change in a variable such as utility or total product.
- The term *ceteris paribus* means "other things being equal" and is used in economics (and other sciences) to rule out independent variables other than the cited one(s), known or unknown, which may have an effect on the dependent variable.

Basic Mathematical Concepts

- A function is like a machine that turns an independent variable into a dependent variable by using an algorithm.
- An algorithm is a set of rules about how the "machine" transforms the input into the output.
- A function can be both a formula and the graphical representation of that formula.

Slopes, Rise over Run

- The slope of any line or curve can be determined graphically by drawing a triangle on the function whereby the hypotenuse is to tangent to a point on the graph. Dividing the rise (i.e. the length of the vertical side of the triangle) by the run (i.e. the horizontal side of the triangle) gives the slope or gradient of the function of the region the triangle encompasses.
- If the function is a line, then the slope will be the same anywhere on it.
- Using differentiation is the correct method for finding the slope of a function for one specific point rather than an area. When faced with non-linear functions this may often be the preferred method over the "rise over run" method.
- The denotation of the derivative of y with respect to x is dy/dx.

Asterisk Sign

- An asterisk sign has to be included with a variable when the value of that variable is optimal, such as Q^* (pronounced "Q star").

The Slope of a Line Segment

$$\text{slope} = \frac{\Delta y}{\Delta x} \tag{1.1}$$

The Rule of the Derivative

$$f'(x) = N \cdot x^{N-1} \tag{1.2}$$

Part I — Consumer Theory

Most of our discussion in Part I of this text focuses on the consumer. Chapter 2 analyses supply and demand and linked to the price elasticity of demand. Chapter 3 then introduces the consumer's basic problem — how to maximise utility. Both Chapters 2 and 3 discuss concepts which are not only vital for the consumer but become important building blocks for Part II and III of this text where we focus on firms. Chapter 4 puts some of the concepts learned in the previous chapter to practice by analysing the decomposition of quantity demanded.

2. Supply and Demand

Introduction

Supply and demand are perhaps the terms that microeconomics is most famous for. In this chapter we firstly explain what we mean by these and related terms, as their usage in everyday language may differ from the economic usage. Then, we discuss the difference between demand and quantity demanded. After this, we analyse the elasticity of demand graphically and quantitatively using specific examples, including perfect substitutes and complements. Before introducing supply, we briefly discuss cross- price elasticity. We combine supply and demand to arrive at the market clearing price and quantity. Other applications discussed are price floors and ceilings, as well as taxation.

Required Background Knowledge

At this stage, it is essential that you have a good working knowledge of the basic terms explained in Chapter 1.

Key Terms

want, demand, supply, demand curve, law of demand, supply curve, exogenous vs. endogenous, quantity demanded/supplied, slide along vs. shift of, (perfect) substitutes, (perfect) complements, price elasticity of demand/ supply, perfectly (in)elastic, unit(ary) elastic, market demand/supply, substitutability, cross-price elasticity, market clearing point, equilibrium quantity, equilibrium price, inverse demand function, inverse supply function, price ceiling, allocative function of price, rationing function of price, price floor, per-unit tax.

2.1 Demand vs. Want

Although the term "demand" may seem very basic, it is nonetheless often misapplied in spoken language, as it is sometimes confused with want. For example, one may be tempted to say that the demand of goods in the world is unlimited, but this is false. The only thing that may perhaps be unlimited is a person's **want**. Your brother wants a Ferrari, you want a castle, and Mary wants a swimming pool. Can we have these things? Perhaps not, as we do not have the money to purchase these items.

Demand incorporates a want, but it is more. It is the combination of the desire to purchase a good and the ability to do so. For example, when the price of CDs is £10, I demand a quantity of five every month, whereas my want may be closer to 50; i.e. that is what I would demand if they were free.

2.2 The Demand Curve

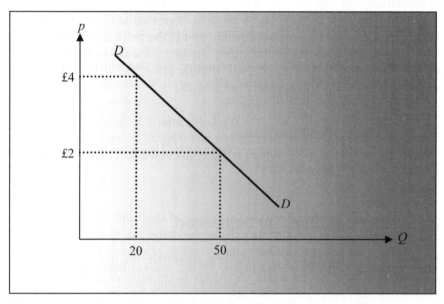

Fig. 2.1. A market demand curve for bagels on Brick Lane on a Saturday night

Let us now look at the graphical representation of demand as depicted in Fig. 2.1, the **demand curve**. In order to avoid abstract discussion, let us pick a specific market that the demand curve applies to: the market for fresh bagels on Brick Lane[1] on a Saturday night.

---

[1] If you haven't been, do go — it's an experience nobody coming to London should miss out on!

Firstly, let us examine the graph a bit more closely. We put price and quantity on the vertical and horizontal axis, respectively. What we see is that the curve represents an **inverse relationship** between the two variables. This simply means that when one is large the other will be low and vice versa. Why this is the case is extremely intuitive. The higher prices are, the fewer people would buy a bagel (or the smaller the average number of bagels bought per person). Picking a ridiculously high price of £100, it is likely that nobody would be willing to buy a bagel! Conversely, if the price was very low, such as a few pence, then it is likely that a very large number of people would demand bagels.

The demand curve itself is a collection of infinitely many price–quantity combinations. In Fig. 2.1, we have picked two such combinations. What does a price quantity combination mean? In our example, if the price of a bagel is £4, 20 people demand a bagel, and if the price is £2, 50 demand one. As you can clearly see, the higher the price, the lower the number of people demanding a bagel, and the lower the price, the higher the number of people who are willing to purchase a bagel.

This inverse relationship will always hold, and it is hence known as the **"law" of demand**. There is only one theoretical exception to this rule, known as the Giffen good, which will be discussed in Chapter 4. There is no need to worry about it now.

2.3 Demand vs. Quantity Demanded

Here is what most people have trouble with at first: the difference between demand and quantity demanded. A change in quantity demanded entails a *slide along the curve*. This is the case in Fig. 2.1, when price changed from £4 to £2 and quantity demanded changed from 20 to 50 as a result. It is false to say that *demand* changed from 20 to 50, so watch the distinction! When the quantity demanded changes, this is attributable to an **endogenous** (i.e. internal) change in the system. This simply means that price changes[2] — there is no other possibility. Hence it only makes sense to speak of quantity demanded in relation to a *specific* price, i.e. quantity demand at price X. In Fig. 2.1, we have quantities demanded of 20 and 50 at prices of £2 and £4, respectively.

---

[2] Generally, an endogenous change within a two dimensional graph entails that the value of one variable changes as a result of a change in the other.

Demand is different from quantity demanded. It is represented by the entire curve, which means that if there was a change in demand, a *shift of that curve* would occur. A change in demand is always attributable to an **exogenous** (i.e. external) change, meaning that there is something other than price that changes. Such a shift is shown in Fig. 2.2. In this graph, we can see the original demand curve *DD*, which is identical to that in Fig. 2.1. What is new is the second demand curve *D'D'*, which is parallel to *DD*. Looking at the new demand curve, for a price of £4 only 6 bagels rather than 20 are demanded. Similarly, when the price is £2, only 35 rather 50 bagels are demanded. This means that generally, for any price, the quantity demanded is lower — in other words demand has gone down. This is also indicated by the arrow in the graph.

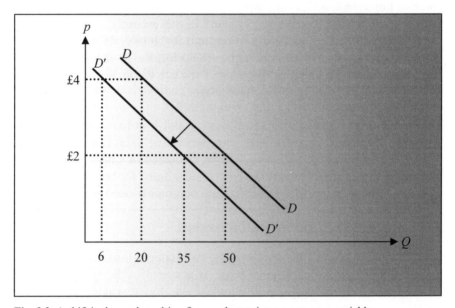

Fig. 2.2. A shift in demand resulting from a change in an exogenous variable

What could cause such a shift? Reasons for this are plentiful. Firstly, there could have been a shift in **tastes**. Perhaps consumers switched to kebabs or more conventional fast food. Another possible reason for the shift in demand might be the **season**. If the demand curve *DD* was compiled using data from the summertime, then we would not be surprised to see a lower demand when we used data 6 months later, when people avoid stepping outside due to low temperatures. Another reason might be that the bagel shop stopped **advertising,** or perhaps the local **news** printed an unfavourable story about the shop.

In addition, a change in **income** has the potential to make the demand curve shift. Income is a bit of a special case. Interestingly, an increase in income will not always make the demand curve shift outwards. Think to yourself: if you were rich, how much pizza would you eat? The answer is likely to be less than now. But don't worry about changes in income now, as Chapter 4 discusses this in detail.

Moreover, the demand curve will be affected by prices of **substitutes and complements**. As the name suggests, substitutes are products that can be substituted for one another (such as petrol from two different petrol stations, two kinds of mineral water, or spaghetti and rigatoni). Complements are the opposite, and represent goods which are commonly used together (such as knives and forks, cars and fuel, or pencils and erasers).

Let us come back to the context in which we raised the two concepts: when the price of *Coke* rises sharply, for example, the demand curve of *Pepsi* (being a very close substitute to *Coke*) is likely to shift outwards. Conversely, when the price of hamburger patties rises, the demand for buns (a complement of the patties) will go down.

> Substitutes are goods that can be substituted for one another.
> Complements are goods that are commonly used together.

Another determinant of demand may be the **expectations** about future incomes and prices that consumers have. If you expect the price of cars to double next year, you will try to purchase one today. Taking another example, if you expect to get promoted next month (which is connected to an increase in income), you are likely to spend more today than you otherwise would have done.

Lastly, demand is influenced by the size of the **population**. The market for hamburgers in London is naturally much larger than that in Lake Arthur, New Mexico. Hence, when the size of the population changes, the demand curve is likely to shift.

> A change in demand is attributable to a change
> exogenous to the graph (something other than Q or p)
> and results in a shift of the curve.
> A change in quantity demanded is attributable to a change
> endogenous to the graph (price)
> and results in a slide along the curve.

2.4 Price Elasticity of Demand

Let us now have a look at Fig. 2.3, which is similar to Fig. 2.1. What is different, however, is that there are now three demand curves instead of one. These three demand curves belong to three different people. Demand curve D_1D_1 is that of Toby, demand curve D_2D_2 belongs to Dominik, and demand curve D_3D_3 is Frank's (a mutual friend of Toby and Dominik). To make sense of the units, let us also change the time frame to one year rather than one specific night.

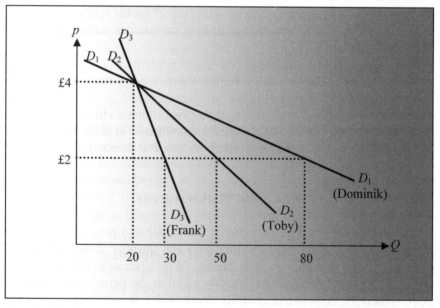

Fig. 2.3. The demand curves for three different individuals show that their responsiveness in quantity demanded to a change in price varies among each other

As you know from your own experience, different people exhibit different patterns of demand. Somebody who is a bagel fan will buy lots of bagels even when they are relatively expensive. Of course, when the price is high, their quantity demanded will be lower than if the price is low (due to the law of demand), but the rate at which their quantity demanded drops when the price changes is lower than that of somebody without a strong preference for bagels. In other words, different people have different price sensitivities for the goods they consume.

In Fig. 2.3 we start off from the same point — all three consumers have a quantity demanded of 20 when the price of bagels is £4. But when the price falls to £2, things are a bit different. Dominik's quantity demanded is 80, Toby's quantity demanded is 50, and Frank's quantity demanded is 30. What you are witnessing is the price elasticity of demand in action. But what is it in the first place?

Think of the analogy of a rubber band. Imagine you are trying to pull this imaginary rubber band. If it is elastic, your force will have a large effect on the distance that you can pull it apart. If the rubber band is inelastic, the same force will result in a smaller distance that you can pull it apart. The price elasticity of demand is similar. The "force" on the rubber band is the change in price, while the response in how far you can pull it apart is the quantity demanded.

So, when some change in price brings about a more than proportionate change in quantity demanded, we say that demand is *elastic*. When a change in price brings about a less than proportionate change in quantity demanded, demand is *inelastic*. When some change in price brings about an equal change in quantity demanded, we say that demand is *unit* or *unitary elastic*.

Expressing Elasticity of Demand Mathematically
The way we calculate the price elasticity of demand is by looking at the relative percentage changes in quantity demanded and price. For example, if price increases 1/2-fold (50% increase) and quantity demanded halves (50% decrease), demand is unit elastic. Why? Because the percentage change in quantity demanded is exactly equal to the percentage change in price. When the response in quantity demanded is less than 50%, demand is inelastic, and when it is more than 50%, demand is elastic. Let us look at the general expression of elasticity of demand:

$$|\eta| = |\frac{\Delta Q/Q}{\Delta p/p}|$$ (2.1)

Firstly, η is the symbol that we use for the elasticity of demand. On the right side of the equation, there is no new information — rather, something we already know is expressed mathematically. ΔQ divided by Q is the percentage change in quantity demanded, while Δp divided by p is the percentage change in price[3]. Hence, the whole right-hand side is the percentage of quantity demanded divided by the percentage change in price, or, in other words, the percentage change in quantity demanded *relative* to the percentage change in price. To put it yet differently, the right-hand side measures the responsiveness of quantity demanded to a change in price expressed in relative terms.

We can now combine this knowledge with the definition of the terms of elastic, inelastic and unit elastic. When $|\eta| > 1$, demand is elastic, when $|\eta| < 1$, demand is inelastic, and when $|\eta| = 1$, demand is unit elastic. These three conditions are very logical, because if the response to a price change is larger than the change in price, $|\eta|$ will be larger than 1, and hence the price elasticity of demand is elastic. If the change in quantity demand is smaller than the change in price, $|\eta|$ will be smaller than 1, and the price elasticity of demand is inelastic. Finally, if the changes are equal, $|\eta|$ will be 1 and so the price elasticity of demand is unit elastic. Often, one will abbreviate statements of this kind to "demand is elastic", for example which is also correct.

The Absolute Sign Around Eta
One thing on the side: What about the absolute sign in $|\eta|$? This is a convention, as the change in price and the change in quantity demanded *always* go in opposite directions. So, either the denominator or the numerator will be negative, making η always negative. The absolute sign therefore helps us to steer clear of confusion.

Defining the Variables on the Right-Hand Side
There is one last thing that we still need to discuss regarding Equation 2.1, and that is the explanation of the variables on the right-hand side. Firstly, as you are probably already aware, Δ is commonly used to show a change in a variable. Hence, ΔQ and Δp are the changes in quantity demanded and in price, respectively. What about Q and p then? These are absolute values

---

[3] We will take up the definition of these four variables in a little while.

of quantity and price respectively. But are these variables to be taken before or after the change in price? The answer is: "both, in a way!"

We simply take the average of the old price and the new price, and the average of the old quantity demanded (before the price change) and the new quantity demanded (after the price change). Why this approach is correct will be explained shortly. First, let us look at what we just discussed mathematically:

$$|\eta| = \left| \frac{\dfrac{\Delta Q}{(Q_{OLD} + Q_{NEW})/2}}{\dfrac{\Delta p}{(p_{OLD} + p_{NEW})/2}} \right| \tag{2.2}$$

Rewriting the Price Elasticity Equation
Now that we have covered and understood all elements of Equation 2.1, let us develop this equation a bit further. Let us take a step back and recall what Equation 2.1 told us: it stated that the elasticity of demand is the percentage change of quantity demanded over the percentage change of price. Since Equation 2.1 is a double-fraction, we can take p up to the top and Q down to the bottom and things become a bit more orderly. We also write the expression using separate fractions:

$$|\eta| = \left| \frac{\Delta Q}{\Delta p} \frac{p}{Q} \right| \tag{2.3}$$

Not only is Equation 2.3 more orderly than Equation 2.1, it also has an important meaning: $\Delta Q / \Delta p$ is the slope of the demand curve. Remember the principle of rise over run? To illustrate what we mean, we have shown it in Fig. 2.4 where the demand curve $D_1 D_1$ introduced in Fig. 2.3 is depicted. The bold part of the demand curve is the region for which the slope is calculated. Since $D_2 D_2$ happens to be linear, the slope is the same anywhere on the demand curve. But if $D_2 D_2$ was curved, $\Delta Q / \Delta p$ would represent the *average slope of the demand* curve *over that region*.

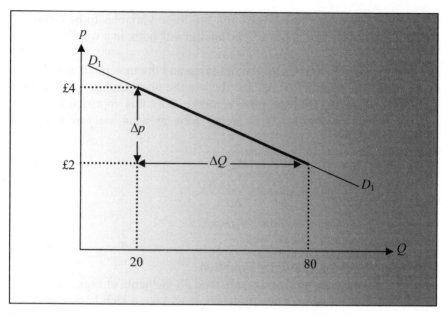

Fig. 2.4. Dominik's demand function with the change in price and quantity demanded emphasised by the vertical and horizontal arrows respectively

Now, that we have knowledge of the meaning of $\Delta Q/\Delta p$, let us switch back to Equation 2.2 and bring it into that form:

$$|\eta| = |\frac{\Delta Q}{\Delta p}\frac{(p_{OLD}+p_{NEW})/2}{(Q_{OLD}+Q_{NEW})/2}| \qquad (2.4)$$

You may remember that we promised to explain what the rationale behind using the average of price and quantity demanded was. The solution lies in the fact that we are analysing a region on the graph as shown in Fig. 2.4. When the demand curve is linear, $\Delta Q/\Delta p$ is constant, but p/Q is not. Very close to the vertical intercept, Q is close to zero and p/Q approaches infinity. And when we come close to the horizontal intercept, p is close to zero and so p/Q approaches 0.

Price Elasticity of Demand Changes Along the Demand Curve

This of course influences $|\eta|$ because $\Delta Q/\Delta p$ is multiplied by p/Q. As we have just shown, *the price elasticity of demand changes along the demand curve*. Its absolute value is equal to infinity at the vertical intercept and equal to 0 at the horizontal intercept. At the midpoint it is 1. This relationship is shown in Fig. 2.5.

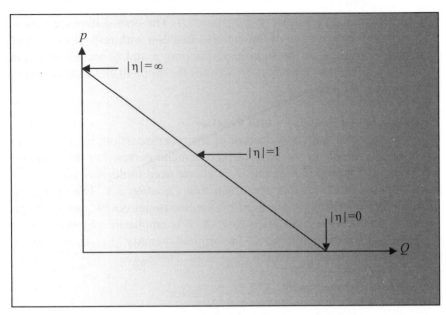

Fig. 2.5. The price elasticity of demand is infinity at the vertical intercept, 0 at the horizontal intercept, and 1 halfway along the demand curve

To cut a long story short: since the elasticity of demand changes along the curve, we have to use the averages of p and Q in order to arrive at the average elasticity of demand for the analysed region.

> On a linear demand curve, elasticity of demand is different at any point on that demand curve.

Moreover, in our case in which the demand curve is linear, we can calculate the elasticity of demand on any point on the demand curve by using specific ps and Qs. This is *not* possible when the demand curve is not linear and we only have two data points. In such an instance, we require the demand function, take its derivative with respect to price, which dQ/dp, and multiply this by the ratio of price over quantity p/Q:

$$|\eta| = |\frac{dQ}{dp}\frac{p}{Q}| \qquad (2.5)$$

This equation is very similar to Equation 2.3. The only difference here is that we take the derivative of the demand function with respect to p rather than writing $\Delta Q / \Delta p$. In the right-hand fraction, p and Q are not averages anymore because the derivative constitutes the slope of the demand curve on one particular point.

Putting Learned Principles into Practice
Now that we have had a fair amount of abstract discussion, let us return to the original example of the three agents' demand curves. For this purpose, we take a look at Fig. 2.4 again. Now all we need to do is to identify the values of the variables and plug them into Equation 2.4. The change in quantity ΔQ (which is emphasised by the horizontal double-arrow on the graph) is 60, the change in price Δp (which is emphasised by the vertical double-arrow on the graph) is -2, the original quantity Q_{OLD} is 20, and the quantity after the change in price Q_{NEW} is 80. Therefore:

$$| \eta | = | \frac{60}{-2} \frac{(4+2)/2}{(20+80)/2} | = 1.8 \tag{2.6}$$

By following these steps, we find that the elasticity of demand for Dominik is 1.8. Since this is larger than 1, we know that, by definition, Dominik's price elasticity of demand for the examined region is elastic. Hence, when the price goes down, his reduction in quantity demanded is more than proportionate to this change in price. Let us now move on to Toby using the values from Fig. 2.3 while employing the same method as before:

$$| \eta | = | \frac{30}{-2} \frac{(4+2)/2}{(20+50)/2} | \approx 1.29 \tag{2.7}$$

Toby's elasticity in the analysed region of demand is less elastic (or more inelastic — whichever way of putting it you prefer) than Dominik's, although it is still some way away from unit elasticity. Finally, let us perform our calculation for Frank:

$$| \eta | = | \frac{10}{-2} \frac{(4+2)/2}{(20+30)/2} | = 0.6 \tag{2.8}$$

Since $|\eta|$ for Frank is smaller than 1, his elasticity of demand for the analysed region is inelastic. In other words, for Frank, a change in price brings about a less than proportionate change in quantity demanded.

We can now summarise our findings of the analysis of Section 2.4 so far: Looking back to Fig. 2.3 and comparing the results we got from equations 2.6, 2.7 and 2.8, we find that *the steeper a demand curve, the more inelastic demand is and the closer $|\eta|$ will be to zero.*

When the percentage change in quantity demanded is larger (smaller) than the percentage change in price, the price elasticity of demand is (in)elastic, $|\eta|$ is larger (smaller) than 1, and the demand curve is relatively flat (steep).
When the percentage change in quantity demanded is equal to the percentage change in price, the price elasticity of demand is unitary elastic, and $|\eta|$ equals 1.

Market Demand
Although implicit in the discussion thus far, the distinction and connection between individual agents' demand curves and the market demand has to be made explicit. Fig. 2.3 exhibited three agents' demand curves, while Fig. 2.1 showed a demand curve for the whole market. The market in this example was very tightly defined around only one bagel shop during one Saturday night.

While the demand curves of Dominik, Toby and Frank belonged to one night, the industry demand belonged to a whole year. So, assuming the price of one bagel is £4, the quantity demanded by Dominik, Toby and Frank is 20 divided by 52 (i.e. the number of Saturdays in one year) which is about 0.38. This means that, on average, these three agents demand 0.38 bagels every Saturday night from the particular bagel shop in question. Together they demand 1.15 bagels at £4 per Saturday night.

Now looking at the demand curve in Fig. 2.1, we know that *all agents* demand a quantity of 20 at that price. Hence, the market demand is simply an aggregation of everybody's individual demand. This not only counts for a price of £4, but for any possible price.

In order to draw the real demand curve, one would have to ask every person in London about their individual quantities demanded for every price, and then the quantities demanded for each price would be added up to arrive at the industry demand.

Note that although we have stated that market demand is the "aggregation" of individual agents' demands, market demand is distinct from aggregate demand. The latter is a term from macroeconomics which has a special meaning distinct from how we treat demand in microeconomics.

2.5 Elastic and Inelastic Goods

It is useful to discuss at this point what the determinants of the demand for certain goods are. When is the demand for a good considered elastic or inelastic for an agent or the entire industry? So far we have named only one explanation: preference. The differences in quantity demanded for the three agents when the price fell from £4 to £2 was explained by the fact that each agent has a different preference for bagels. Of course, a bagel lover is more tolerant to high prices than somebody who is not such a fan. While such an explanation may be perfectly adequate in some situations, it is by no means a complete picture of the underlying reasons for individual or market demands. So, what other factors influence demand?

One such factor is the *proportion of total expenditure* the good constitutes for a consumer. The price elasticity of demand is likely to be a lot higher (i.e. more elastic) for cars or houses than for matchboxes or pens. Secondly, the **degree of necessity** also influences price elasticity of demand. A price increase in flights to Madrid is likely to result in a drastic decrease in quantity demanded from the weekend traveller consumer segment (for which such a trip is regarded as luxury), whereas the business traveller segment (for which the flight is considered a necessity) would exhibit much less of a reduction in quantity demanded.

Moreover, **consumer loyalty** may also have an important role in whether demand is elastic or inelastic. When consumers have spent a long time searching for a product they like and that meets their requirements, they are unlikely to exhibit a strong price elasticity of demand. Consumer loyalty may, however, have nothing to do with how long consumers searched for the good. Some people, for example, simply purchase the same washing powder every time they go shopping, out of habit. Prices are not checked regularly, and so an increase in price may not bring about a large reduction in quantity demanded.

Another factor to consider is whether a product is *consumed together with another very expensive good*. When that is the case, the first good's demand tends to be inelastic. Imagine you just bought yourself a new Ferrari, and after your purchase the price of petrol increased considerably. Would this influence your decision on how much petrol to buy? It is likely that the increase in the price of petrol would reduce your quantity demanded by only a very small margin, if at all.

2.5.1 Substitutability

The degree of substitutability also has a determining role in whether a good would be considered elastic or inelastic. The implication of the fact that a good has close substitutes is that it is very price sensitive. Most people would switch from McDonald's to Burger King or vice versa if the price of burgers at one of the restaurants, say, doubled. Fast food restaurants are aware of their consumers' highly elastic demands and hence special deals and new promotions matched to their rivals' offers.

High Substitutability
Now let us consider an extreme case of substitutes: two *identical* products. An example of this is the petrol from two different petrol stations. One is as good as the other. They are therefore **perfect substitutes**. When this is the case, the demand for the gas from both stations will be **perfectly elastic**. This means that if one station has a slightly higher price than the other, the effect will be that you purchase *all* of your petrol from the other station[4]. In effect, your quantity demanded has dropped to zero from a tiny increase in price. This is synonymous to saying that demand is perfectly elastic.

This situation is shown in Fig. 2.6, in which we can observe a horizontal demand curve. This means that a certain price $p*$ is given as a standard. The consumer will only consume at that price and consume nothing at all if the price is higher, even if the difference was as little as 1 pence! Instead, the consumer would then purchase a substitute product as, by definition, the perfect substitute would be just as good. The consumer is so sensitive to a change in price in this example that $|\eta|$ is infinite. We will pick up Fig. 2.6 in Chapter 9 again in which we discuss perfect competition.

---

[4] This is ignoring the fact that these petrol stations may be located at different places, which would add varying amounts of effort cost to the economic transaction, but it keeps things much simpler.

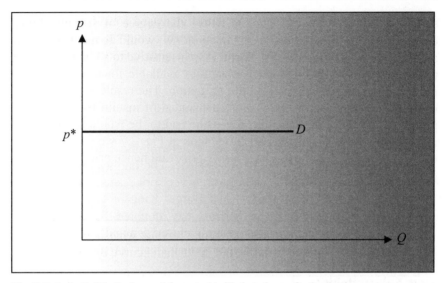

Fig. 2.6. An individual's demand for petrol is likely to be perfectly elastic

You might wonder how much you would be willing to consume if the price was p^*. Technically a horizontal demand curve as we see it in Fig. 2.4 would imply that you would consume *any* quantity. Of course, this is of little practical value. We ask you to suspend your curiosity for a little while. When we introduce the concept of supply, there will be a solution!

When agents perceive products to be identical, they are considered perfect substitutes. The demand curve is horizontal and hence demand is perfectly elastic.

Low Substitutability
We have just had a look at a situation in which the degree of substitutability was very high, such as petrol from two different petrol stations. Now, let us consider a reverse situation in which the degree of substitutability is extremely low. This would be the case for goods that you consume and that cannot easily be replaced with other goods. The price elasticity of food, for example, is very low. Of course, if food prices doubled, perhaps you would eat a little less but generally your quantity demanded of food is not strongly dependent on price.

Going to the extreme, an example where the degree of substitutability could be zero (even in a very short time window) would be medicine; such as insulin for a diabetic. Such a person is so insensitive to a change in price that his $|\eta|$ is zero. There are no substitutes available for insulin whatsoever, and consuming less is also not an option. The result is that the diabetic has no response in the quantity demanded of insulin to a change in price. After all, his life depends on it! If he had to, he would spend all his income on insulin. Therefore, when we look at Fig. 2.7 we notice that the quantity demanded does not change with price and hence price elasticity of demand is **perfectly inelastic.**

When there are no substitutes for a product whatsoever, its demand is perfectly inelastic and the demand curve is vertical.

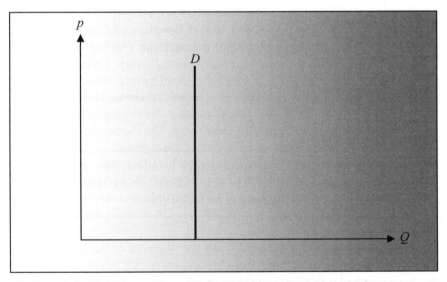

Fig. 2.7. The demand of insulin by a diabetic is likely to be perfectly inelastic

Quantifying Substitutability

Within the discussion of substitutability, we can quantify our analysis by using the concept of **cross-price elasticity of demand**. The cross-price elasticity of demand is defined as the proportional change in quantity demanded of one good resulting from a proportional price change in a second good. Hang on a second! So far, we have discussed only the own price elasticity of demand, that is the change in quantity demanded of a specific good resulting from a change in price of that *same* good.

Now we will look at how the quantity demanded of one good changes when the price of *another* good changes. Whether there is such a response and how big it is will depend on the degree of substitutability of one good for another. Mathematically, the cross-price elasticity of demand is denoted as:

$$\eta_{12} = \frac{\Delta Q_1 / Q_1}{\Delta p_2 / p_2} \qquad (2.9)$$

Equation 2.9 states that the percentage change in quantity demanded of good 1 resulting from a percentage change in price of good 2 equals the cross-price elasticity of good 1, i.e. η_{12}. Let us use an example. The cross-price elasticity of *Coke* is the change in quantity demanded of *Coke* resulting from a change in price of *Pepsi*. This will always be positive, as these two goods are substitutes. If the price of *Pepsi* goes up, the quantity demanded of *Coke* will go up as well, and if the price of *Pepsi* goes down, the quantity demanded of *Coke* also goes down (as *Coke* drinkers switch to *Pepsi*).

The larger the response in quantity demanded to a price change is within the cross-price elasticity of demand, the higher the degree of substitutability. In the extreme case of perfect substitutes, the change in quantity demanded from a change in price of the other good would be infinite, as we already discussed above. When dealing with substitutes, the change in quantity demanded of one good will always move in the same direction as the change in the price of the other. In other words, the cross-price elasticity of two substitutes is positive.

To complete our analysis, let us discuss the opposite of substitutes: **complements**. So, what is a complement? Cars and petrol, left shoes and right shoes, bacon and eggs, forks and knives. These are all examples of goods that are usually consumed together, and this is precisely what the definition of a complement is. As was the case with substitutes, using the word perfect in front of "complement" makes it an extreme case. That means **perfect complements** are goods that can only be consumed together. Two of our examples were perfect complements: cars and petrol, and left shoes and right shoes. It is easy to see how these pairs have little use on their own[5].

Let us now apply the concept of complements to cross-price elasticity. Say the price of petrol doubled overnight. What would happen to the demand for cars? Given that this price increase is not temporary, it seems very likely that the demand for cars would go down, as prospective car buyers might change their minds and switch to public transport. Generally, when dealing with complements, a change in price of one good will always result in a change in quantity demanded of the other good in the opposite direction. The cross-price elasticity of complements is therefore negative.

> The cross-price elasticity of substitutes is positive, whereas the cross-price elasticity of complements is negative.

2.5.2 The Influence of Market Definition on Substitutability

Earlier we stated that *Coke* and *Pepsi* may be good substitutes for each other, meaning that the own-price elasticity of demand for both of them would be very high (while the cross-price elasticities would also be very high). So far so good. But there is another thing that must be considered. Price elasticity of demand is dependent on how we define the market. The market for *Coke* may be extremely price elastic, but what about the market for soft drinks in general?

This market definition is much wider, as it would encompass not just *Coke* but also *Pepsi* and indeed all sodas, fruit juices etc. Therefore, a wider market definition is likely to be associated with more inelastic demand. If the price of *Coke* goes up, you will drink *Pepsi*, but if the price of all soft drinks went up collectively, would you switch to beer or water? We could drive this even further. If you defined your market as beverages then demand would be even more inelastic. After all, people need to drink *something*.

---

[5] We ignore the fact that petrol can be used in other motorised vehicles and the fact that a few people may require only one shoe.

The degree of substitutability has progressively decreased in this example. So, as you can see, without going into too much detail about the definition of a market, we can still ascertain that the market that we define is all important for the price elasticity of demand, and hence an appropriate definition is invaluable. We take this discussion up again in Chapter 8.

2.6 Supply

So far we have not spoken about supply at all. Instead, we have focused entirely on the various aspects of demand and discussed these in a reasonable amount of detail. As you will see, there are quite a lot of similarities to demand.

No In-Depth Discussion at this Point
As demand is a concept that focuses on the consumer, supply is about firms and production. As such, this is not a topic we wish to analyse in Part I and as a result the following discussion is on a relatively high level. As you can imagine, supply is influenced by an abundance of variables. And while we mention the most important ones here, an in-depth understanding should be gained from Parts II and III.

The Basics
While supply has many similarities to demand, let us firstly look at the most important differences. In a way, supply is the opposite of demand. While demand is the amount of a certain good that consumers are willing and able to buy at various prices during a certain time frame, supply is that amount of a good that firms are willing and able to produce at various prices during a certain time frame.

As we can see in Fig. 2.8, the demand curve slopes downwards while the supply curve slopes upwards. As was the case with quantity demanded, the quantity supplied is a function of price. However, the quantity supplied reacts to price in a fashion opposite to how quantity demanded does. The higher prices are, the higher the quantity supplied. The reason for this is that when prices are very low, only few producers find it worthwhile, given their capabilities, to offer a certain good. By contrast, when prices are very high, many more producers seek to find buyers for their good as they are lured into the market by the carrot of higher prices.

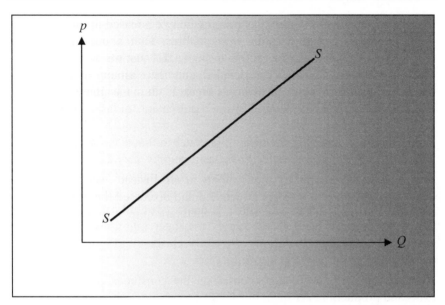

Fig. 2.8. In contrast to the demand curve, the supply curve is upward sloping

Since we have mentioned supply and quantity supplied above, it is worth-while noting that our discussion within demand regarding exogenous and endogenous changes applies equally to supply: a change in price results in a slide along the supply curve, while a change in any other variable results in a shift of the entire supply curve.

Moreover, the elasticity of supply functions in the same way the elasticity of demand does. When some change in price results in a larger than pro-portionate change in quantity supplied, supply is considered elastic. When a change in price results in a less than proportionate change in quantity supplied, it is considered inelastic. Finally, when a change in price results in an equal change in quantity supplied, supply is considered unit elastic. When there is ambiguity as to whether elasticity of demand or supply is meant, one can simply differentiate between η_D and η_S, which refers to the elasticity of demand and supply, respectively.

Price Elasticity of Supply
Price elasticity of supply basically indicates the ease and the cost with which a firm can alter its quantity of a certain good it produces. There are lots of factors influencing supply but we will only raise the most important points here. An example of inelastic supply may be the amount of wheat a farmer produces. Since he will need to wait for the wheat to grow, there

may be a considerable time lag in production of additional wheat. And if the farmer is not certain whether prices will stay high, he may not increase the production at all. Hence, in this example the quantity supplied hardly reacts to a change in price. Factors influencing the elasticity of supply may be the variability in the price of **input factors**[6], the time frame (as implicitly assumed in the above example) and requirements of large investments.

When supply is perfectly inelastic, η is equal to 0 and the supply curve is vertical. An example of perfectly inelastic supply may be the amount of iron ore a mine can produce over a specific time frame. Once at full capacity, the miners cannot extract any more iron ore from the soil unless they somehow enlarged the mine, which of course would take some time. On the other hand, perfectly elastic supply translates into a horizontal supply curve and an η equal to infinity. Perfectly elastic supply means that any quantity can be produced at a specific price[7].

Determinants of Supply
Having talked about the slope of the supply function (i.e. the elasticity of supply), let us now discuss determinants of supply. As was the case with demand, the supply curve may shift for a number of reasons. Most importantly, supply depends on the **cost of production**. This includes factor prices (capital and labour) as well as the production technology. A change in the production costs would make the supply curve shift. Indeed, as we shall see in Section 2.9, an imposition of a tax levied upon the producer (which is equal to an increase in production cost) makes the supply curve shift. Production costs are considered in Part II in more detail.

In addition, **expectations of producers** determine a firm's supply. When a producer expects the wage rate to rise sharply next year, for example, she will try to produce as much as possible in the present and store the excess. Moreover, if the prices of goods are expected to change in the future, this will also influence supply in the present, possibly involving the utilisation of inventory.

The Supplier's Environment
Another determinant of supply is the environment the producer finds herself in. As analysed in Chapter 8, the term "environment" may entail a

---

[6] i.e. the materials and labour used for production. The term is discussed in more detail in Chapter 5.
[7] In other words, every unit costs the same to produce, so a firm would be willing to supply an infinite amount at this cost.

number of factors, including geography, the size and characteristics of the market and more. Although this may sound surprising at first, **weather** may influence supply as some production processes such as those for food stuffs are heavily dependent on the weather, and so a change in the weather conditions may result in a shift in the supply curve. Lastly, the **number of suppliers** can also influence the supply[8].

2.7 Market Clearing

Recall that we said earlier that when there is a specific price, quantity demanded can be read from the demand curve. The same is also true for the quantity supplied and the supply curve. Despite all of this knowledge, we can still not ascertain what the market price will be.

We can find this by combining the supply and demand curves in one graph. The result is Fig. 2.9, perhaps the most famous type of graph in introductory microeconomics. What does it show us? The point at which the demand and supply curves cross each other determines the price for the good in the market as well as the quantity demanded and supplied (which equal each other).

This point is known as the **market clearing point**. This term is useful, as when quantity demanded is equal to quantity supplied the market is literally "cleared": there is no excess demand or supply. The market clearing point is also known as the equilibrium.

> The market clearing point or equilibrium is the point at which supply and demand curves cross and where quantity demanded and quantity supplied are equal.

---

[8] This does not imply that industry profits would be higher when there are more suppliers. In fact, the contrary is likely.

Now that we have seen market clearing graphically, let us look at this in a mathematical context as well. Let us assume the following **inverse demand function**[9]:

$$p_D = \frac{16}{3} - \frac{2}{30} Q \qquad (2.10)$$

Equation 2.10 is the function that we used to plot the very first demand function of this chapter shown in Fig. 2.1. It is now replicated in Fig. 2.9 with the addition of the supply curve. One last point about Equation 2.10: 16/3 is the vertical intercept (i.e. the price at which no quantity would be demanded) while the negative sign in the equation is consistent with the fact that demand functions are always downward sloping.

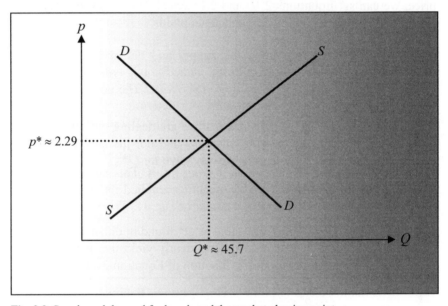

Fig. 2.9. Supply and demand for bagels and the market clearing point

Having discussed the demand function, let us move to the **inverse supply function**[10]:

---

[9] You may wonder why we are utilising an *inverse* demand function in Equation 2.10. This is a convention in economics, as price is denoted on the vertical axis. Hence, expressing the demand function as an inverse allows us to draw it. The subscript *DD* is used to clarify that the equation pertains to demand and not supply. A regular demand function (rather than an inverse function) would be denoted as Q_D.

[10] The same argument as in the previous footnote applies.

$$p_S = \frac{1}{20}Q \qquad (2.11)$$

Here, a subscript of SS is used to signify that this function pertains to supply. Unlike in Equation 2.10, in Equation 2.11, there is no negative sign. This means that the supply curve slopes upwards, which is consistent with what we already know.

Solving for Optimum Price and Quantity
Remember how we defined the market clearing point? It is that point at which quantity demanded and quantity supplied are equal. Moreover, it is that point that determines the market price. Since there is only one such price, we can set Equations 2.10 and 2.11 equal. We do so in order to arrive at the optimum quantity demanded/supplied.

$$p_S = p_D \qquad (2.12)$$

$$\frac{1}{20}Q^* = \frac{16}{3} - \frac{2}{30}Q^*$$

The asterisk sign on the Q indicates that we are dealing with the optimum quantity (i.e. the market clearing quantity) and not just any quantity. By rearranging Equation 2.12 slightly we can solve for Q^*:

$$Q^* = \frac{320}{7} \approx 45.7 \qquad (2.13)$$

Now we simply need to plug the value of Q^* found in either Equation 2.10 or Equation 2.11, as both would independently yield the market clearing price. Let us use the inverse supply function of Equation 2.11:

$$p^* = \frac{1}{20}\frac{320}{7} = \frac{16}{7} \approx 2.29 \qquad (2.14)$$

Hence, simply by making the inverse demand function and the inverse supply functions equal, we have found the price and the quantity demanded/supplied at which the market clears. At market clearing in our example, a quantity of about 45.7 is supplied and demanded at a price of about 2.29.

2.8 Price Ceilings and Price Floors

So far, in our analysis we have discussed supply and demand within a system in which the only agents participating were producers and consumers. Now, let us talk about situations in which the government artificially keeps a lid on prices (below equilibrium price) or imposes an artificially high prices (above equilibrium). These actions are usually motivated by a concern for the poor.

2.8.1 Price Ceilings

Let us firstly look at a situation in which the government imposes a price below equilibrium — a price ceiling. This means that some price lower than the market clearing price is imposed by law to be the highest price that suppliers are allowed to charge. Of course, prices lower than this price ceiling could be charged, but producers will have no incentive to do so as we will soon see. Perhaps the most prominent example of a price ceiling is rent control. This is presented graphically in Fig. 2.10.

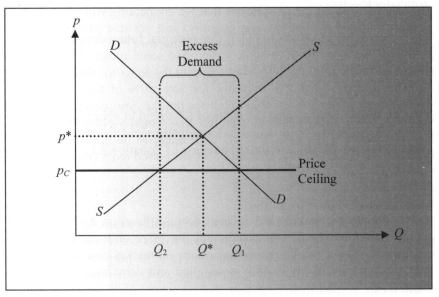

Fig. 2.10. A price ceiling of $p_C < p^*$ that results in excess demand of $Q_1 - Q_2$

What we can see is that the price ceiling p_C is below the equilibrium price p^*. This results in excess demand. Why? If you consider the demand curve in isolation for one moment, you will notice that the quantity demanded at price p_C is equal to Q_1. Now, have a look at the supply curve in isolation. At price p_C the quantity supplied is only equal to Q_C, which is much lower than Q_1. The difference between the two, that is $Q_1 - Q_2$, is the excess demand as it is the precise additional quantity demanded over and above the quantity supplied at a price p_C.

> A price ceiling is a maximum price in a market below the equilibrium price, imposed by the government.

In a competitive market (i.e. a market without intervention by the government), producers would notice that excess demand is present and so they would increase prices to p^*, at which point the quantity demanded is exactly equal to the quantity supplied. However, with the existing price ceiling they cannot (lawfully) do so, and hence the quantity supplied is at this artificially low level.

The problem that results from this is that potential future development projects may be abandoned. Imagine if you had some money to invest in a project and were thinking of buying a certain flat to let to somebody. Now, all of a sudden, if you can only ask for, say, 70% of the rent that you would otherwise have been able to get for the flat, you would perhaps invest your money elsewhere, in a project that would yield a better return. For the market as a whole, resources are likely to be guided away from housing to other projects as a result of the decreased rents landlords expect to receive.

The Allocative Function of Price
The allocative function of price is disturbed in this example. What do we mean by this? It is what Adam Smith meant by his concept of the invisible hand that guides resources (for production) to those projects for which the price exceeds the cost (including opportunity cost). Therefore, in this case it will mean, at least to some extent, that resources are directed away from housing.

> The allocative function of price is the process whereby resources are directed towards production processes for which prices lie above cost and away from production processes for which prices lie below cost.

So what does this mean in practical terms? A reduction in allocated resources may not only imply a cessation of new housing developments, but might also mean that existing housing units will be less well maintained. Imagine you were a landlord and a price ceiling was suddenly imposed by the government. The result of this is that there are now many people who would be willing to live in your flat for that price. Knowing this, you now have no incentive to spend money on maintenance on your property whereas before you were able to charge a premium for things like "a nice view", secure locks, furnishing and central heating. None of these frills can be used as arguments in the pricing of the flat any longer. Hence, nobody bothers!

The Market Finds a Way
Since landlords in rent controlled cities cannot charge a price equal to the economic value of the property (i.e. the equilibrium or market clearing price of a competitive market), it is not uncommon to see side payments disguised as "key deposits" or "finder's fees". Since the landlords cannot charge the market clearing price they find another way to receive payments. And they can do so because of the excess demand!

The Rationing Function of Price
The price ceiling interferes with market forces in a second way. Having discussed the implications for the producer (the landlord), let us now focus on the consumer (the tenant). In a competitive market, i.e. one without price controls by the government, price serves a **rationing function**. This is simply another way of saying that the person who values something the most will get it.

> The rationing function of price is the process by which existing supplies are directed towards those consumers who value them most highly.

Imagine you have just graduated from university, got yourself a good job and now you earn a respectable salary. In a competitive market, you could use that money and rent a high quality flat in a good location. Only having rent controlled flats to choose from, however, would be quite a nuisance. Not only might you not be able to attain the quality you are looking for, but because of the excess demand it would be extremely difficult to get a hold of any sort of flat. The person who values the property most highly might *not* get it when rent control is in place.

Imagine a large flat with five rooms occupied by only a husband and wife. If all their children have left home, the couple would, in a competitive market, be likely to vacate the flat because they would be able to save money by moving to a smaller place. But because there is no monetary incentive to do so, they simply stay in their flat.

Solving the Problem
Recall that the goal of rent control in the first place was to enable low income individuals to find a place to live. Instead, if the government simply deposited some money in these individuals' bank accounts, the negative side effects of excess demand can be avoided altogether!

Let us assume that fiscal policy (paying a lump sum to the poor) is not an option. How then could the problem of excess demand be rectified? Generally, there are two things that could be done that would move the market back to an equilibrium position.

Increase Supply
Firstly, supply could be increased. This is shown in Fig. 2.11 where supply shifts outward from SS to $S'S'$. This rightward shift of the supply curve allows for a new equilibrium price of p_C, and a new equilibrium quantity of Q^*_{NEW} to be found. At this new equilibrium, there is no excess demand or supply.

But how could one increase supply? The government may be able to fund new developments in outskirts of the city or perhaps redevelop derelict or otherwise unused sites into dwellings. Recall that private individuals may not have an incentive to build new developments as the allocative function of price cannot be realised. If the government is serious about its rent control plans, the funding for such new developments may be a necessary measure to remove tensions in the market and hence reduce unwanted side-effects.

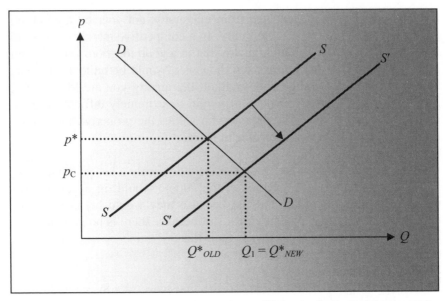

Fig. 2.11. An increase in supply allows a market equilibrium to be reached despite a price ceiling

Decrease Demand

Secondly, one may arrive at an equilibrium if demand drops, as shown in Fig. 2.12 by the leftward shift of DD to $D'D'$. This shift of the demand curve allows for a new equilibrium price of p_C and a new equilibrium quantity of Q^*_{NEW} to be found. Notice, when you compare Figs. 2.11 and 2.12, that while the new equilibrium price is in both cases p_C, in this second case, the market clearing quantity Q^*_{NEW} is much less in Fig. 2.12 than in Fig 2.11.

Therefore, whereas in the previous case we solved the problem of excess demand by satisfying that demand, now we solve the problem by slashing demand by such an amount that quantity demanded is equal to quantity supplied again.

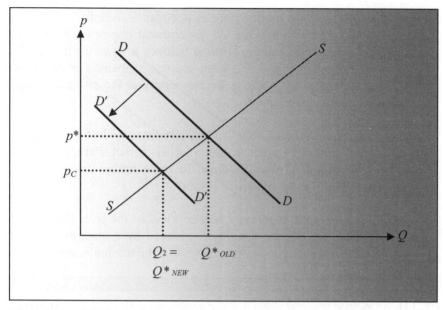

Fig. 2.12. A reduction in demand from DD to $D'D'$ allows a market equilibrium to be reached at price p_C and a quantity $Q^*{}_{NEW}$ despite the existence of a price ceiling

But how would the government go about reducing demand? Rent control could be restricted to confined areas; if this was the case, wealthier individuals could find accommodation elsewhere which would lift the excess demand on individual flats. Secondly, the government could give special discounts to people who decided to move to an outskirt region of the city, which would then also have the effect of a reduction of demand. However, these options seem difficult to exercise in practice.

2.8.2 Price Floors

As you might have guessed, a price floor is the opposite of a price ceiling. Rather than a maximum price that is imposed by the government in a certain market, a price floor is a minimum price that is imposed. Of course, this minimum has to be above the market clearing price for it to make sense.

> A price floor is a minimum price in a market above the equilibrium price, imposed by the government.

Similar to a price ceiling, a price floor is intended to benefit low income individuals. Let us assume that the US government imposes a price floor for cotton with the goal of helping farming families to sustain a living. The price floor is shown in Fig. 2.13. What we see happening is that now, rather than excess demand, there is excess supply at the artificially high price imposed by the government.

In a competitive market, each supplier would want to undercut the current price by a small amount in order to gain a larger market share. If this was to happen, other suppliers would reduce the price further and eventually the price would fall to the competitive level $p*$.

Now suppliers are forced to charge a higher price. At the price floor p_F the quantity supplied exceeds the quantity demanded by a quantity equal to $Q_1 - Q_2$. So what are we to do in order to resolve the tension in the market?

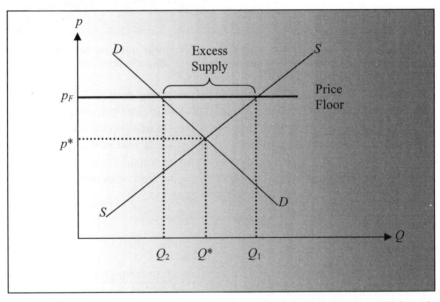

Fig. 2.13. From the imposition of a price floor, excess supply equal to Q_1 - Q_2 is brought about

Reduce Supply

Firstly, one could try to reduce supply. Perhaps this could be done by issuing licenses for farming. This does not appear a satisfactory solution as the goal was to help low income farmers and not to put them out of business. Another possibility may be to put high tariffs on imports of cotton from foreign countries. This would result in fewer sellers of cotton in the market place and this would hence shift the supply curve to the left from SS to $S'S'$ as shown in Fig. 2.14. At the new market clearing point, equilibrium price is equal to p_F and the new equilibrium quantity is equal to Q^*_{NEW}. There is no excess demand or excess supply at this point.

Increase Demand

Another way of solving the problem of excess supply is to increase demand. Since it would be difficult to force individuals to buy more cotton, the government itself would have in and become a buyer. This is shown in Fig. 2.15. We can observe that through the extra purchases by the government, the demand curve DD shifts outwards to become $D'D'$. The new demand curve $D'D'$ resolves the tension in the market and the new market equilibrium is reached for a price of p_F and a quantity of Q^*_{NEW}.

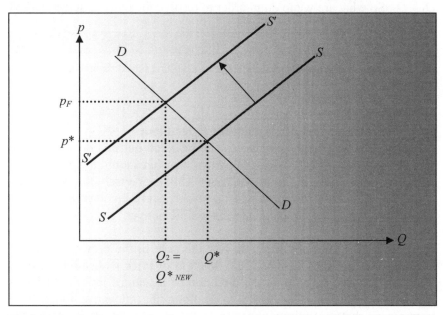

Fig. 2.14. A reduction in supply allows a market equilibrium to be reached at p_C and Q^*_{NEW} despite a price floor

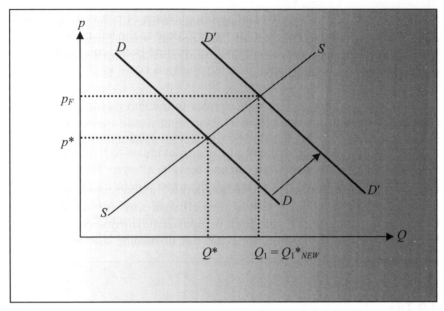

Fig. 2.15. The excess supply created by the price floor is resolved through an increase in demand

Further Problems Resulting from the Price Floor

The tension in the market might now be resolved but this does not mean that the arrangement is flawless. In particular, what should the government do with all the cotton it had to purchase? This is precisely the weak point of this policy, and in instances when perishables are involved they are often left to decay if the government fails to find a buyer.

The problems do not end here. As was the case in the previous example with the price ceiling, the allocative function of price is disturbed. Recall that the allocative function is the direction of resources towards different production processes. Due to the price floor, the allocative function of price means that inefficiencies occur. In the absence of a price floor, the labour, machines, fertiliser etc. that are used for the production of cotton when the price floor exists, would then be used for production of other crops or different products altogether. For example, a person that would "naturally" go out of business in the farming sector might become an office clerk. Hence, some of the resources used for cotton production with a price floor are used in a sub-optimal way (i.e. they would yield a higher return elsewhere).

In addition, one side-effect of a country-wide artificially high price is that *everybody* producing cotton benefits, and not just small, family run farms. Many of the other producers are highly profitable agribusinesses that have no need of governmental support.

Lastly, the price floor entails higher prices to the end consumer. Clothing and other products that use cotton as their input would inevitably become more expensive, as the businesses producing those consumer products would have to pay higher prices for their inputs.

Once again, the intervention in the competitive market has failed to produce an entirely satisfying outcome in an efficient way. As was the case in the previous example, the utilisation of transfer payments, i.e. aid, would by far be more efficient in meeting the end of helping low income individuals pay their bills.

2.9 Tax

In this section, we will examine what will happen when a per-unit tax is levied upon the market. We can graphically present such a per-unit tax in two ways, both of which yield the same outcome. One may assume that the tax is paid either by the producers or by the consumer. Fig. 2.16 represents a situation in which a tax t is levied upon the producer. Since he needs to pay this tax, it is in effect similar to a price increase of production. This "price increase" results in a leftward shift of the supply curve from SS to $S'S'$. The vertical distance from SS to $S'S'$ is equal to the amount of the tax t.

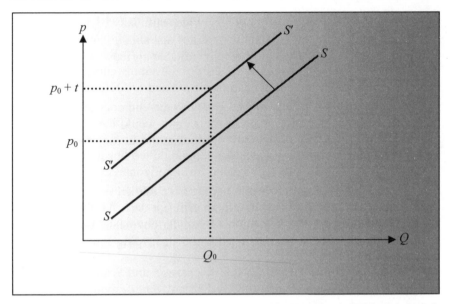

Fig. 2.16. A per-unit tax *t* levied upon the producer results in an upward shift of the supply curve. The vertical distance of the shift is equal to amount of the tax

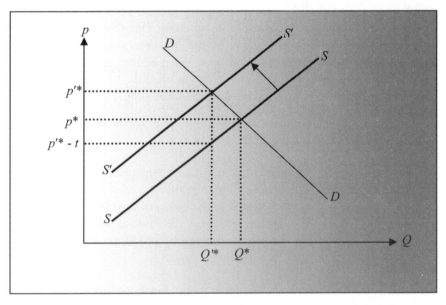

Fig. 2.17. The equilibrium price and quantity with a tax *t*

Now we add the demand to find out who is going to pay the tax. This is shown in Fig. 2.17. Let us start our analysis in a simple way: p^* and Q^* are equilibrium price and quantity when there is no tax. Recall that the imposed tax had the result of an upward shift of the supply curve. This results in a new equilibrium price and quantity of p'^* and Q'^*. Hence, as a result of the tax, price rose and the equilibrium quantity fell.

As mentioned before, the vertical distance from SS to $S'S'$ is equal to the amount of the tax t. Hence, if we add a vertical dotted line at the new equilibrium price p'^* and quantity Q'^* and draw a horizontal dotted line where p'^* hits the original supply curve SS, we get a third price on the vertical axis. Since the vertical difference of SS and $S'S'$ is t, the corresponding price of where the lowest horizontal dotted line intercepts the vertical axis is $p'^* - t$.

What do we learn from this? Both supply curves S and S' are needed in our analysis. If you wanted to treat the tax like any other production cost you would only look at $S'S'$ and DD and forget about everything else. What interests us, however, is who bears the burden of the tax. In effect, we use two prices here. One is the price that the buyer pays, which is whatever it would have been without the tax p^*, and secondly the equilibrium price at which we arrive when the tax imposed p'^*. A naive look would suggest that the consumer pays $p^* + t$, but this is not correct.

Look at Fig. 2.17 again. The tax resulted in a shift of the supply curve to $S'S'$, and so *the new price that is paid by the consumer rose* from p^* to p'^*. In other words, the amount of the tax burden paid by the consumer is equal to $p'^* - p$, or put differently, the new (higher) price minus the old price. We can see graphically that $p'^* - p^*$ is less than t.

What about the producer then? You might say: "the price paid by the consumer is exactly the same amount of money that the producer receives." In essence it is, but as we are interested in the effect of the tax, we ignore that in reality there really is only one price, i.e. the price at which the good is sold. Instead, we say that the prices received by producers and paid by the consumer *differ* by exactly the amount of the tax t.

So, what is the tax burden the producer pays? Since we already calculated the burden the consumer pays and know the total amount of the tax t, we could simply subtract the former from the latter, but let us determine this graphically in the same way we did for the consumer. The price the producer now receives is less than what it was in the non-taxed market. To be more precise, the difference is the equilibrium price $p* - p'* - t$ or $p* - (p'* - t)$.

If you are getting confused by the different prices, think about it like this: Tax reduces the amount of money that agents have. For this reason, when a tax is imposed, a consumer will need to *pay more* compared to a situation without tax, and a producer will *receive less* compared to a situation without tax, as the increase in price implied a reduction in quantity demanded. The sum of the two will always be equal to the total amount of the tax t.

As we have seen in our analysis, although one agent (the producer) makes the transfer of the payment of the tax to the government, both parties share the burden. The proportion of the burden taken by producers and consumers will depend on the relative price elasticities of supply and demand. If, for example, price elasticity of demand is very inelastic compared to the price elasticity of supply, then the consumer bears a larger share of the tax.

This can be verified both intuitively and graphically. The intuition is that, if the consumer is not able to escape a higher price, she will pay a larger share of the tax burden than the producer. After all, the producer is assumed to have knowledge of the consumer's preferences and can therefore charge a price that entails a large share of the tax by the consumer without being "punished" for it via a significant reduction in quantity demanded.

Graphically, a very steep demand curve will have the result that the equilibrium price $p*$ of the non-taxed market will vertically be very close to $p'* - t$. This means that the burden $p'* - p*$ paid by the consumer will be large, as $p'* - t$ takes up only a small portion of the total burden t.

2.10 Chapter Summary

The Basics of Demand
- Demand is distinct from a want, as a demand is the want *and* the willingness to purchase a certain good.
- The demand curve is a graphical representation of demand.
- It depicts an inverse relationship between quantity demanded and price, known as the law of demand.

Demand vs. Quantity Demanded

- A change in quantity demanded is always attributable to a change in the endogenous variable of price.
- A change in demand, however, is brought about by an exogenous change and results in a shift of the entire curve.
- Reasons for a change in demand might be changes in tastes, season, advertising, income, prices of substitutes and complements, expectations, and population.
- Substitutes are goods that can be substituted for another (such as *Coke* and *Pepsi*).
- Complements are goods that are commonly used together, i.e. complement each other (such as cars and petrol).

Price Elasticity of Demand

- The price elasticity of demand measures the responsiveness of a change in quantity demanded to a change in price.
- Mathematically, it is the percentage change in quantity demanded divided by the percentage change in price. This measures the price elasticity of demand for an entire region rather a specific point on the demand curve.
- When some change in price brings about a more than proportionate change in quantity demanded, (price elasticity of) demand is elastic, $|\eta| > 1$, and the demand curve relatively flat.
- When a change in price brings about a less than proportionate change in quantity demanded, (price elasticity of) demand is inelastic, $|\eta| < 1$, and the demand curve relatively steep.
- When some change in price brings about an equal change in quantity demanded, we say that demand is unit or unitary elastic and $|\eta| = 1$, and the demand curve has a gradient of 1.
- The price elasticity of demand equation can be rearranged so that $|\eta|$ is the product of the gradient of the demand curve $\Delta Q / \Delta p$ and p/Q. p and Q are the averages of price and quantity demanded before and after the change in price respectively.
- The average has to be taken because unless the demand curve has a very special shape, the elasticity of demand changes along the curve.
- Price elasticity of demand can be calculated for stationary points as well. When the demand curve is straight, $\Delta Q / \Delta p$ times p/Q can be used again. When it is not straight, the derivative of the demand curve with respect to p i.e. dQ/dp has to be taken. In both instances p and Q are not averages. They are a specific price and quantity for

the point at which we want to calculate the price elasticity of demand.

- The market demand is the aggregation of each consumer's quantity demanded for all relevant prices.

Elastic and Inelastic Goods

- Whether the demand for a good is considered elastic or inelastic depends on many factors including preferences, the proportion of total expenditure the good constitutes, how necessary the good is considered to be, how loyal consumers are, and whether the good is consumed with another, very expensive good.
- Goods that are regarded as identical by agents are known as perfect substitutes. The price elasticity for such goods is perfectly elasticity (i.e. the demand curve is a horizontal line) and $|\eta|$ is infinite. This means that when the price of one good is ever so slightly higher than the price of the other, *only* the cheaper good will be demanded.
- As we will learn in Chapter 9, this is an attribute of perfectly competitive industries.
- When there are no substitutes for a product whatsoever, its demand is perfectly inelastic. The demand curve is vertical and $|\eta|$ is equal to 0.

Quantifying Substitutability

- The cross-price elasticity of demand is defined as the change in quantity demanded of one good resulting from a price change in a second good.
- When dealing with substitutes, the change in quantity demanded of one good will always move in the same direction as the change in price of the other good. Hence, the cross-price elasticity is positive.
- Complements are goods that are usually consumed together.
- When dealing with complements, the change in quantity demanded of one good will always move in the opposite direction of the change in price of the other good. Hence, the cross-price elasticity is negative.

Market Definition

- The (cross-)price elasticity of demand is dependent on how the market is defined.

Supply

- Supply is that amount of a certain product that firms are willing and able to produce at various prices during a certain time frame.
- Many concepts of demand are similar in supply, including the difference between supply and quantity supplied and the price elasticity of supply.
- Opposite to demand, the supply curve is upward sloping because the higher the price, the higher the quantity supplied.
- The elasticity of supply depends on the ease with which a producer can change the amount of a specific good produced.

Market Clearing

- At the market clearing point (or equilibrium), quantity demanded and quantity supplied are equal. It is obtained by drawing a supply and demand curve on the same graph. Doing so also determines the price of the specific good in the specific market.
- Using inverse demand and supply functions is a convention that allows us to draw these functions on a graph.

Price Ceilings

- A price ceiling is a maximum price in a market below the equilibrium price imposed by the government.
- The allocative function of price is the process whereby resources are directed towards production processes for which prices lie above cost, and away from production processes for which price lies below cost.
- The rationing function of price is the process by which existing supplies are directed towards those consumers who value them most highly.
- Poorly maintained flats, a disincentive to build new developments, side-payments and a failure of those with the greatest desire to obtain the property are all unintended effects of rent control.
- Excess demand can be solved by increasing supply or by decreasing demand.

Price Floors

- A price floor is a minimum price in a market above the equilibrium price imposed by the government.
- The excess supply caused by a price floor can be resolved by either decreasing supply or increasing demand.

Tax

- When a per-unit tax is levied on a market, the consumer pays an amount of tax equal to p'^* minus p^*, where p^* is the equilibrium price without tax and p'^* is the equilibrium price with tax, attained by shifting the supply curve upwards by a vertical distance equal to the tax t.
- The producer pays an amount of tax t equal to $p^* - (p'^* - t)$.
- The way the burden of the tax is shared between producer and consumer depends on the relative elasticities of supply and demand. That agent who can least escape it (i.e. who has the least elastic supply/demand) pays the larger portion of the tax.

Price Elasticity of Demand (General)

$$|\eta| = |\frac{\Delta Q}{\Delta p}\frac{p}{Q}| \tag{2.3}$$

Price Elasticity of Demand (Over a Region)

$$|\eta| = |\frac{\Delta Q}{\Delta p}\frac{(P_{OLD} + P_{NEW})/2}{(Q_{OLD} + Q_{NEW})/2}| \tag{2.4}$$

Price Elasticity of Demand (On a Point)

$$|\eta| = |\frac{dQ}{dp}\frac{p}{Q}| \tag{2.5}$$

3. Rational Consumer Choice

Introduction

Chapter 3 is divided into two parts. Firstly, fundamental principles relevant for rational consumer choice are introduced in Sections 3.2 through 3.4. These principles will be implicitly and explicitly used in discussions in the rest of this chapter and throughout the text. Secondly, from Section 3.5 onwards, we focus on the application of rational consumer choice in the context of finding optimal consumption bundles using budget lines and indifference curves.

Required Knowledge

The reader is expected to have an understanding of the basic terms discussed in Chapter 1. Moreover, the ability to perform basic differentiation is also required.

Key Terms

cost–benefit analysis, explicit cost, implicit cost, opportunity cost, reservation price, monetary equivalent, consumption bundle, commodity space, budget, budget constraint, budget line, income, rotation, shift, composite good, utility function, marginal utility (MU), diminishing marginal utility, Cobb–Douglas utility function, indifference curve, marginal rate of substitution (MRS), indifference map, perfect substitutes, perfect complements.

3.1 Introducing Rational Choice

What Is a Consumer?

The term "consumer" appears so basic, that is easy to take it for granted without giving much thought to what it actually means. While the term is frequently used in everyday language, here the consumer is defined as an economic agent whose goal it is to maximise her utility. We already know this from Chapter 1. Let us now analyse the consumer's behaviour.

What Is Rational Choice?

As the name suggests, rational choice entails an assumption that the consumer behaves rationally. In the following section, we examine a scenario in which a rational choice would be to engage in activities which yield a benefit higher than the associated cost (where cost may not necessarily be confined to explicit cost). As we will see in Sections 3.3 and 3.4, there are two more considerations that a rational consumer should make. However, before we get started with cost–benefit analysis, it is worth examining the concept of consumer rationality a bit further.

Are Rational Consumers Really Rational?

Consumer rationality assumes that individuals behave in a purely self-interested way. While this may seem plausible at first sight, upon closer inspection such an assumption may lead to bizarre outcomes. If exhibited by consumers, this assumption would mean that individuals would, for example, not engage in social contact unless some measurable gain was attached to it. A purely self-interested person would not give money to charity, be nice to strangers, or leave their phone number when accidentally scratching somebody else's car in a parking lot — unless, of course, there was some kind of gain to be reaped from such behaviour. It is easy to see that a person who is purely self-interested does not at all seem like somebody you would want to be friends with. Yet, this is the kind of person that economists think of when they talk about a "rational" consumer.

It is unlikely that many of these selfish individuals really exist, but analysing the rational consumer still proves to be a valuable exercise for us. Remembering our discussion from Chapter 1, we know that while certain models in economics may not seem realistic all of the time, their internal validity is not to be disputed in the sense that the predictions a model makes using assumptions and scope conditions cannot be argued with — as long as the logical process is not flawed. The concept of the rational consumer (who is sometimes also referred to as *Homo economicus*) can therefore help us to find out what consumers *should* do if their goal is to maximise their well-being.

The degree of such well-being, or more precisely the utility, may not purely be derived from the attainment of some form of monetary payoff. An agent may derive utility in the form of personal satisfaction from giving to charity, or from the good feeling of knowing that one has done "the right thing". Some individuals might prefer these feelings to monetary payoffs while others might not. And so the economic concept of utility is remarkably flexible, as behaviour is "rational" so long as it helps the agent achieve a certain goal, whichever one it might be. Abandoning a life of luxury and giving away all your possessions is a rational pursuit if your aim above all other competing interests is to be a kind, selfless person. Conversely, if the pursuit of wealth is the primary objective in your life, you would, for example, only behave nicely towards others if you thought you might need them at some point!

3.2 Cost–Benefit Analysis

Perhaps the most basic way of thinking like an economist is the cost–benefit analysis. You find it applied virtually everywhere around you in situations economic and non-economic alike. Decisions based on cost–benefit analysis are made by everyone, from economics professors to individuals who have never heard of the subject. Economics is therefore relevant to all of us, on a daily basis, whether we are aware of it or not.

In the most simple terms, cost–benefit analysis states that if the benefit of some action exceeds the cost of that action, one should always engage in that action. This principle is as simple as it is important. Do not be fooled by the terms "cost" and "benefit", as their meaning may vary from situation to situation. Neither a cost nor a benefit have to necessarily be expressed in monetary terms. Say you are faced with the decision of whether or not to visit your grandparents. The cost of doing so might be the effort of walking to their house while the benefit would be the utility (in the form of joy) you derive from seeing them.

Although introduced in the context of consumers, cost–benefit analysis can be extended to firms as well. A company might try to find out whether it should invest money in a new project or not. Unless there are competing alternative projects, the firm should invest if the associated cash flow from doing so[1] is larger than the cost associated with it. Cost–benefit analysis may be extremely simple or very complicated, depending on the circumstances and the relevant variables. In order to understand cost–benefit analysis better, let us focus our attention on "cost" in Section 3.3.

---

[1] Expressed as the net present value NPV. This term is explained in Chapter 6.

3.3 Explicit Cost vs. Implicit Cost

Two Options
Suppose it is your day off and you are considering different leisure activities. Option 1 is to go to the movies and option 2 is to see friends in the park. What is the cost of going to the movies? The intuitive answer is: "What ever the price of the admission ticket is!" But, this is only part of the story.

Almost all the time in your life you need to make decisions about what to do, and often doing one thing means not being able to do another. Therefore going to the movies costs you, say, £10 admission fee plus the foregone opportunity of a level of utility you might have derived from going to see your friends. In this example, the lost utility from not being able to see your friends is an **opportunity cost**[2].

Two Types of Cost
You will have noticed that the cost of the admission ticket and the opportunity cost (not being able to see your friends) are quite different. One is an explicit (or monetary) cost, i.e. the amount of money you pay out of your pocket, while the other is an implicit cost in the form of a foregone opportunity — the opportunity cost. Again, the concept of opportunity cost is something that applies to individuals and firms alike.

> An opportunity cost is the cost of foregoing benefit that would have been derived from an alternative activity.

Finding the Opportunity Cost
Back to our movie and park scenario. What should we do? As it stands, we are not unable to answer this question. The reason is that we have not yet specified how big the opportunity cost is. This element in the cost–benefit analysis is subjective, and is likely to vary from person to person. There is no price tag attached to the amount of utility you derive from seeing your friends. So, in order to be able to solve our problem we ask: "How much

---

[2] We looked at the opportunity cost very briefly in Chapter 1, but we will discuss it here in much more detail.

would somebody have to pay you to stay in your house and not to go and see your friends?" This question might seem silly but it serves a useful purpose. We will assume that staying in your house will not give you any utility, positive or negative, and that there is no effort cost associated with seeing your friends.

So, how much? What about 1 pence? Unless you really don't care much for your friends, you would turn that proposition down straight away. £1? You would probably still go. How about £1000? Hmmm, it is very likely that you would stay home, even if you value your friends highly — after all, £1000 is a large sum of money. We can therefore deduce that somewhere between £1 and £1000 is a price which made you switch your decision from going to staying at home.

For this amount of money, it was worthwhile not seeing your friends and wasting the afternoon (remember, we said that at home you derive no utility). For the sake of argument, let us assume that the critical amount of money was £70. If somebody was to offer less you would still see your friends, if somebody offered you more you would stay at home. If the offer was equal to £70, you would be indifferent between taking the money and seeing your friends. In our example, this £70 is known as the **reservation price**. You could remember the term this way: you would essentially be reserved, or in other words be hesitant, to take the money at £70 due to your indifference.

> The reservation price is that amount of money one would have to be given in order to be indifferent between two activities.

Let us use what we have just learned and put it back into the original scenario. We noted that £70 is what you would have to be paid (or to be more precise, £70 plus 1 pence) in order for you *not* to see your friends. In other words, you value seeing your friends at £70. In economics, that amount of money that we let some utility be equal to is known as the **monetary equivalent**. Hence, the monetary equivalent of the utility derived from seeing your friends is £70.

You have just found your opportunity cost of going to the movies — it is the foregone benefit of not being able to see your friends, or rather the monetary equivalent thereof.

Making A Decision

Now let's recall what our goal was. We started out wanting to know whether we should go to the movies or not. There is only one thing missing, which is the monetary equivalent of our utility of going to see the film. We use the same reasoning as above. How much would someone have to pay you for not going to the movies and sitting at home instead (where you derive a utility of zero)? Let's say that this would be £40. Finally we can answer the question by writing up a simple equation in words:

$$\text{Net benefit of going to the movies} = \text{utility derived from doing so} \quad (3.1)$$
$$- \text{admission fee} - \text{opportunity cost}$$

Putting £-values to it this we get:

$$\text{Net benefit of going to the movies} = £40 - £10 - £70 = -£40 \quad (3.2)$$

As we can see, the net benefit of going to the movies would be minus £40, which means you should definitely not go to the movies. Intuitively this £40 is also the net (positive) benefit of seeing your friends in the park. This can be verified by rearranging Equation 3.1 and solving for the net benefit of meeting your friends. Alternatively, you may simply use your logic and formulate a new equation applying a simple cost–benefit analysis.

$$\text{Net benefit of seeing friends} = \text{utility of seeing them} - \text{net oppor-} \quad (3.3)$$
$$\text{tunity cost}$$

We have to recognise that this time there is one further complication in the step, which is the fact that the opportunity cost we are using is a **net effect**. What does this mean? Well, pretty much the same as before only that going to the movies is not just a utility but also carries some explicit cost (in excess of the implicit opportunity cost of not being able to see your friends). This explicit cost is the admission fee. So let us assign £-values to Equation 3.3:

$$\text{Net benefit of seeing friends} = £70 - (£40 - £10) = £40 \quad (3.4)$$

Equation 3.4 has helped us to verify our intuition. The net benefit of seeing your friends is £40.

Reasonable Calculations?

Your likely reaction to the calculations that we just made might be something along the lines of: "Who would actually do this in real life? This is some academic mumbo jumbo that has nothing to do with real life whatsoever!" If this is indeed what you are thinking then you would not be alone in your opinion. But let us tell you this:

Calculations like the ones above happen every day. However, most people are not aware that they are making what are, in essence, economic decisions. Your mind is a calculating machine, whether you like it or not. It may not be able to give you these exact calculations in an explicit form (if you haven't studied economics before) but it does give you an indication of the net benefit of some activity. Not as a number, but in the form of a feeling which is then used to make a decision. It happens in all our daily lives on a constant basis.

Say, for instance, you are working on an extremely important project for university, and the deadline is only days away. One of your good friends has just flown in from New York and is in town only for the weekend. She asks you to come out for drinks and to chat about the "olden days". If you did indeed go out, your project would suffer and there would be a chance that you would not be able to complete it in time. What should you do? You think about the issue for a while, and most pressingly in your head is the fact that you might not get the degree classification that you were hoping for.

Your stomach starts growling at the thought of not doing the project and your decision is made. The negative feelings of possible failure have increased your cost of working on the project (because of a rise in the opportunity cost) and you decide not to go out because of the possibility of the lost future benefit (or alternatively, the pain of a bad grade).

As you can see, the learned concepts find application in a variety of ways in real life. What you should take away from this section is the following: *In order to make economically sound decisions it is important that one always takes into account implicit and explicit costs alike.*

3.4 Sunk Costs

The concept of sunk cost is also a very important one. As was the case with opportunity cost in the previous section, sunk cost applies to consumers and firms alike. A sunk cost is a cost that one has already incurred. Unlike the scenarios above in which cost *changes depending on the course of action that we take*, when we deal with sunk costs our decisions *do not affect the sunk cost* as it has been occurred prior to that point in time at which the decision is taken.

The intuition that follows from the above finding is vital, as errors involving sunk cost are very common. Whenever a sunk cost is involved, we must ignore it in our decision making. In order to understand what we mean by this, consider the following example.

Picture any band whose music you enjoy. Now assume that a friend gave you a free ticket for one of their concerts which is taking place tonight. Unfortunately there is a tube strike and delays to Wembley stadium are severe. Would you still go to the concert? There is no right or wrong answer to this question as this will depend on your own preferences and net benefit. Answer the question for yourself and make a mental note of it.

Now, consider a very similar scenario. In fact everything stays the same, except that the ticket was not given to you for free. Instead of you purchased it for £50. Given the tube strike, what would your decision be now? If you are like most people, you would be more likely to go to the concert if you purchased the ticket than if it was given to you. Most people can justify such decision-making in a very articulate way.

From a purely economic perspective, however, and this must be said clearly, *your decision should not vary across the scenarios.* In fact, your cost–benefit calculations should not even show the cost of the acquisition of the ticket at all. That money is spent and gone[3], so to speak. The only thing you should take into account is the cost and (net) benefit you derive from travelling to and attending the concert that evening. As mentioned before, sunk cost errors are very common, so do keep this concept in mind[4].

---

[3] We assume that the ticket cannot be resold.

[4] Sunk cost errors have been the centre of discussion for authors such as Thaler (1980) and Kahneman & Tversky (1979).

3.5 Understanding Consumption Bundles and Budget Constraints/Lines

Let us now start the more formal analysis for which we have developed the intuition up to this point. What follows is the intuitive continuation of the consumer's optimal choices analysed in the above sections.

3.5.1 Consumption Bundles

So far, we have only dealt with situations where an agent is taking the decision to follow one course of action or to consume one good. Now, we are interested in scenarios in which the consumer consumes multiple goods at the same time. For now we will stick to two goods, but later we will learn how to manage situations with any number of goods.

We can illustrate a two-good world graphically by showing the goods on the axes of a graph such as Fig. 3.1. Here, the axes are labelled Q_F and Q_S, representing the quantities of food and shelter, respectively[5]. These units could be loafs of bread and square metres in a flat, for example.

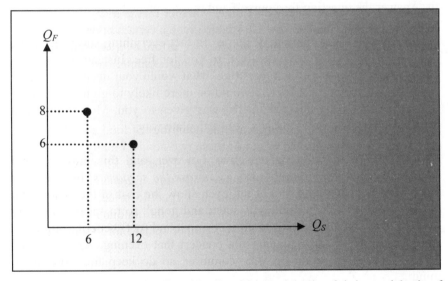

Fig. 3.1. Two consumption bundles of 8 units of food and 6 units of shelter, and 6 units of food and 12 units shelter, respectively, shown in commodity space

---

[5] Some authors may use X to represent the quantity of a good (e.g. X_F).

Any one point within **commodity space** (this is what we call the area en-compassed by the axes in graphs such as Fig. 3.1) represents some combi-nation of the two goods in question. Two such combinations are shown in via dots in commodity space. One consumption bundle encompasses 8 units of food and 6 units of shelter, whereas the other contains 6 units of food and 12 units of shelter. The term **consumption bundle** is very intui-tive as it can be viewed as a basket that is filled with specific quantities of two goods. Note that it is not necessary for a combination of two goods to actually be consumed for them to be graphed in a "consumption" bundle. As we will see later, certain bundles may not be affordable and will there-fore never be consumed.

3.5.2 Budget Constraint and Budget Line

Generally, the more one has of a certain good, the better off one is[6]. There-fore, the wants of consumers are unlimited. However, very few people are so well endowed that they can consume everything that they want to con-sume. No matter how poor or wealthy, consumers are constrained by their **budget** in some way. A budget is a certain amount of income an agent has available over a certain period of time, whether that is a day, a week or a year. While some bundles are affordable given a certain budget, others are not. In order to show us which bundles are affordable, we introduce the concept of the budget constraint, which in our example can be expressed as:

$$p_F \cdot Q_F + p_S \cdot Q_S \leq M \qquad (3.5)$$

As we recall, variables Q_F and Q_S are the quantities of food and shelter, re-spectively. p_F and p_S are the prices of these two goods. Finally, M is the in-come that we have available — our budget. Equation 3.5 shows us what we have already understood in principle, only now in a mathematical way. Each unit of each good is purchased at a specific price. Together, the spending on the two goods must not exceed the amount of income M available. This is very intuitive as you cannot spend more than you have and we utilise the $\leq$ sign here.

---

[6] We can think of cases in which this statement is not true. Are you likely to enjoy the last one of ten beers in a single night? We will, however, follow a convention that a good is something of which you would *always* like to have more.

Budget Line

The budget constraint can also be shown on a graph but before we can do so, we have to introduce another related concept: the **budget line**. A budget line is the collection of consumption bundles that are *just afford-able*. This means these are only bundles which when consumed require the entire income *M*. Expressing this mathematically, all we need to do is to replace the ≤ sign of Equation 3.5 with an = sign:

$$p_F \cdot Q_F + p_S \cdot Q_S = M \qquad (3.6)$$

As we can see, the budget line is a subset of the budget constraint. It should be noticed that some authors do not make a distinction between the two terms and use them interchangeably.

A budget constraint is the collection of all affordable sets of the consumer given a certain income *M*.
The budget line is the collection of consumption bundles that are just affordable given a certain income *M* of the consumer.

Finding the Intercepts

So let us put the concept of the budget line into practice in Fig. 3.2. How can it be drawn? Say that your weekly income is £100. In such a case, how many units of food Q_F would you be able to buy if you decided to consume only food and no shelter? This is easy. It is simply the income $M = £100$ divided by the price of food p_F. Suppose that p_F is equal to £6, to pick a random price, we would be able to buy around 16.7 units. As we just mentioned, this is a situation in which we have no shelter and so by necessity this point must lie on the vertical axis (as any point on the vertical axis represents a consumption bundle containing no shelter). Therefore, we know that the vertical intercept is 16.7.

As a next step we need the horizontal intercept, which can be found using the same logic. If we use all of our income on shelter and none of it food, the largest number of units of shelter Q_S we can afford is M/p_S. Suppose the price of shelter is £8, then the intercept would be 100/8 = 12.5

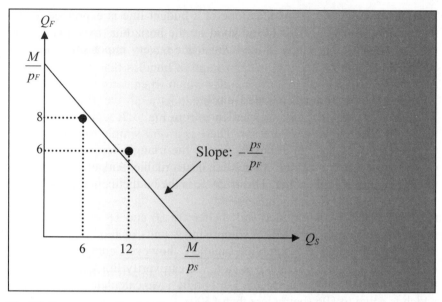

Fig. 3.2. Two consumption bundles and a budget line with a vertical intercept of M/p_F and a horizontal intercept of M/p_S. The area encompassed by the budget line and the axes is known as the budget constraint and incorporates all affordable bundles. A bundle of 8 units of food and 6 units of shelter is affordable, a bundle of 6 units of food and 12 units of shelter is not

Drawing the Line

Now that we have the two intercepts on the axis, we can combine these by simply drawing a straight line and voilà — we have our budget line. But there is additional insight to be gained, namely the slope of this line. Recall from Chapter 1 that the slope of *any* line can be determined by its "rise over run", where "rise" refers to the height of the triangle and "run" refers to its length. The rise is M/p_F (the horizontal distance) whereas the run is M/p_S (the vertical distance). Dividing the rise by the run we get:

$$-\frac{M/p_F}{M/p_S} \tag{3.7}$$

Since the rise is negative, as we move from left to right, a negative sign is included in the equation. Simplifying, we get:

$$-\frac{p_S}{p_F} \tag{3.8}$$

Therefore, in general terms the slope of a budget line is expressed as the negative ratio of the prices of the good on the horizontal axis and that on the vertical axis. The slope of the budget line is very important as we will soon see.

Affordable and Non-affordable Bundles
There is one last thing that we can learn from Fig. 3.2: which bundles are affordable and which ones are not. There is a very simple rule that can be followed: any consumption bundle within the triangle formed by the axis of commodity space and the budget line is affordable. Any bundle which is outside of this triangle is not. This triangle is the budget constraint.

Given that the prices for food and shelter are £6 and £8 respectively, we note that consumption bundle 1 comprising 8 units of food and 6 units of shelter is affordable. Consumption bundle 2, however, comprising 6 units of food and 12 units of shelter, is not. We can verify this easily by using the left-hand side of Equation 3.5. For bundle 1 we calculate £6 · 8 + £8 · 6 which is equal to £96 (being less than £100). For consumption bundle 2 we calculate £6 · 6 + £8 · 12 which is equal to £132 (being more than £100).

3.5.3 Change in Price

Let us now look at a minor extension of the above ideas. Assume that the housing market in London continues to move the same way it has for the last couple of years, and so the price of shelter rises. The new price of shelter $p_{S(NEW)}$ will be £10 per unit, which is effectively an increase of £2 per unit.

This change in the price of shelter is shown in Fig. 3.3, where the new (grey) budget line under the increased price is steeper than the original (black) budget line. Recall that the slope of the budget line is influenced by the prices of both goods as shown in Equation 3.8. Knowing this we automatically expect that the slope of the budget line must change. But how exactly will it change? Recall that the intercept on the axis is simply the income divided by the individual prices. Since the price of food has remained unchanged, the vertical intercept is untouched.

However, what has changed is the price of shelter, and so the horizontal intercept changes as well. Since we know that $p_{S(NEW)} > p_{S(OLD)}$, we deduce that $M/p_{S(NEW)} < M/p_{S(OLD)}$. This simply means that the number of units of shelter that we could buy, if we devoted all of our income to it, shrinks. This is what you would expect when the price of a good rises.

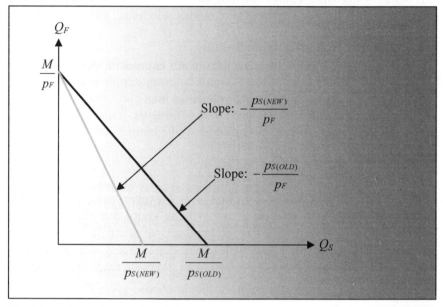

Fig. 3.3. A change in the price of shelter from $p_{S(OLD)}$ to $p_{S(NEW)}$ results in a change of the slope of the budget line making it steeper

In general terms, an increase in price will result in the budget line rotating around the intercept of the axis pertaining to that good which does not change in price. Should the price of both commodities change, then there would be two new intercepts and the net effect of the rotation (clockwise or anti-clockwise) would be ambiguous. If both goods changed in equal proportions, e.g. both increased by, say, 10%, then there would be a parallel **shift** in the curve. Note that such a shift would also occur if income changed.

3.5.4 Multiple Goods

In our analysis we have assumed so far that consumers choose between two goods. You may have already criticised this assumption in the process of working through this chapter. Of course, in reality, consumers will not just consume food and shelter. They will consume hundreds if not thousands of individual items in addition to food and shelter over a given time period.

In order to visualise the existence of more than 2 goods without using multiple dimensions, we may analyse *one good* vis-à-vis *all others*. How does this work? Rather than using food and shelter we can simply look at the affordability of food vis-à-vis shelter, movies, clothing, and in fact everything else consumed.

This amalgamation of goods is known as the **composite good**. The composite good is defined as *the consumption of all goods other than X*, where *X* is a single good used in the analysis such as food[7].

3.6 The Utility Function

So far, our discussion has taken us to understand what bundles are. We have also developed tools to show these on a graph, and with the help of the budget line we are also able to show which bundles are affordable and which ones are not. However, this is not yet entirely satisfying as it does not give us a deep insight into the decision-making processes of the consumer. In order to make our analysis more interesting, we want to be able to find out which bundles consumers *should* choose given their individual preferences.

Assumptions About Consumer Preference
Before we go any further at this point, we must qualify the term "preference" a bit further. Economists make four assumptions about consumer preferences which are quite intuitive. Firstly, the **completeness** assumption states that when faced with two different bundles, a consumer must *always* be able to state which bundle she prefers over another. She simply cannot have no opinion about her preferences. Secondly, **more is better**. This assumption is implicit in the definition of a good. A bundle consisting of more of both goods or simply of more of one good and at least as much of the other will *always* be better than the original bundle.

---

[7] The definition may seem strange at first as we refer to the composite good as *a* "good". If we assume that of, say, £1000 income per month we buy 10 units of food at £10 each, and the remaining £900 on, say, going out, clothing, books and shelter, the meaning of the composite good becomes clearer. "All consumption of goods other than food" is here simply the amalgamation of the named goods. And so under this definition we would have bought 10 units of food and one unit of the composite good while the respective prices of each good are £10 and £900.

Thirdly, the **transitivity** assumption states that when a consumer prefers some bundle A to some other bundle B but also prefers C to A, it must follow that the consumer also favours C over B. If you prefer a homemade burger to fast food burger, and you prefer lobster over a homemade burger then it would be absurd to think that you would prefer a fast food burger over lobster. For this reason, transitivity is sometimes also referred to as rationality. The fourth assumption is that **consumers prefer combinations of goods**. Since this is less obvious than the other three assumptions, we will validate this assumption intuitively in this section by working through an example.

Back to the Intuition
While in theory it is simple to say that a consumer must be able to choose between any two bundles, how would we go about this in reality? Let us reuse our bundles from before: bundle 1 comprising 8 units of food and 6 units of shelter and bundle 2 comprising 6 units of food and 12 units of shelter. Ignoring the fact that one of these bundles was previously not affordable given the income level M, which one of these bundles would you choose solely based on the fact that you want to maximise your utility? While you would know that you would always prefer 3 pizzas to 2 pizzas or a large flat to a small flat, or even a bundle consisting of 3 pizzas *and* a large flat to one consisting of 2 pizzas and a small flat, bundles 1 and 2 cause us a little more trouble. From the completeness assumption we know that the consumer must have some preference between the bundles but how is this preference arrived at?

3.6.1 Introducing the Utility Function

In order to answer the question of which bundle is better, we need exact utilities for each good. Using the intuition that we developed in Section 3.3, let us assume that the utility derived from the consumption of each unit of food is equal to 10, whereas the utility derived from the consumption of each unit of shelter is 8. Hence, the utility from bundle 1 would be:

$$U_1 = 10Q_F + 8Q_S \tag{3.9}$$

$$U_1 = 8 \cdot 10 + 6 \cdot 8 = 128$$

Similarly, the utility from bundle 2 would be:

$$U_2 = 6 \cdot 10 + 12 \cdot 8 = 156 \tag{3.10}$$

As we can see, the utility of bundle 2 exceeds the utility of bundle 1. We have therefore solved the problem of which bundle the consumer should choose with relative ease by using **utility functions**. But what is a utility function in the first place? As discussed in Section 1.7.1, a function is like a machine that is fed with one thing (the independent variable) and spits out another (the dependent variable). Here the dependent variable is the utility derived from consumption, while the independent variables are the numbers of units of food and shelter consumed. So are we done now?

Unfortunately the answer is no, because the above analysis assumes that the utilities derived from units of food and shelter are constant irrespective of the number of units previously consumed. This is not a realistic assumption, as we will see in the following subsection.

3.6.2 Marginal Utility — A Framework for Improving the Utility Function

A Diversion Without a Loss in Focus
This subsection may at first seem to take us further away from our quest of working with the utility function. However, we ask you to be patient and to let us explain the principle of marginal utility to you first. Once this is completed, there is an important insight as to how we can improve the utility function.

Introducing the Concept
As you know, in economics we are often interested not only in the entire benefit an agent derives, but also in the amount of benefit the agent derives on the margin. In the context of the consumer and his utility, we are interested in the change of total utility resulting from a one-unit change in the number of units consumed. This change in total utility is known as **marginal utility**. For example, a question may be: "by how much does the consumer's utility increase when he consumes 12 instead of 11 units of food?" The increase in total utility is then the marginal utility.

The definition of marginal utility should sound familiar. A change in one variable resulting from a change in another reminds us of the concept of the derivative. And this is precisely what the marginal utility is: the derivative of the utility function, with respect to that good the quantity consumed of which is altered. Therefore, we require the utility function in order to calculate marginal utility. In general, the marginal utility of good 1 MU_1 of a consumption bundle consisting of some quantities of good 1 Q_1 and good 2 Q_2 is denoted as:

$$MU_1 = \frac{\partial U(Q_1, Q_2)}{\partial Q_1} \qquad (3.11)$$

Now let us return to our aim of studying the utility function. Our hypothesis was that a utility function of the kind shown in Equation 3.9 is unrealistic, as every additional unit of food would yield the same increase in utility. In other words, the marginal utility would be constant. That this is the case with Equation 3.9 can be verified mathematically. If we take the partial derivative of Equation 3.9 with regards to Q_F, we get 10. This is the marginal utility of food, i.e. that additional amount of utility derived from an additional unit of food consumed. Since there are no variables included in the derivative, we know that this it is constant. Let us think about this for a second.

The marginal utility is the change in total utility resulting from a one-unit change in quantity. Alternatively, the marginal utility can be defined as the partial derivative of the utility function with respect to the quantity consumed of one good.

Diminishing Marginal Utility

If the marginal utility of food really was constant, then the first pizza in one month, for example, would give you exactly the same utility as the tenth or hundredth pizza. We argue that this is unrealistic and show this to be true in the following scenario.

If you had no food whatsoever and we offered you one pizza, it is likely that this first pizza would yield an amazing utility for you as you would be quite hungry not having *any* food. If you already had one pizza today, how much utility would you gain from the second, third or fourth? Chances are that each additional pizza would yield a diminishing amount of additional utility as you simply aren't that hungry any more after you have already had some food. And this brings us to the concept of **diminishing marginal utility**. Diminishing marginal utility simply means that with an increase in the consumption of a good, total utility keeps increasing but at a decreasing rate.

From now on, we shall assume that *all* goods that are consumed exhibit some sort of diminishing marginal utility. To account for the existence of diminishing marginal utility in the utility function, the exponent on the variable pertaining to the good(s) (i.e. Q_F and Q_S in our case) *must be smaller than 1* (but larger than zero[8]). You will see why the exponent must be smaller than 1 when we try it out. Let us take Equation 3.9 again and put exponents of 1/2 instead of 1 on Q_F and Q_S:

$$U(Q_F, Q_S) = 10Q_F^{1/2} + 8Q_S^{1/2} \qquad (3.12)$$

Let us now calculate the marginal utility of food by calculating the partial derivative of Equation 3.12 with respect to Q_F. This is denoted as MU_F, and so:

$$MU_F = 5Q_F^{-1/2} \qquad (3.13)$$

What is most interesting to us in Equation 3.13 is the exponent on Q_F, which is $-1/2$. Its significance can be shown by plugging in three randomly chosen numbers for Q_F. If Q_F is equal to 1, the marginal utility of food MU_F will be equal to 5; if Q_F is equal to 2, MU_F will be roughly equal to 3.54; and if Q_F is equal to 3, MU_F will be roughly equal to 2.89.

As you can see, the larger Q_F is, the smaller MU_F will be — the definition of diminishing marginal utility. The rate at which total utility is increasing from an increase in food is decreasing — or, in other words, it is increasing but at a decreasing rate. Hence, we were able to show what we wanted: we require an exponent smaller than 1 on the goods' variable in order to account for diminishing marginal utility, which we intuitively verified to be realistic. You may think that the utility function must surely be perfect now, but we are not quite there yet.

3.6.3 Finalising the Utility Function

The original utility function (Equation 3.9) was still somewhat unrealistic not only for the fact that it ignored diminishing marginal utility but also for another reason. The original function also implicitly assumed that the utility derived from the consumption of one good was entirely independent of the utility derived from the consumption of the second good, which was signified by the plus sign in the equation. In other words, if the coefficients

---

[8] If it was smaller than 0, then an increase in the consumption of some good would always result in a reduction in total utility which, as discussed in the previous footnote, is erroneous.

for both goods were equal, you would not care in which way an arbitrary collection of, say, 10 units would be allocated between the two goods. Bundles consisting of 10 units of food and 0 units of shelter, 5 of each, or only shelter and no food would, according to that function, all yield the same utility. Surely this cannot be the case[9]!

Say that you found yourself in a situation with 5 units of food and 5 units of shelter. If we offered you a flat twice the size in return for all your food, would you take us up on the offer? Or to put it differently: do you think you would be just as well off in both cases? Certainly not! We could offer you Buckingham Palace and you wouldn't trade it for all your food, as naturally you need food to live.

Unless we are dealing with the special case of perfect substitutes, the utility one derives from the consumption of a good is always linked to how much of the other good is consumed. Consumers simply prefer combinations of goods rather than extreme bundles. This was the fourth assumption that we made at the beginning of this section and now we have shown that it is intuitively correct. It's all about the right balance, isn't it?

Finally a Realistic Utility Function
So what is the implication of this newly gained knowledge for our utility function? It means that utilities of the two goods have to be multiplied rather than added. It is the only way of accounting for the fact that consumers prefer mixtures of goods. Let us thus replace the plus sign in Equation 3.9 by a multiplication sign:

$$U(Q_F, Q_S) = 80Q_F^{1/2} \cdot Q_S^{1/2} \tag{3.14}$$

So how is this more realistic? Let us try it out and see. Suppose you had no shelter and only food. You would be homeless, living in a box on the street with no bed, no shower and… nothing really, apart from food. The above utility function would assume that your utility would in fact be 0 (as we would plug in 0 for Q_S). This seems realistic as, living on the street, you are not likely to be at all happy, even if you had lots and lots of food[10].

---

[9] There is only one very special case in which such an assumption (i.e. plus sign in the utility function) is correct, and that is when the goods in question are perfect substitutes. Bundles consisting of 10 units of gas from Shell and none from Elf, 5 from each or 10 from Elf and none from Shell would indeed all yield constant utility.

[10] We assume that food cannot be traded for money or shelter.

Equally, if you had a magnificent mansion but no food whatsoever, we suspect that you would be quite unhappy. In fact, if your lack of food were prolonged, you would not just be unhappy, you would be dead! Being dead also gives you no utility (at least in this world), and so it is easy to see why you wouldn't exchange your small apartment with a fridge full of beans and toast with Buckingham Palace devoid of sustenance.

Let us again use a collection of 10 units that can be allocated by the consumer among the two goods as she sees fit. The different ways in which this can be done is represented in Table 3.1. It also shows the varying levels of utility that are attained from the different bundles using the utility function presented in Equation 3.14.

Table 3.1. Examples of combinations of food and shelter and their respective total utility

Units of food	Units of shelter	Total # of Units	Total Utility
0	10	10	0
1	9	10	240
2	8	10	320
3	7	10	366.6
4	6	10	391.9
5	5	10	400
6	4	10	391.9
7	3	10	366.6
8	2	10	320
9	1	10	240
10	0	10	0

What can be seen quite clearly from the table is what we have already developed intuitively. The largest total utility is reached when we evenly divide the allowance of total units of 10 among the two goods. As we have just confirmed, consumers want combinations of goods!

The Cobb–Douglas Utility Function
Equations like 3.14 are known as Cobb–Douglas utility functions. The term Cobb–Douglas might be most familiar from production (as you will learn in Chapter 5) but it also finds application in consumer theory. Its general form is:

$$U(Q_1, Q_2) = Q_1^{\alpha} \cdot Q_2^{\beta} \tag{3.15}$$

where Q_1 and Q_2 are the quantities of the two goods, and α and β are exponents on the goods. Let us zero in on the latter. So far we know that due to diminishing marginal utility, which we assume to be present in all consumption processes, α and β should each be smaller than 1 (but larger than 0), but this is not all that we can take away from the Cobb–Douglas utility function.

The Sum of α and β Always Equals 1

The sum of the exponents is also critical. α and β always have to be equal to 1[11]. There is a very good practical reason for this. In Equation 3.14 exponents were 1/2 each, and when we did our calculations we found out that equally dividing our allocation of ten units between the two goods yielded the highest utility. The fact that the proportion by which the 10 units were divided up and the exponents in Equation 3.14 are equal to each other (i.e. 1/2) is no coincidence. If, say, the exponents on Q_F and Q_S in Equation 3.14 were 1/4 and 3/4 respectively, the best combination of goods would have been to consume 2.5 (i.e. 1/4 of 10) units of food and 7.5 (i.e. 3/4 of 10) units of shelter. As you can see, when α and β are equal to 1, you can easily determine what portion of the utility maximising bundle should consist of good Q_1, and what portion should consist of Q_2[12].

Monotonic Transformation

If the exponents on Q_1 and Q_2 were, say, 12 and 18, it would be impossible to see at the first glance which proportion of the bundle should consist of each good. But even if the Cobb–Douglas function did exhibit such exponents, there is no need to despair! We can use a trick known as **monotonic transformation**. In general, the term refers to the act of scaling a set of numbers upwards or downwards using one or more mathematical operations such as multiplication or division.

In our case, we would like to scale α and β down so that their sum is equal to 1. We simply add both of them (which is 30) to find a common denominator. Now we take both sides of the equation to the power of 1/30, which results in α being equal to 2/5 and β being equal to 3/5, and there we go: we can tell straight away what proportion of each good the bundle should consist of in order to maximise the agent's utility.

---

[11] Note that the Cobb–Douglas production function (as opposed to the utility function) is governed by different rules. For the production function, the sum of the exponents is only equal to 1 when returns to scale are constant.

[12] Note that being able to tell the proportions in the bundle at the first glance only works when the prices are equal. In Section 3.8, we will look at a case in which exponents are equal but prices are not.

You might critically add that $U(Q_1, Q_2) = Q_1^{12} \cdot Q_2^{18}$ is not the same as $U(Q_1, Q_2) = Q_1^{2/5} \cdot Q_2^{3/5}$, as $U(Q_1, Q_2)^{1/30} = Q_1^{2/5} \cdot Q_2^{3/5}$. You are of course correct, but in practical terms it makes no difference. Why?

Well, let us think about utility a little more abstractly. Utility as a number is actually meaningless. Whether it was 10, 100 or 1,000 does not give us any insight whatsoever *unless* we can compare it with another utility that is smaller or bigger than the one we are looking at. Such a comparison is known as an ordinal ranking.

Therefore, if we change the entire function as we have done above, the comparison between two sets of utilities remains the same, i.e. the ordinal ranking is unchanged. No matter by how much we scale the equation up or down, the preferences between 2 budgets of, say, (8,12) and (6,13) remains the same. Thus, we can happily change $U(Q_1, Q_2) = Q_1^{12} \cdot Q_2^{18}$ to $U(Q_1, Q_2) = Q_1^{2/5} \cdot Q_2^{3/5}$, without changing the rankings of the bundles. Doing so will change the value of the utilities, but since we are interested only in comparing the rankings of the utilities, this is not a problem. We are not able or interested in saying that a consumer would, for example, be twice as well off with bundle 1 than with bundle 2.

Coefficients — The "Perfect" Utility Function
For precisely the same reason (i.e. the focus on ordinal rankings), coefficients in the Cobb–Douglas function are also unnecessary and can therefore be excluded altogether[13].

After having accounted for diminishing marginal utility, the fact that consumers prefer combinations of goods, and applying monotonic transformation (by dividing by 80), we have found a "perfect" utility function in the Cobb–Douglas form:

$$U(Q_F, Q_S) = Q_F^{1/2} \cdot Q_S^{1/2} \tag{3.16}$$

Coefficients and Perfect Substitutes
Although the coefficient will always be 1 in the Cobb–Douglas form of the utility function, in the case of perfect substitutes coefficients other than 1 may be used. Let us take the example of Shell and Elf petrol again. A litre of petrol from Shell gives us the same utility as a litre of petrol from Elf.

---

[13] Equations can be scaled up or down by means of a monotonic transformation not only by changes in exponents but also by changing the coefficient. Equation 3.14 can be refined by dividing the right-hand side by 80.

No coefficients are required. But think of a case in which one thing is as good as another but not in the same proportion. To illustrate this example, let us assume that the units at Shell are measured in gallons whereas the units at Elf are measured in litres.

Clearly, one unit from one petrol station is *not* as good as petrol from the other, and so the utility function will have to be changed. In order for the utility function to be correct, we need to include a coefficient of 3.79 (the conversion rate between litres and gallons) in front of the variable pertaining to units of petrol consumed at Elf[14]. 3.79 litres of Elf petrol are as good as 1 gallon of Shell petrol.

3.7 Introducing Indifference Curves

The concept of the indifference curve is perhaps the most important principle that you should take away from this chapter, and indeed from consumer theory. What we have seen in Table 3.1 is that utility varies with different combinations of goods. We have also had a look at a general Cobb–Douglas utility function as shown in Equation 3.15, and a specific example of it is our final, "perfect" utility function represented by Equation 3.16.

What we can actually do now is to slightly rewrite the Cobb–Douglas utility function so that the consumer's preferences can be drawn in commodity space. Remember, commodity space is simply the name of the area that a graph with two goods on its axes encompasses.

If you have a look at Equation 3.16, you might have trouble imagining how you would be able to draw anything in a two-dimensional space. After all, there are three variables: the utility $U(Q_S, Q_F)$, the amount of shelter Q_S, and the amount of food Q_F. In order to be able to represent such a function two-dimensionally, we have to pick a constant for one of these three variables. Since we already mentioned that we want to use commodity space, none of the two goods must be constant, and so the only thing that we can do is to pick a constant $\bar{U}$ for the utility. We therefore rewrite our utility function slightly:

$$\bar{U} = Q_1{}^{\alpha} \cdot Q_2{}^{\beta} \tag{3.17}$$

---

[14] Alternatively, one may include a coefficient of 1/3.79 in front of the variable reserved for the units of Shell petrol, but doing so would be less elegant.

If we assume that good 1 is shown on the vertical axis, we would then solve for Q_1^α which is:

$$Q_1^\alpha = \frac{\bar{U}}{Q_2^\beta} \tag{3.18}$$

In order to account for the exponent, we simply take both sides to the power of $1/\alpha$, and we have the general Cobb–Douglas formula solved for Q_1:

$$Q_1 = (\frac{\bar{U}}{Q_2^\beta})^{1/\alpha} \tag{3.19}$$

Since the last two steps might have been a little bit abstract, let's simply try this out with the example of Equation 3.16. Firstly, since Q_F and Q_S both have an exponent of 1/2, we square both sides so that we get:

$$\bar{U}^2 = Q_F \cdot Q_S \tag{3.20}$$

When solved for Q_F, this gives:

$$Q_F = \frac{\bar{U}^2}{Q_S} \tag{3.21}$$

Alternatively, we could have used Equation 3.19 and plugged in 1/2 for α and β, which would have yielded the same as Equation 3.21. Now, in order for us to be able to graph this function we need a value for $\bar{U}$, so let us pick 1 to keep things simple:

$$Q_F = \frac{1}{Q_S} \tag{3.22}$$

Whenever the independent variable is at the bottom of a fraction, as is the case in Equation 3.21, we will get a convex curve[15]. Using Equation 3.22, we can now finally represent the utility function graphically, as is done in Fig. 3.4. The resulting curve with the constant utility in commodity space is known as an **indifference curve**. Most indifference curves will look similar to that shown in Fig. 3.4. Such convex indifference curves are often referred to as "well-behaved" indifference curves as indifference curves can have various shapes. The two relatively common special cases of perfect substitutes and perfect complements are analysed in Section 3.9.

---

[15] When a function is convex we mean that is curved or bulging outwards. It is the mathematical way of expressing the assumption that consumers prefer combinations of goods rather than extreme bundles.

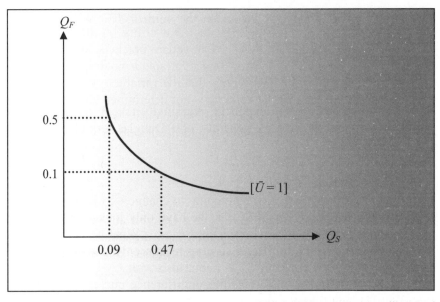

Fig. 3.4. An indifference curve in commodity space with a constant exogenous utility equal to 1

The Meaning of the Indifference Curve

Let us come back to understanding what we learn from an indifference curve in the first place. The indifference curve is a vital concept, as it passes through *all possible consumption bundles for which utility is equal to some constant level*. In Fig. 3.4 this constant utility level is $\bar{U} = 1$. Although we have only explicitly shown two bundles, the collection of consumption bundles that lie on the indifference curve is infinite, because commodity space includes an infinite number of consumption bundles.

Knowing that the utility on any point on the indifference curve is constant, it is not hard to find out why this graphical representation of the consumer's utility is called an "indifference" curve in the first place. With regards to the utility the consumer derives, they will literally be *indifferent* between any of the consumption bundles lying on any given curve. A large house and a small amount of food may be just as good as lots of food and a small flat.

> An indifference curve is a convex function within commodity space representing an infinite collection of consumption bundles, all of which yield the same constant utility.

The Use of Square Brackets
One technical thing on the side: The fact that utility on the indifference curve is constant is signified by $\bar{U} = 1$ in square brackets. We use square brackets whenever we want to show that a variable is not implicitly changing within the graph or, in other words, that the variable is **exogenous**. Exogenous simply means that the variable is not determined within the graph but outside of it. A *slide* along the indifference curve will not change utility; only a *shift* would. Such a shift would occur only if we changed the level of utility $\bar{U}$.

Multiple Indifference Curves
Let us now do precisely that: we are going to change $\bar{U}$, which results in a shift in the indifference curve. So far, we have only looked at one single indifference curve for which we have used $\bar{U}_1 = 1$. What we can do now is to show the consumer's **indifference map** by not only drawing the indifference curve with a constant $\bar{U}_1 = 1$, but also with $\bar{U}_2 = 2$, and another curve with $\bar{U}_3 = 3$. The three resulting indifference curves are shown in Fig. 3.5. The indifference map is defined as a sample of a consumer's preferences. In this instance the indifference map consists of 3 indifference curves, each one of which constitutes an infinite collection of bundles all yielding the same constant utility.

> The indifference map is a collection of indifference curves and represents a sample of a consumer's preferences.

Higher Indifference Curves Mean More Utility
With an indifference map, we can now answer the question of which bundles would be preferred over others in a graphical way and not only mathematically. Specifically, any point that lies on the indifference curve with constant utility $\bar{U}_2 = 2$ will be preferred to all other points that lie closer to the origin (i.e. that lie below this indifference curve), including any point on the first indifference curve with the exogenous constant utility of $\bar{U}_1 = 1$. Remember, theoretically there are infinitely many indifference curves between the curves with utilities $\bar{U}_1 = 1$ and $\bar{U}_2 = 2$. All of these would yield less utility than the latter indifference curve. Generally, the further an indifference curve lies away from the origin, the higher the associated utility and the better the consumer is off.

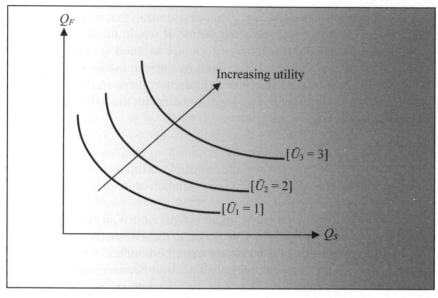

Fig. 3.5. A consumer's indifference map using $Q_F = \bar{U}^2/Q_S$ where the constant utilities $\bar{U}_1$, $\bar{U}_2$, $\bar{U}_3$ are equal to 1, 2 and 3, respectively

Rules of Indifference Curves
Let us examine the concept of the indifference curve a bit further. There are four rules of how indifference curves are drawn which are directly linked to the assumptions that we made about the consumer's preferences at the beginning of Section 3.6. In a way, the rules are a graphical translation of these prior assumptions.

Firstly, arising from the completeness assumption, *every possible combination of goods must have one, and only one, utility associated with it.* This means that you can draw an indifference curve through any possible bundle. As a result, the utility of any bundle must be comparable to the utility of any other bundle. It is therefore possible to graphically show sets of bundles that are preferred to any one specific bundle.

Secondly, arising from the more-is-better-assumption, *indifference curves are always downward sloping*[16]. If an indifference curve was not downward sloping, this would violate the definition of a good which says that more of a good is always preferred to less of a good. Picture an indiffer-

---

[16] There are some exceptions, such as the indifference curves for perfect substitutes, but in most ordinary instances this rule holds true.

ence curve that is shaped like a U. This would mean that there are pairs of bundles which would yield the same utility. It would mean, for example, that 5 units of shelter and 5 units of food are as good as, say, 5 units of food and 10 units of shelter. This cannot be correct, as more of a good is always better than less. Hence, the indifference curve must slope downwards, or to put it differently, the slope anywhere on the indifference curve must be negative.

Thirdly, arising from the transitivity assumption, *indifference curves must never cross each other*. If they did, multiple utilities would be present along the indifference curve, which is in violation of its definition.

Fourthly, and as we have already found out previously, *as we move along the curve it becomes less steep*. This is due to the assumption that consumers prefer combinations of goods over extreme bundles, which is mathematically accounted for by a multiplication sign between individual utilities in the utility function. This rule is also known as the convexity property.

3.8 The Marginal Rate of Substitution

The Purpose of this Section
In this section, we will talk about the slope of the indifference curve. We are interested in this because in Section 3.9 we will calculate a consumer's optimal bundle *given her budget constraint.* As you will see, a bundle is optimal when the budget line and the indifference curve are tangent to each other. While we already know the slope of the budget line in principle, we still need to learn about the slope of the indifference curve — which is what this section deals with.

Previously, we discussed that the concept of diminishing marginal utility means that further increases in the consumption of a good yield ever smaller increases in total utility. This fact translates to the slope of the indifference curve becoming ever flatter as we slide along it (while it never crosses either of the axes). But exactly how is diminishing marginal utility connected to the slope?

Getting Started
Let us assume a specific bundle of food and shelter $B_1 = (10, 2)$. This bundle sits very close to the vertical axis as we can see in Fig. 3.6. Moreover,

this bundle also lies on an indifference curve with a constant utility of $\bar{U} \approx 4.58$, which was derived using the utility function introduced in Equation 3.16[17]. Since this specific bundle consists of a relatively large amount of food, one extra unit of food would only give us a small increase in total utility (small marginal utility) due to the principle of diminishing marginal utility. Not so for shelter. Compared to food, a one unit increase in shelter would give a large increase in total utility (large marginal utility) due to the fact that you possess very little shelter in comparative terms.

Giving Lots of Food for a Little More Shelter
Now let us assume that you slide down the indifference curve to a new bundle. Suppose that all you know is that you give up an amount of food $\Delta Q_F = 2$ and in return you get some amount of shelter ΔQ_S, which is unknown at this point. The amount of utility you lose from not having the food anymore is the marginal utility of food MU_F multiplied by ΔQ_F, while the amount of utility you gain from having more shelter is the marginal utility of shelter MU_S multiplied by ΔQ_S.

Recall the definition of the indifference curve: every point on it presents a bundle that yields the same utility. For this reason, the utility that you give up from the reduction in food must be equal to the utility that you gain from the increase in shelter. We can take this last sentence and put it into an equation. Note that we include a negative sign in front of the marginal utility of food to account for the fact that there is a reduction in total utility stemming from the reduction in the quantity of food consumed.

$$-MU_F \cdot \Delta Q_F = MU_S \cdot \Delta Q_S \qquad (3.23)$$

We know that the marginal utility of food is very low compared to the marginal utility of shelter. Since the left- and the right-hand side are equal in Equation 3.23, this imbalance must be corrected by the fact that ΔQ_S must be smaller than ΔQ_F. That this is true can very easily be verified by looking at Fig. 3.6.

---

[17] We simply plug 10 and 2 into the function.

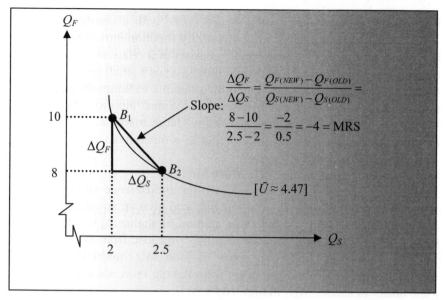

Fig. 3.6. The marginal rate of substitution MRS on an indifference curve shows us the rate at which the consumer has to give up one good in order to gain a unit of another while holding utility constant. Here it is the slope of the hypotenuse of the triangle formed using bundles B_1 and B_2

Due to the steep slope of the indifference curve in the examined area, the change in food (i.e. the vertical distance) is definitely much larger than the change in shelter (i.e. the horizontal distance). The change in shelter that lets the utility remain constant happens to be 0.5. And how do we know this? Since we know that the original bundle is $B_1 = (10, 2)$, that the new bundle is $B_2 = (8, Q_S)$ and that the utility for both bundles has to be the same (as they lie on the same indifference curve), we simply let the utility of the two bundles be equal to each other while including the unknown variable Q_S.

$$10^{1/2} \cdot 2^{1/2} = 8^{1/2} \cdot Q_S^{1/2} \tag{3.24}$$

When we multiply everything out and solve for Q_S we get 2.5. Hence, ΔQ_S is 0.5. This specific example has thus illustrated diminishing marginal utility in practice. In order to get only half a unit of shelter, the consumer was willing to give up 2 units of food because she already had a lot of food compared with shelter.

In this specific example, the consumer was willing, on the margin, to *substitute* 4 units of food for 1 unit of shelter. Hence the **marginal rate of**

substitution MRS is $-4/1$. This also happens to be the slope for the area that we examined in Fig. 3.6[18]. After having seen what it does, the MRS requires little additional clarification. It is simply the rate at which consumers are willing to give up some amount of one good in exchange for another while their utility stays constant, which happens to be the slope of the indifference curve. In our example the rate at which the consumer was willing to give up one good for another was $\Delta Q_F/\Delta Q_S$, and so we can write:

$$\frac{\Delta Q_F}{\Delta Q_S} = \text{MRS} \qquad (3.25)$$

At this point we can make even more connections. $\Delta Q_F/\Delta Q_F$ is not only the MRS but also something else. You will see what if you cross-multiply Equation 3.23. This gives:

$$-\frac{\text{MU}_S}{\text{MU}_F} = \frac{\Delta Q_F}{\Delta Q_S} \qquad (3.26)$$

Equation 3.26 shows us that the (negative) ratio of the marginal utilities is equal to the inverse ratio of the changes in their quantities. So, if we gained a lot of food, and lost a little shelter, we would expect that the marginal utility of food was small compared to the marginal utility of shelter. This has to be the case, as both bundles are located on the same indifference curve. This formula is also interesting for another reason. It will later help us to find the optimal bundle to maximise the consumer's utility. As we will soon see, Equation 3.26 can be used as the indifference curve's derivative with a minor adjustment.

As a note on the side, it must not be forgotten that the subscripts on the two sides of the equation are flipped around! Pulling everything we have learned together, we can write one long final equation:

$$-\frac{\text{MU}_S}{\text{MU}_F} = \frac{Q_{F(OLD)} - Q_{F(NEW)}}{Q_{S(OLD)} - Q_{S(NEW)}} = \frac{\Delta Q_F}{\Delta Q_S} = \text{MRS} \qquad (3.27)$$

Depending on the usage area, parts of this equation can be deleted as appropriate. The subscripts *OLD* and *NEW* refer to the quantity of each good before and after a slide along the indifference curve, as shown in Fig. 3.6.

---

[18] Note that this is not the same as the slope on a single point.

3.9 Finding Optimal Bundles Given Budget Constraints

Our analysis up to this point has taken us quite far. Firstly, we looked at different bundles, their affordability and the related budget constraints. Secondly, we learned about the indifference curve, how it can be used to show preferred sets of bundles, and how to work with its slope.

As foreshadowed at the beginning of Section 3.8, our quest at this instance is to pull together some of the tools that we have acquired thus far. Our goal is to show the budget line and the indifference curve on the same graph. Until now we have been able to say which bundles consumers prefer over others, but what we have completely ignored until now (and which was previously discussed in isolation) is the price of goods and the consumer's income.

The Budget Line
Fig. 3.7 shows us the combination of indifference curve and budget line. As a reminder, the budget line has a slope of the negative of the relative prices of shelter and food, which is $-p_S/p_F$, while vertical and horizontal intercepts are the income M divided by p_F and p_S respectively. Also recall that on any point on the budget line, the following equation will hold true:

$$M = p_F \cdot Q_F + p_S \cdot Q_S \qquad (3.28)$$

Indifference Curve
Now, let us focus on the indifference curve. We will reuse our utility function 3.16 from before, which was $U(Q_F, Q_S) = Q_F^{1/2} \cdot Q_S^{1/2}$. When solved for Q_F, this is:

$$Q_F = \frac{\bar{U}^2}{Q_S} \qquad (3.29)$$

Solving by Intuition
Before coming back to the maths, let us discuss the intuition of what we are trying to do. If you are a rational person, you are not fond of wasting money, and so it is your goal to get the "most bang for the buck", i.e. you want to use your income most effectively. In our context this means that you want to derive the highest utility possible given the limited income M you have at your disposal.

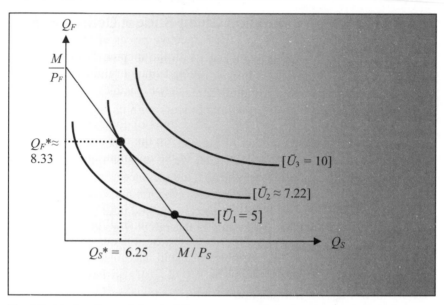

Fig. 3.7. A budget line and three indifference curves. Given the consumer's preferences and the budget line, the optimal bundle consists of roughly 8.33 units of food and 6.25 units of shelter. The associated utility of this bundle is about 7.22

Let's try to understand this graphically. We will assume that you do not want to save any of your income so you will want to choose a bundle that is on the budget line, implying that the entire income is used for consumption. You can therefore choose any bundle, including the corners of M/p_F and M/p_S. But will you be equally well off choosing any point on the budget line? The answer is no, because in all but one case there are other, higher indifference curves that touch the budget line and which yield higher utilities.

In order to find the highest utility given our income and respective prices of goods, we start from the lowest of the indifference curves in Fig. 3.8. It cuts through the budget constraint at some point relatively close to the horizontal axis. Our utility for that specific consumption bundle is $\bar{U}_1 = 5$. Is this the best we can do? No, because by jumping to one of the infinitely many higher indifference curves we will have more utility but can still afford the bundle as long as it cuts through the budget line.

You continue this rationale of jumping to higher indifference curves until you hit that *one* indifference curve that just about barely touches the budget line. This is where the two are tangent to each other. The consequence is that you have found the highest possible utility you can derive from a given level of income and the respective prices of the two goods. You cannot gain more utility than that. With the income M that we have available and from which we draw the budget line, an indifference curve with a constant utility $\bar{U}_X > \bar{U}_2$ including $\bar{U}_3$ is not feasible.

The optimal bundle consists of $Q_F{}^* = 25/3$ units of food and $Q_S{}^* = 6.25$ units of shelter. Remember, the asterisks refer to the fact that these are optimal quantities. How we actually arrived at the optimum quantities is the focus of the remainder of this section.

Defining the Problem Mathematically
Let us pick specific values for p_F, p_S and M. These shall be 6, 8 and 100, respectively. Q_F and Q_S remain undefined because it is our goal to find the optimum values for these two variables that will maximise the consumer's utility $U(Q_F, Q_S)$. Implicitly therefore, $U(Q_F, Q_S)$ also has no value assigned to it yet.

Defining the Slope of the Indifference Curve
Given the prices of the two commodities, an income, and a given utility function, which optimal bundle consisting of $Q_F{}^*$ and $Q_S{}^*$ should the consumer choose? We just found intuitively that this will be the case where budget line and indifference curve are tangent to each other. At the point of tangency their gradients are equal. We know the gradient of the budget line is $-p_S/p_F$, which is equal to $-4/3$. The gradient of the indifference curve will, in our example, be the derivative of:

$$Q_F(Q_S) = \frac{U(Q_F, Q_S)}{Q_S} \qquad (3.30)$$

Equation 3.30 is different from Equation 3.29 as $\bar{U}$ has been replaced by $U(Q_F, Q_S)$, which is the more general form. Also note that it is necessary to write Q_F as a function of Q_S (i.e. $Q_F(Q_S)$) on the left-hand side, as on the right-hand side utility is dependent on Q_F and Q_S. Equation 3.30 is a bit of an obstacle for us. While in principle it is not hard to find a partial derivative of a function, what we are asked to do here is to find a derivative of a function in which another function is embedded. This could get quite messy!

Leaning on Previous Insight
But hang on a second, we have already discussed the slope of the indifference curve. Let us go back in our minds to Section 3.7, in which we dealt

with the slope of the indifference curve. We recall that this was $\Delta Q_F / \Delta Q_S$, which was equal to the marginal utility of shelter and the marginal utility of food, respectively, as expressed in Equation 3.26. This is repeated here again for the sake of convenience:

$$-\frac{MU_S}{MU_F} = \frac{\Delta Q_F}{\Delta Q_S} \qquad (3.31)$$

The Δs signify the fact that the term shows us the slope for an area. Let us make the Δs infinitesimal so that we can calculate the slope for one specific point[19], which is necessary for finding the tangent to the budget line. Hence, we can rewrite the previous equation where the Δs have been replaced with ds. Let us also switch the left- and right-hand sides, as the focus of the discussion has changed:

$$\frac{dQ_F}{dQ_S} = -\frac{MU_S}{MU_F} \qquad (3.32)$$

Now, as a final step, you may remember the definition of marginal utility in mathematical terms. It is simply the derivative of the utility function with regards to the relevant good. And so we arrive at our final equation to show us the slope of the indifference curve in general terms:

$$\frac{dQ_F}{dQ_S} = -\frac{\partial U(Q_F, Q_S)/\partial Q_S}{\partial U(Q_F, Q_S)/\partial Q_F} \qquad (3.33)$$

In plain words, Equation 3.33 says that the gradient of the indifference curve is the negative of the partial derivative of the utility function, with respect to the good on the horizontal axis divided by the partial derivative of the utility function, with respect to the good on the vertical axis. That is it.

Solving the Problem Mathematically
In our case the utility function was $U(Q_F, Q_S) = Q_F^{1/2} \cdot Q_S^{1/2}$, and so the slope of the generic indifference curve pertaining to that utility function is:

---

[19] We omit the mathematical treatment of the formula, which would be rather lengthy without giving additional economic insight. If curiosity arises, the mathematical steps are well explained in Varian's *Intermediate Microeconomics*, sixth edition, in the appendix of Chapter 4.

$$\frac{dQ_F}{dQ_S} = -\frac{(1/2)\cdot Q_S^{-1/2} Q_F^{1/2}}{(1/2)\cdot Q_S^{-1/2} Q_F^{1/2}} \qquad (3.34)$$

$$\frac{dQ_F}{dQ_S} = -\frac{Q_S^{-1/2}\cdot Q_F^{1/2}}{Q_S^{-1/2}\cdot Q_F^{1/2}}$$

$$\frac{dQ_F}{dQ_S} = -\frac{Q_F}{Q_S}$$

Now, in order to find the point of the optimal bundle, we set the derivative of the indifference curve (i.e. the last line of Equation 3.34) equal to the gradient of the budget line. This gradient is in principle given by Equation 3.8. As we know from the prices given in our specific example, it is equal to −4/3. We set the gradient of the budget line and the derivative of the utility function equal as this resulting equality holds at the point of tangency. This helps us to identify the quantities of each good:

$$-\frac{Q_F\,*}{Q_S\,*} = -\frac{4}{3} \qquad (3.35)$$

$$\frac{Q_F\,*}{Q_S\,*} = \frac{4}{3}$$

$$Q_F* = \frac{4}{3}Q_S\,*$$

Therefore, optimally we will want to buy 4/3 times as many units of food as shelter. This much, we now know. What we don't know, however, is how many units in total we will buy, and not surprisingly this has to do with our income M. Hence, we use the equation used to draw the budget line and fit in the optimal quantities of the two goods. We can do this because we know that the formula holds true anywhere on the budget line, including the point at which it is tangent to the indifference curve. And so, we state that:

$$100 = 6Q_F* + 8Q_S* \qquad (3.36)$$

Now we plug the last line of Equation 3.35 into Equation 3.36, which gives us the optimal number of units of shelter to consume:

$$100 = 6 \cdot \frac{4}{3}Q_S* + Q_{S*} \qquad (3.37)$$

$$100 = 16Q_S*$$

$$Q_S^* = 6.25$$

Putting this solution into the last line of Equation 3.35, we also find the optimal number of units of food that are consumed:

$$Q_F^* = \frac{4}{3} \cdot 6.25 \qquad (3.38)$$

$$Q_F^* = \frac{25}{3} \approx 8.33$$

Therefore, we found that we should optimally buy 6.25 units of shelter and about 8.33 units of food in order to gain the most utility from our income of £100.

Summary

Summarising what we have learned in this section, we can state that two conditions hold true in order for the consumer to derive a maximum utility $\bar{U}$ from the consumption of goods 1 and 2. Firstly,

$$\frac{\partial U(Q_1, Q_2)/\partial Q_2}{\partial U(Q_1, Q_2)/\partial Q_1} = \frac{p_1}{p_2} \qquad (3.39)$$

must hold. This is simply saying that the budget line and indifference curve have to be tangent to each other. Moreover, the budget has to be entirely devoted to consumption, which is expressed as:

$$M = p_1 \cdot Q_1 + p_2 \cdot Q_2 \qquad (3.40)$$

Comment

Thinking about it, what we found is quite interesting. Given one specific consumer's preferences, their income, and prices of two goods, we can determine how much of each good the consumer will want to buy. Of course, no consumer (except perhaps some very keen economists) would think about their own consumption in this elaborate way, but it is nonetheless a calculation that happens implicitly in everyday life as individuals think about the choices they make regarding their consumption.

Proportions of Goods, Exponents, and Prices

In Section 3.6, we asserted that as long as exponents α and β of the general Cobb–Douglas utility function add up to 1, one would be able to read off what proportion of the bundle would consist of each good. As you may have noticed, in the above example, the exponents were 1/2 each, yet 4/3 times as much food is consumed as shelter in optimality. The reason for this is the price of the two goods. Shelter is 4/3 times as expensive as food. Hence, the price influences the proportions with which the two goods are consumed. Only when prices are equal can we read off the proportions with which each good is consumed from exponents at the first glance.

3.10 Two Special Indifference Curves

To finish our discussion of this chapter, let us look at two special cases in which the indifference curve looks different to what we are used to. These special cases arise when we are dealing with perfect substitutes or perfect complements.

3.10.1 Perfect Substitutes

At the end of Section 3.6, we discussed perfect substitutes and explained that the utility function includes an addition rather than a multiplication of individual utilities. Since the example was already discussed in sufficient detail, we limit ourselves to the technical analysis. Remember how 3.79 litres of Elf petrol were as good as 1 gallon of Shell petrol? Therefore, our utility function is:

$$U(Q_E, Q_S) = Q_S + 3.79 Q_E \qquad (3.41)$$

Let us now solve for the good on the vertical axis (Elf petrol):

$$Q_E = \bar{U} - 3.79 Q_E \qquad (3.42)$$

Now we substitute constant utilities of $\bar{U}_1 = 1$ and $\bar{U}_2 = 2$ into Equation 3.42 so that we can draw two indifference curves, which we can see in the right-hand panel of Fig. 3.8. The consumer is as well off at any point on each line as on any other, including the intercepts. Applying the concept of using the optimal bundles as learned in Section 3.8, one of three things could happen. If the budget line is steeper than the indifference curve, the consumer will only want Elf petrol; if it is flatter, the consumer will only want Shell petrol; and if it is of the same gradient as the indifference curve, the consumer is equally happy with any bundle lying on the indifference curve, including the intercepts. The first two instances are known as **corner solutions**.

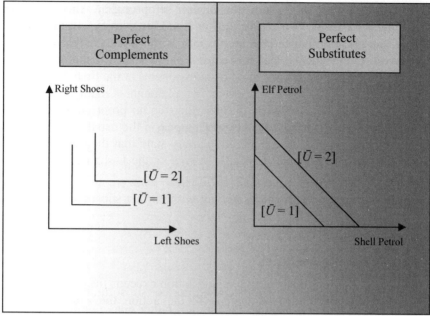

Fig. 3.8. Indifference curves for perfect complements and perfect substitutes are L-shaped and straight lined, respectively

3.10.2 Perfect Complements

When we are dealing with perfect complements, the argument about the preferences of consumers regarding combinations of goods is different. Here, the combination is all important. Before, we go into the analysis of the indifference curves, let us firstly discuss what is meant by a perfect complement.

As we know from Chapter 2, perfect complements are goods that *can only be consumed together*. Right and left shoes are a commonly stated example, as they are only produced in pairs and hence *only* consumed as a pairs. The rate at which perfect complements are consumed need not necessarily be 1:1, however. For the sale of a tuxedo, for example, given that it is sold as a set, shoes and trousers may be a perfect complements, at a rate of 2:1.

How can we now translate perfect complements into our indifference curve framework? If you have one right shoe and one left shoe you gain some utility $\bar{U}_1$. If, however, we were to give you two right shoes and only one left shoe, it is not very likely you would be any better off than before. Hence, the additional right shoe yields no extra utility whatsoever. It is, essentially, useless. It is like that Alanis Morissette song in which the lyrics go: "It's like 10,000 spoons when all you need is a knife." In order to be placed on a higher indifference curve, goods must be consumed in **fixed proportions.** This can be seen in the left-hand panel of Fig. 3.8.

Finding the optimal bundle for perfect complements is mathematically (in principle, at least) problematic because there is no point on an L-shaped curve which is tangent to a budget line shaped in the usual way. We shall not let this anomaly bug us here, and simply state that the optimal bundle lies where the budget line *touches* the corner of the L-shaped indifference curve.

3.11 Chapter Summary

Cost–Benefit Analysis
- Generally, if the benefit of some action exceeds the cost (both implicit and explicit) associated with that action, the action should be undertaken, given there is no competing activity which would yield a higher net benefit.
- Cost–benefit analysis applies both to consumers and to firms. This type of analysis is used by agents in an implicit way all the time, whether they are conscious of it or not.

Explicit Cost vs. Implicit Cost
- An explicit cost is some £-amount that the agent pays out of their pocket.
- An implicit cost is a cost associated with an action that is not necessarily monetary. Frequently, an implicit cost of an action is the opportunity cost of performing that action.
- An opportunity cost is a foregone benefit of not being able to engage in a different action as a result of participating in the first action.
- The reservation price is that amount of money one would have to be given in order to be indifferent between two activities.
- We use the concept of monetary equivalent to measure utility. It is that amount of money one would have to be paid not to engage in a certain activity (assuming that one would not derive any utility from not doing so).
- In order to make economically sound decisions, implicit and explicit costs must be taken into account alike.

Sunk Cost
- A sunk cost is a type of cost that has already been incurred and which cannot be changed by making choices.
- Since the sunk cost cannot be changed, it should never enter an agent's decision-making process.

Consumption Bundles
- A consumption bundle is a basket filled with quantities of two specific goods.

Budget Constraint and Line
- A budget is the amount of money an agent has available over a certain period of time.
- A budget constraint is the collection of all affordable bundles of the consumer given a certain income M.
- Graphically, the budget constraint is the area encompassed by the axis of commodity space and the budget line.
- The budget line is the collection of consumption bundles that are just affordable given a certain income M of the consumer.
- The intercepts of the budget line on each axis is the income divided by the price of the good on that axis.
- The slope of this line is the negative of the price on the horizontal axis divided by the price of the good on the vertical axis.

Changes in Price
- An increase in price will cause the budget line to rotate around the intercept of the axis pertaining to that good which does not change in price.
- If both goods change in price, the rotation (i.e. clockwise or anti-clockwise) is ambiguous.
- If both goods change in price by an equal amount, the budget line shifts parallel to the original budget line.
- A change in income has the same effect.

Composite Good
- The composite good is defined as the *consumption of all goods other than* X, whereby X is a single good used in the analysis such as food.
- The definition of the composite good entails that only one unit of this "good" is consumed.

Utility Functions

- A utility function for a consumer is an equation that takes into account their preferences about specific goods. By plugging in values for the number of units of each good consumed, we can calculate the total utility a consumer derives from a specific consumption bundle.
- When dealing with perfect substitutes, individual utilities of both goods are simply added.
- In all other cases, they are multiplied. Utility functions exhibiting this feature are known as the Cobb–Douglas utility functions.
- A realistic utility function requires the exponent on the variable(s) pertaining to each good to be less than 1, reflecting diminishing marginal utility of each good.
- We assume that all goods exhibit diminishing marginal utility because, intuitively, equal increases in the consumption of a good yield ever smaller increases in total utility.
- Both exponents should always add up to 1. If they don't, they can always be made to add up to 1 by the process of monotonic transformation.
- Monotonic transformation can also be used to make the coefficient equal to 1.
- Marginal utility of a good X is the partial derivative of the utility function with respect to good X. It can also be defined as the change in utility resulting from a one-unit change in the quantity of good X consumed.

Indifference Curves

- When solving for the good which is drawn on the vertical axis and using some constant for utility, this new function can be used to draw an indifference curve.
- An indifference curve is a convex function within commodity space representing an infinite collection of consumption bundles, all of which yield the same constant utility.
- An indifference map is a sample of indifference curves.
- The higher the exogenous constant utility is, the farther to the north-east of the origin the indifference curve lies and the better the consumer is off.

Four Rules of Standard Indifference Curves

- Every possible combination of goods must have one, and only one, utility associated with it.

- Indifference curves are always downward sloping.
- Individual inference curves must never cross each other.
- As we move along the curve it becomes less steep. This is due to the diminishing marginal utility present in all goods (also known as the convexity rule).

The Marginal Rate of Substitution (MRS)
- The marginal rate of substitution is the rate at which the consumer is willing to give up one good in exchange for another without altering the level of utility.
- The MRS is the slope of the indifference curve.

Finding An Optimum Consumption Bundle
- The optimal bundle for the consumer (provided that the entire income is to be spent) is where the budget line and the indifference curve are tangent to each other.
- Mathematically this can be found by equating two expressions. The first is the derivative of the utility function with respect to one good divided by the derivative of the utility function with respect to the other good (slope of the indifference curve). The second is the price of the other good divided by the price of the one good (slope of the budget line).

Indifference Curves for Perfect Substitutes and Perfect Complements
- Indifference curves for perfect substitutes are straight lines.
- The optimal bundle for a perfect substitute is either one of two corner solutions, or instead any point on the indifference curve.
- Indifference curves for perfect complements are L-shaped curves.
- The optimal bundle is where the budget line touches the corner of the curve.

Budget Constraint

$$p_F \cdot Q_F + p_S \cdot Q_S \leq M \qquad (3.5)$$

Budget Line

$$p_F \cdot Q_F + p_S \cdot Q_S = M \qquad (3.6)$$

Slope of the Budget Line

$$-\frac{P_S}{P_F} \tag{3.8}$$

Marginal Utility

$$MU_X = \frac{\partial U(X,Y)}{\partial X} \tag{3.11}$$

The Cobb–Douglas Utility Function

$$U(Q_1, Q_2) = Q_1^{\alpha} \cdot Q_2^{\beta} \tag{3.15}$$

The Slope of the Indifference Curve:

$$-\frac{MU(Q_S)}{MU(Q_F)} = \frac{Q_{F(OLD)} - Q_{F(NEW)}}{Q_{S(OLD)} - Q_{S(NEW)}} = \frac{\Delta Q_F}{\Delta Q_S} = MRS \tag{3.27}$$

4. Decomposition of Quantity Demanded

Introduction
This chapter will show you how to analyse the change in quantity demanded[1] following a change in the price of a good. Firstly, we discuss what happens when income changes — the effect of a price change will be dealt with separately. We then apply these aspects and show how to decompose quantity demanded graphically, and how to account for it in a quantitative framework. In this context, we also introduce the Slutsky and Hicks decomposition and the Slutsky equation.

Required Knowledge
It is vital that you have worked through Chapter 3 (especially from 3.5 onwards) prior to reading this chapter. We assume a good working knowledge of budget constraints/lines and indifference curves.

Key Terms
normal good, inferior good, nominal income, real income, income consumption curve, income effect, substitution effect, Giffen good, Hicks decomposition, Slutsky decomposition, pivot vs. shift, Slutsky equation.

4.1 Introducing Normal and Inferior Goods

The Connection to Chapter 3
Before we jump straight into a new discussion, it is useful to review where we have left off in the last chapter. While the first half of Chapter 3 constituted the introduction of a mental framework for economic problem solving, the second half (from Section 3.5 onwards) revolved around the specific concepts of indifference curves and budget constraints. We combined and applied these two concepts to help the consumer make optimal decisions regarding their consumption.

---

[1] Some authors use "demand" rather than "quantity demanded" in this context.

While Chapter 3 served as an introduction to specific *principles* supported by a few applications, this chapter constitutes another specific *application* of these methods.

Getting Started

The utilisation of the term "good" has by now become second nature to us. What we have not discussed until this point, however, is the fact that there are different *types* of goods. In this section we will show the properties of these goods before naming them.

Suppose you are a student in London with an income M equal to £100 per week (due to the generosity of your parents). Without considering prices for the moment, we will assume that at this specific income, you decide to consume 1 DVD per week.

Normal Good

Imagine now that, since you have been awarded a grant based on your stellar performance in EC100 (which pays out weekly), your income has all of a sudden doubled to £200. Let us say that with this new income you now decide to buy 2 DVDs per week instead of only 1.

As if fortune wasn't already on your side, your parents win the lottery and hence decide to triple your pocket money so that in total your weekly income has climbed to £400. With this new level of income you consume 4 DVDs. The pairs of income and quantity consumed are summarised in Table 4.1. What we find is quite simple: With an increase in income, the quantity demanded also increases. For this reason the DVD is considered a **normal good**.

Table 4.1. For normal goods, the particular consumer's preferences yield an increase in quantity demanded when their income increases

Income (in £/wk.)	100	200	400
Number of DVDs consumed	1	2	4

Inferior Good

Let us now have a look at a different type of good. In the context of this analysis, we can scale the consumer's income up exactly the same way as we have done in the previous example. The only difference now is the good analysed: we will talk about pizzas now.

Let us now say that when your income is £100 per week, your quantity demanded for pizzas is 1. As your income doubles, we will assume that your quantity doubles. So far this is exactly the same as above. Now, with the final increase in your income to £400 your quantity demanded for pizzas is 1. Our findings are summarised in Table 4.2.

Table 4.2. The particular consumer's preferences yield an increase in quantity demanded when their income increases from £100 to £200, but decreases when their income rises from £200 to £400

Income (in £/wk.)	100	200	400
Number of pizzas consumed	1	2	1

The values for quantity demanded in Table 4.2 may raise a few eyebrows. In the last example, when we had more income we bought more DVDs so surely when we have more income we would also like to buy more pizza? No, not always — but why is this so?

The Logic Behind Inferior Goods
To answer this question, we pose a second (albeit rhetorical) question: "Does the Queen eat pizza?" Our guess is that she probably doesn't[2], and we can think of many reasons why, one of which has to do with her income. The Queen has enough money to eat any type of food she wants, even something as ostentatious as lobster, for example. Take yourself. If you are like many London students, you are reasonably well endowed, but not rich. Pizza is considered "sort of expensive" and it is therefore not the type of food that you could afford every day. Hence your quantity demanded is relatively low at an income of £100.

Now, if you had slightly more income, you can buy more pizza. If, however, you had even more income, then you could purchase something else instead of pizza that you might enjoy eating even more, such as lobster perhaps. It is no wonder that your quantity demanded of pizza decreases (when your income increases from £200 to £400). Your greater income means you can purchase something better than pizza. And this is precisely the vital difference between pizzas and DVDs in our example when income rises from £200 to £400.

If an increase in income means that the quantity demanded of a certain good decreases, we are dealing, by definition, with an **inferior good**. This

---

[2] If you happen to know if she does, please get in touch (with us, not the Queen!)

is the case with pizza when income changes from £200 to £400. Once again, if we give you more money and you demand less of a certain good, that product is inferior. And it's quite easy to remember too: it must literally be "inferior" to something else, because if you have a higher income, you buy less of it as you can afford something better.

Also note that a good does not necessarily have to be normal or inferior for all levels of income. In our example, pizza is a normal good in the income range from £100 to £200 and an inferior good from income £200 to £400.

Consumer Preferences
Finally, whether a good is considered normal or inferior also depends on the individual consumer. For example, Toby likes pizza but prefers other foods. If his income increased he would be likely to switch away from pizza to eating more frequently at London's Club Gascon where the taster menu with matching wines is offered for £65 per person. Tom, our copy editor for this book, is quite different. He tells us that upon an increase in his income his quantity demanded for pizza would not change at all.

> A normal good is a good for which the quantity demanded increases when income rises.
> An inferior good is a good for which quantity demanded decreases when income rises.

The Engel Curve
We can show whether a good is normal or inferior using the Engel curve, as done in Fig. 4.1. In the left- and right-hand panel we use income on the vertical axis. The horizontal axis of the left-hand panel shows the quantity demanded of DVDs Q_D and the horizontal axis of the right-hand panel shows the quantity demanded of pizzas Q_P. For the entire income range depicted, we assume DVDs to be a normal good while pizzas are an inferior good. As we expect from the definition of normal and inferior goods, the curve in the left-hand panel is sloping upwards whereas the curve in the right-hand panel slopes downwards.

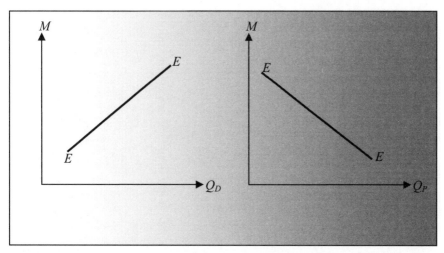

Fig. 4.1. Two Engel curves for a normal (left) and an inferior (right) good. The change in quantity demanded for DVDs moves in the same direction as the change in income, whereas the change in quantity demanded for pizzas moves in the opposite direction to the change in income

4.2 Shift and Rotation of the Budget Line

Recap
In Section 3.5.3 we showed in Fig. 3.3 how the budget line rotates upon a change in the price of one good. We also mentioned that a change in income results in a shift of the entire curve rather than a rotation. We have not yet shown this on a graph because it was not immediately applicable in Chapter 3. This is now different.

Showing an Income Change on a Graph
Let us have a look at Fig. 4.2. We resume our example of DVDs, and as in Chapter 3, we find ourselves in commodity space. The horizontal and vertical axes represent the quantity of DVDs Q_D and the quantity of the composite good Q_C, respectively. Moreover, we can observe two budget lines B_1 and B_2. As we learned in the last chapter, the budget line is derived by finding the intercepts on the vertical and horizontal axis and connecting these with a straight line. Thus, budget line B_1 is derived by dividing income M_1 by the price of DVDs p_D to find the vertical intercept. Then we divide M_1 by the price of the composite good p_C to find the horizontal intercept and connect the two intercepts.

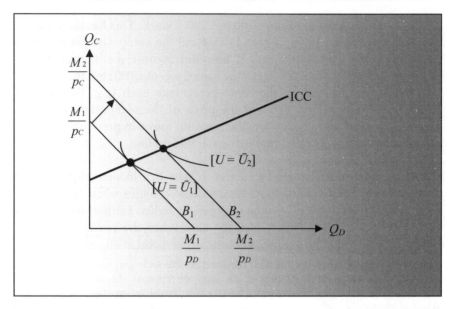

Fig. 4.2. A shift in the budget line brought about by an increase in income from M_1 to M_2

So what is up with the second budget line that lies further away from the origin? The only difference of B_2 compared with B_1 is that it has been derived using a different income $M_2 > M_1$. Remember, commodity space consists of infinitely many consumption bundles, and hence the outward shift of the budget line means that a whole new range of additional affordable bundles is now open to us.

As explained in Section 3.8, we can now find optimal consumption bundles by looking for the points of tangency between the indifference curves and the budget lines. Not surprisingly, it turns out that the indifference curve tangent to budget line B_2 is further away from the origin than the other indifference curve being tangent to B_1. Hence, the consumer derives a higher total utility $\bar{U}_2 > \bar{U}_1$ from more income. So far, this discussion has largely been a repetition of Chapter 3.

Changes in Price and Income Are Interconnected
As indicated before, a change in income may be considered the same as a proportional change in prices. But even if only one good changes in price, there will be an effect on income, albeit on real income and not on nominal income. Let us explain:

Say your income changes from £100 to £200 a week. This has the same effect as a halving the price of both DVDs and the composite good. And it works the other way round, too. If **nominal income**, i.e. the number of monetary units that you hold, stays the same (e.g. at £100) but the prices of the two goods changed by the same percentage each (e.g. the price of DVDs rises from £10 to £12 and the price of the composite good rises from £50 to £60), the budget constraint would move in precisely the same way as it did before, parallel to the original budget line.

In such an instance, it would be correct to state that income changed. Not nominal income but **real income**. Real income changes when the purchasing power of every unit of income changes, i.e. when £1 buys more or less than it did previously. This is also the case when the price of only one good changes, assuming we buy anything of the good at all.

Income Consumption Curve
It is worth noting that when you draw a line combining the optimal bundles (the points of tangency between the indifference curves and the budget constraints), what you get is an income consumption curve[3] (ICC). It can potentially be formed in any way, straight, curved or other, depending on the particular consumer's tastes. One example of an ICC has already been seen in Fig. 4.2.

For an Inferior Good, the ICC Looks Different
While the specific example of Fig. 4.2 showed an increase in the consumption of *both* goods as income increased, we can deduce from Section 4.1 and the example of pizzas that the ICC must not necessarily always move towards the north-east region of commodity space. In other words, the quantity demanded of a good can actually decrease when you have more income, which implies that we are dealing with an inferior good.

Let us redraw Fig. 4.2 in Fig. 4.3 using pizzas instead of DVDs on the horizontal axis. We assume that we are dealing with the same consumer as in Section 4.1 and income increases from M_1 to M_2. The bundle representing the tangency on budget line B_2 and the optimal indifference curve with utility $\bar{U}_2$ is now located closer to the horizontal axis than the tangency on B_1 and *its* optimal indifference curve. Think about what this means. All the statement is saying is that the quantity demanded of pizza is less at a higher income than it is at lower income. We already knew this, but now

---

[3] The ICC is also sometimes referred to as the "income offer curve" or the "income expansion path".

we also have a very elegant way of showing this graphically! By looking at diagrams such as Figs. 4.2 and 4.3 we can now say at the first glance what type (i.e. normal or inferior) of good we are dealing with.

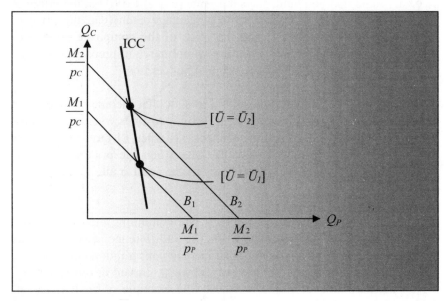

Fig. 4.3. The income consumption curve ICC for pizza (assumed to be an inferior good) is downward sloping. As income increases from M_1 to M_2, its quantity demanded decreases

A Change in Price Shown on a Graph

In Section 3.4.3 we showed what happens to the budget line when the price of one good changes holding income constant. In Fig. 3.3, the budget line rotated clockwise around the vertical intercept as the price of the good on the horizontal axis changed. This is replicated in the top-left panel of Fig. 4.4.

As we can see in the remaining three panels, there are more ways in which the budget line can rotate when the price of one good changes, holding the price of the other good and income constant.

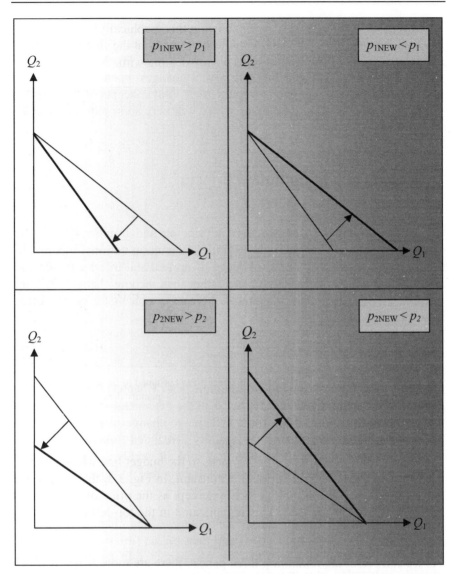

Fig. 4.4. Clockwise starting from the top-left panel: A increase in the price of good 1 results in a clockwise rotation of the budget line around the vertical intercept. When the price of good 1 decreases, the budget line rotates around the vertical intercept *anti*-clockwise. In a similar fashion, when the price of good 2 decreases the budget line rotates around the horizontal axis in an clockwise fashion, whereas it rotates around this axis in an anti-clockwise fashion when the price of good 2 increases

Teaching Methods
Without having been shown immediate applications, you may wonder what the purpose of the examples in Section 4.2 was. We wanted to familiarise you with the budget line and how it changes when income and/or prices change before we plunge into the most vital concepts of this chapter in the following section. Rest assured; we will very soon put into practice what we have just learned.

4.3 Income and Substitution Effects

Change in Price (Again)
In Sections 4.1 and 4.2 we have seen, in principle and graphically, how the quantity demanded changes as a result of a change in nominal income. In this section, we will use our knowledge of normal and inferior goods and apply this to situations in which price rather than income changes. We are interested in how the quantity demanded reacts to a change in price, which is denoted as:

$$\frac{\Delta Q_1}{\Delta P_1} \qquad (4.1)$$

You may remember this kind of equation from Chapter 2, in which we dealt with supply and demand. Rather than the percentage change in quantity demanded resulting from some percentage change in price, Equation 4.1 denotes the *absolute* change in quantity demanded following a change in price. As simple as this equation may look, it entails more than meets the eye. It comprises two effects, as we will elaborate on below.

Substitution Effect
Figs. 4.5, 4.6 and 4.7 show the *decomposition* of the change in quantity demanded of DVDs (normal good) and then pizzas (inferior good). What we mean by decomposition is that we can in fact split up the change in quantity demanded into two separate effects: the income effect and the substitution effect.

If the relative price of a good rises, for example, then becomes less attractive vis-à-vis to other goods whose prices have remained constant. For instance, if your local supermarket sells *Coke* and *Pepsi* and the price of *Coke* suddenly increases, then *Coke* becomes, relatively speaking, less attractive. Therefore, one would *substitute Coke* (or any other good with positive cross-price elasticity[4]) with *Pepsi*. The change in quantity demanded resulting from only a change in price (or to be more precise, a change in relative prices without the change in real income) is known as the substitution effect.

> The substitution effect is that change in the quantity demanded of a good following a change in the price of that good that is solely attributable to a change in relative prices.

Income Effect
Something else happens when the price of a good changes: the consumer's real income is affected. The change in quantity demanded resulting from a price change solely attributable to a change in real income (which, as we shall see later, is illustrated by a hypothetical adjustment of nominal income) is called the income effect. We know that the quantity demanded following a change in nominal income depends on what kind of good we are dealing with. The income effect for a normal good moves in the opposite direction as the price change, and for an inferior good it moves in the same direction as the price change. This follows from the definition of these two types of goods, and we illustrated this earlier using the example of pizzas and DVDs.

> The income effect is that change in quantity demanded of a good following a change in price of that good solely attributable to the change in real income.

Intuition of the Decomposition of Quantity Demanded for a Normal Good
Consider Fig. 4.5. The top arrow indicates that there is a decrease in price. However, the change in price could just as well be an increase. The thing that matters to us is the direction of the arrows (specially those pertaining

---

[4] By definition, any two goods that exhibit negative cross price elasticities to each other are substitutes. The concept was introduced in Section 2.4.

to income and substitution effects) relative to each other.[5] For a normal good the simple rule always holds that *income and substitution effects reinforce each other in moving in the opposite direction of a change in price.*

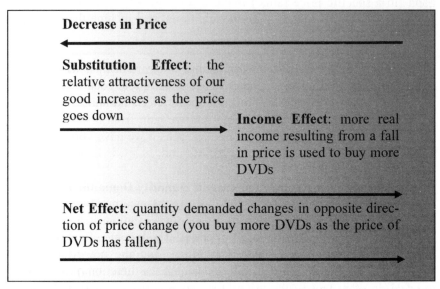

Fig. 4.5. A decrease in the price of a normal good, such as DVDs, results in both income and substitution effects to reinforce each other. The quantity demanded increases following a fall in price

Intuition of the Decomposition of Quantity Demanded for an Inferior Good

Let us now look at Fig. 4.6, which functions in the same way as Fig. 4.5. The difference now is that we are dealing with pizza — which we assumed to be an inferior good. As we can see, a change in income results in the substitution effect moving in the opposite direction to the change in price. This is no different from what we saw for the normal good. Therefore, we can state that the substitution effect will *always* move in the opposite direction to a change in price. If the price of pizzas decreases, other goods will now be relatively less attractive, and we would, for this reason, substitute them with pizza[6].

But there is also something else that has happened as a result of the change in price of pizzas: our real income has increased. And this leads us to the

---

[5] The absolute length of the arrow has no special meaning.
[6] This is why we speak of the "substitution" effect.

crucial difference between normal and inferior goods. As the substitution effect always moves in the opposite direction to the price change, the determining factor of whether we are dealing with a normal or an inferior good (in a specific price range) is the income effect. When the price decreases, what would you do with the additional real income that you have gained?

If the answer is "Spend it on something else!" we are dealing with an inferior good. And now we have come a conceptual circle back to the beginning of the chapter, where we first introduced DVDs and pizza. In our example of pizza, the extra real income that we gain from a fall in price is used for the consumption of other goods. It is as if we gave you extra cash, and you went off to buy a different type of good.

Inferior Goods — A Partial Decrease in Quantity Demanded
Let us now have a closer look at Fig. 4.6. As the income effect is moving in the same direction as the change in price, in isolation, it decreases the quantity demanded following a fall in prices. The income effect, however, only *partially* offsets the substitution effect, and the net effect of the change in quantity demanded is still opposite to the direction of the change in price. In other words, the price falls and quantity demanded increases. This is what we are used to from Chapter 2, in which we saw downward sloping demand curves. For a normal good this will, of course, always be the case.

Intuition of the Decomposition of Quantity Demanded for a Giffen Good
While in the above example the change in quantity demanded moved in the same direction as the change in price, it has to be noted that when dealing with inferior goods, the effect of a price change on the quantity demanded is *ambiguous*. This means we cannot say whether the quantity demanded of a good increases or decreases when its price falls. Look at Fig. 4.7 to see what we mean. Here, the income effect is so large it overrides the substitution effect and turns the net effect of quantity demanded in the same direction as the change in price. This seems strange because it means that if prices fall we demand less of the good. In fact, this is in violation of the "law" of demand.

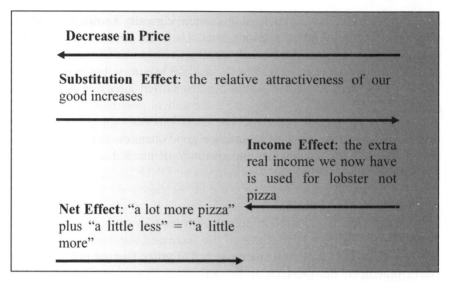

Fig. 4.6. A decrease in the price of an inferior good, such as pizza, results in the substitution effect to move in the opposite direction of the change in price whereas the income effect moves in the same direction. Hence, the two effects partially offset each other so that the net effect in the quantity demanded is opposite to the change in price (as is the case with normal goods)

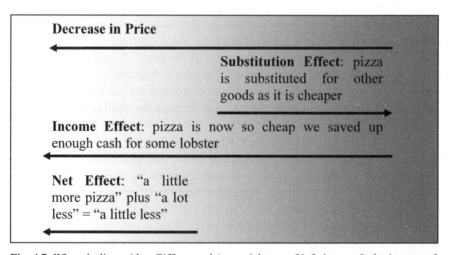

Fig. 4.7. When dealing with a Giffen good (a special type of inferior good) the income effect overrides the substitution effect, so that the change in quantity demanded moves in the same direction as the change in price

If this is the case, we are facing a theoretical curiosity known as a **Giffen good**, which is a subset of inferior goods. There are not (m)any useful examples of Giffen goods. Supposedly potatoes used to be Giffen goods during the potato famine in Ireland in the mid 19th century, but even this example is disputed, so that it is possible that Giffen goods do not exist in practice at all. Nonetheless, they are a theoretical possibility and it is important to understand the concept. The most important thing to take away here is that when the price of an inferior good changes, at least in theory, we are unable to say whether the quantity demanded increases or decreases.

Summarising Our Findings

As we have seen, the crucial difference between normal and inferior goods is that for the inferior good, some of the increased purchasing power you newly acquired is devoted to *other goods* that you could not previously afford (remember, the Queen eats lobster rather than pizza) while for the normal good, the increase in real income is used to buy more of that good (e.g. DVDs). Finally, for the Giffen good the effect of a change in real income resulting from the price change (the income effect) overrides the substitution effect.

The substitution effect always moves
in the opposite direction of the price change.

The income effect for normal goods reinforces the substitution effect in moving in the opposite direction as the change in price.

The income effect for an inferior good moves in the same direction as the change in price and hence the total effect of the change in quantity demanded is ambiguous.

4.4 The Hicks Decomposition

Combining What We Have Learned so Far

We already know the components of a change in quantity demanded following a change in price: the income and substitution effects. You can show the decomposition of the entire change in quantity demanded (also referred to as the price effect) analytically using either the **Slutsky** or the **Hicks decomposition**[7]. Although the methods are slightly different, they work equally well, and their mechanisms are very similar. Let us start with the Hicks decomposition.

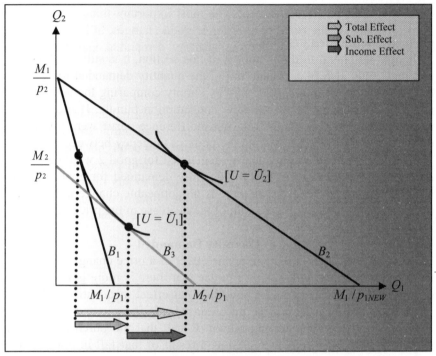

Fig. 4.8. Hicks decomposition of quantity demanded for a normal good. Income and substitution effects reinforce each other, as shown by the arrows underneath the horizontal axis

An Anti-Clockwise Rotation of the Budget Line

Fig. 4.8 incorporates directional arrows to highlight the decomposition of quantity demanded brought about by a change in price into income and substitution effect. But let us start with the basics: Fig. 4.8 shows a decrease in the price of good 1 from p_1 to p_{1NEW} and a subsequent anti-clockwise rotation of the budget constraint from B_1 to B_2. Also included are the indifference curves, which are tangent to the original budget line (with an exogenous utility $\bar{U}_1$), and the new budget line (with an exogenous utility $\bar{U}_2 > \bar{U}_1$).

---

[7] Named after economists Eugene Slutsky (1880–1948) and Sir John Hicks (1904–1989), who independently devised these methods.

Total Change in Quantity Demanded of Good 1
The horizontal distance between the optimal bundles on B_1 and B_2 (indicated by the left-most and right-most blobs, respectively) shows us the total change in quantity demanded brought about by a change in price. This distance is shown by the large light-grey arrow underneath the horizontal axis. This distance is the change in Q_1, i.e. the change in the amount of good 1 consumed.

Quantity Demanded of Good 2
Although peripheral to the argument of this section, it is still worth noting that there may also be a change in Q_2, the quantity demanded for good 2. This can be shown in a similar way by simply comparing the *vertical* difference of the original and the new consumption bundle. If the point of tangency between B_2 and the relevant indifference curve were lower (i.e. closer to the horizontal axis) than the point of tangency between B_1 and *its* indifference curve, then the quantity demanded for good 2 would have decreased. If it were higher, then the quantity demanded for good 2 would have *increased*. In our example there is no noticeable change in the quantity demanded for good 2 as a result of the decrease in the price of good 1.

Decomposing the Change in Quantity Demanded
We have now discussed the composite effect of a price change for good 1, but looking at the graph, you will notice that there is more going on. The following is an explanation of how the total effect in quantity demanded following a fall in price can be decomposed into income and substitution effects using the Hicks decomposition. Recall that the purchasing power (i.e. the real income) has increased as a result of that fall in price. While nominal income was unaffected, let us now pretend that our real income *was still the same*! We do this by hypothetically reducing nominal income from M_1 to M_2.

But how much should we decrease nominal income by? We simply move the budget line parallel to B_2 back until it is tangent to the original indifference (of utility $\bar{U}_1$) curve. With the hypothetical reduction in nominal income that gave us the new and final budget line B_3, we are now just as well off as we were in the beginning. Why? Because we are on the same indifference curve, which we know yields the same utility anywhere on it. As the price of good 1 has changed, the final bundle on B_3, albeit yielding the same utility as the first bundle, contains different combinations of the two goods compared with the first bundle.

Substitution Effect in Action

The reason for moving the budget line back was to find out which part of the change in quantity demanded is solely due to the change in relative prices. We have achieved this by ignoring the effect that the change in real income had on the quantity demanded, and this is equivalent to isolating the substitution effect. Graphically, it can be shown as the horizontal difference between the original and the final bundle, indicated by the medium-grey arrow in Fig. 4.8.

Income Effect in Action

By definition, then, the remaining change in quantity demanded is the income effect (dark-grey arrow). As this is a normal good we are dealing with, the income effect moves in the opposite direction to the price change and reinforces the substitution effect.

Decomposing Quantity Demanded for an Inferior Good

Now, let us do the same thing again, but this time for an inferior good. We have previously learned that the crucial difference between an inferior and a normal good is the fact that the income effect for an inferior good moves in the same direction as the change in price. In other words, if you were given more money and you wanted to buy less of the good as a result, this would mean that, for you, the good is inferior.

Consider Fig. 4.9. We have an original budget line B_1 that rotates outwards to B_2 as the price of good 1 decreases from p_1 to p_{1NEW}. The final step is to move the budget line back (by decreasing nominal income) until it is just tangent to the original indifference curve with utility $\bar{U}_1$.

What is making good 1 inferior is the fact that the income effect is pointing in the same direction as the change in price. Graphically, the horizontal position of the point of tangency between the indifference curve with utility $\bar{U}_2$ and B_2 is to the left rather than to the right of the point of tangency between B_3 and the original indifference curve with utility $\bar{U}_1$. Just as we have conceptually shown in Fig. 4.6, the income effect partially offsets the substitution effect. The reason for this partial offset is to be found in the shape of the indifference curves that we use in Fig. 4.9, which in turn is a result of the consumer's preferences.

Drawing the Decomposition for a Giffen Good

In this text, we omit the depiction of the decomposition of the quantity demanded for a Giffen good. It is firstly very difficult to do, and secondly Giffen goods are rarely if ever found in real life. If you wish to draw the decomposition for a Giffen good you need to draw the indifference curves in such a way that when the budget line is moving outwards (i.e. anti-clockwise), the point of tangency between B_2 and the indifference curve must lie further to the right than the point of tangency between B_1 and the other indifference curve. Should you choose to try this out, you will find out that the indifference curves must be formed in a very special way.

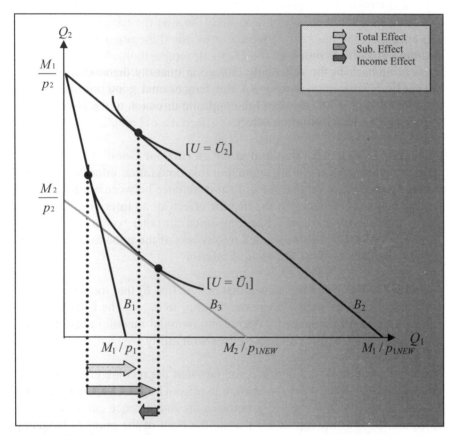

Fig. 4.9. Hicks decomposition of demand for an inferior good. The substitution effect is partially offset by the income effect

4.5 Doing it the Slutsky Way

The Slutsky decomposition is almost identical to the Hicks decomposition, except that now we *isolate the change in quantity demanded solely attributable to a change in relative prices (the substitution) by theoretically ad-*

justing income in such a way that the old bundle is just affordable, in contrast to adjusting income so that the old utility level is reached. As a result we end up requiring a third indifference curve. Although this may seem more complicated, it is in many ways more convenient, especially because the quantitative illustration of income and substitution effects becomes very transparent, as we shall see in Section 4.6.

For now, let us concentrate on Fig. 4.10. As was the case in the previous two examples, the budget line rotates outwards if the price of good 1 falls. But here is the difference to the Hicks decomposition: As we move the budget line back by hypothetically adjusting nominal income, we move it not until it is tangent to the original indifference curve, but until the budget line passes through the original bundle. In other words, we adjust nominal income so that the consumer could just afford the old bundle, if she wished to do so.

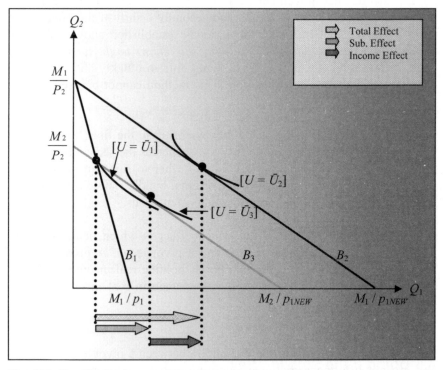

Fig. 4.10. The Slutsky decomposition of quantity demanded for a normal good. The decomposition entails a pivot of the budget line around the original consumption bundle and hence a third indifference curve with utility $\bar{U}_3$ is drawn

However, it turns out that the consumer does not want to choose the old bundle; because prices have changed, she now prefers a different bundle. This new bundle gives a higher utility, and this is seen by the point of tangency between B_3 and a third indifference curve with utility $\bar{U}_3 > \bar{U}_1$. By allowing the consumer to choose her original bundle and noting the *actual* bundle consumed, we can observe the change in quantity demanded due to a change in price only (disregarding the fact that real income also changes when the price changes). Thus, the horizontal difference between the original and the third bundle is the substitution effect. By definition, the remaining change in quantity demanded is attributable to the change in real income, which is the horizontal difference between the third and the second bundle. This is represented by the dark-grey arrow.

The Pivot and Shift Method
Taking a look at Fig. 4.10 again, we can separate out the change from B_1 to B_2 into two distinct movements. Firstly a pivot of the budget line around the original bundle from B_1 to B_3, and secondly a shift of the budget line from B_3 to B_2. Remembering the rationale established above, *the pivot shows us the substitution effect while the shift shows us the income effect*[8]. This method is vitally important in being able to quickly analyse graphs showing the Slutsky decomposition. This method cannot be used in conjunction with the Hicks method.

For a price decrease, the pivot will always result in the final bundle being located further away from the vertical axis, whereas the second bundle (i.e. the bundle on B_2) could be located still further to right, in between the other two bundles or to the left of the original bundle. These cases respectively correspond to normal, inferior and Giffen goods.

Rather than blindly remembering which effect is which, it makes more sense to keep in mind what a shift and a pivot *mean*. A pivot means a change in relative prices of the two goods holding real income stable (by adjusting nominal income). A shift is a change in real income, holding relative prices constant.

Pivot vs. Rotation
It is essential to make clear the distinction between a pivot and a rotation. We are not offering a dictionary definition, but for the purpose of this

---

[8] A way this may be remembered is to think of a letter sent by one economist to the other with a P.S. after the main body. P(ivot) and S(substitution effect) go together.

chapter we will define a **pivot** to be a movement of a line around a bundle. By contrast, a **rotation** is a movement of the budget line around a fixed point on either of the two axes. In the latter case only one rather than two intercepts change.

4.6 Deriving the Slutsky Equation

We complete our analysis of the effect of a change in price on quantity demanded by illustrating the quantitative approach. The Slutsky equation shows us mathematically what we have already learned in principle: the effect on quantity demanded resulting from a price change is made up of a change in quantity demanded solely attributable to a change in relative prices (the pivot), as well as that change in quantity demanded solely attributable to a change in real income (the shift). This is expressed in general terms in Equation 4.11, but before discussing this formula, let us derive it. Since the derivation of the Slutsky equation can be perceived as rather demanding, we would recommend you work through these steps yourself on a piece of paper as you are reading on.

Step 1: Change in Nominal Income to Consume Original Bundle
Our starting point is to quantify the most vital elements of a decomposition of quantity demanded. Let us use Fig. 4.10[9] as an example. As we move along, it will become evident as to why we do this. Firstly though, we can state that the original budget line B_1 is given by:

$$M_1 = p_1 \cdot Q_1 + p_2 \cdot Q_2 \qquad (4.2)$$

We are used to equations of this kind from Chapter 3. Secondly, let us look at the formula for budget line B_3 that we get when we hypothetically adjust nominal income after a price change so that the original bundle can be consumed. This is:

$$M_2 = p_{1NEW} \cdot Q_1 + p_2 \cdot Q_2 \qquad (4.3)$$

As we have already learned conceptually, we can see in Equation 4.3 that relative to the original budget line shown in Equation 4.2, the price of good 1 and the level of income have changed.

Now let us quantify the change in nominal income that is necessary to consume the original bundle, i.e. that change in income that we need to shift

---

[9] Although Fig. 4.10 is a normal good, the following steps are also correct for inferior or Giffen goods.

the budget line back (after it rotated following the price change) until it crosses the original bundle. The change from M_2 to M_1 (i.e. $M_2 - M_1$) can be expressed as ΔM. This is simply Equation 4.3 minus Equation 4.2. Therefore:

$$\Delta M = p_{1NEW} \cdot Q_1 + p_2 \cdot Q_2 - (p_1 \cdot Q_1 + p_2 \cdot Q_2) \qquad (4.4)$$

$$\Delta M = p_{1NEW} \cdot Q_1 - p_1 \cdot Q_1$$

$$\Delta M = Q_1 \cdot (p_{1NEW} - p_1)$$

$$\Delta M = Q_1 \cdot \Delta p_1$$

where Δp_1 is the change in price. This new equation gives us the change in nominal income that we need so that we are able to consume the original bundle located on B_1. That is the original quantity demanded of the good multiplied by its change in price. In this simplified form, the equation is intuitive. If the price of the good decreases, this is the "saving" the consumer would get.

Step 2: Proving a Hypothesis
Our next step is to quantify the hypothesis that the change in quantity demanded is the sum of income and substitution effects. So far we have simply assumed that this is true, as it is intuitive. However, now we will also prove it.

Recall, the substitution effect is that change in quantity demanded that results from a change in relative prices, holding real income constant. This can be expressed as:

$$\Delta Q_S = Q_1(p_{1NEW}, M_2) - Q_1(p_1, M_1) \qquad (4.5)$$

where the left-hand side is the change in quantity demanded attributable to the substitution effect, the first term on the right-hand side is the quantity demanded at the point of tangency between B_3 and the final indifference curve, and the second term on the right-hand side is the quantity demanded of the bundle lying on B_1. What we are basically doing here is changing the consumer's income to keep the old bundle just affordable.

Moving on to the second effect, we remember that the income effect is that change in quantity demanded resulting from a change in real income while holding relative prices constant. Mathematically this is:

$$\Delta Q_N = Q_1(p_{1NEW}, M_1) - Q_1(p_{1NEW}, M_2) \qquad (4.6)$$

where the left-hand side is the change in quantity demanded attributable to the income effect, the first term on the right-hand side is the quantity demanded at the point of tangency between B_2 and the second indifference curve, and the second term on the right-hand side is the quantity demanded of the bundle lying on B_3. This corresponds to the shift of the budget line B_2 (which was arrived at by the change in price of good 1) back to that budget line B_1 crossing the original bundle. What this says is that a decrease in the price of a good increases real income. Therefore, to keep the original bundle affordable we need to decrease nominal income.

As we have seen graphically, we also know that the entire change in quantity demanded following a change in price is simply:

$$\Delta Q_1 = Q_1(p_{1NEW}, M_1) - Q_1(p_1, M_1) \qquad (4.7)$$

where the first term on the right-hand side is the quantity demanded of good 1 represented by the bundle on B_2, while the second term on the right-hand side is the quantity demanded of the good shown by the bundle on B_1. This means that the original quantity demanded is subtracted from the final quantity demanded and not vice versa. It is now easy to see that the total effect is the sum of income and substitution effects:

$$\Delta Q_1 = \Delta Q_S + \Delta Q_N \qquad (4.8)$$

As mentioned at the beginning of Step 2, we can verify from intuition that this equation is true. However, with the formulae developed in Step 2, (i.e. Equations 4.5, 4.6 and 4.7) we can now also prove this mathematically fairly easily. By plugging the expressions into Equation 4.8 we get:

$$Q_1(p_{1NEW}, M_1) - Q_1(p_1, M_1) = Q_1(p_{1NEW}, M_2) - Q_1(p_1, M_1) + \qquad (4.9)$$
$$Q_1(p_{1NEW}, M_1) - Q_1(p_{1NEW}, M_2)$$

The first and third term of the right-hand side cancel each other out and so we know that the equation is true. For this reason we can confidently use Equation 4.8 in Step 3!

Step 3: Deriving the Final Equation
Since Equation 4.8 shows us the absolute changes of quantities demanded, we can also divide each term of the equation by Δp_1 so that we can work with a formula that shows us the *rates of change*:

$$\frac{\Delta Q_1}{\Delta p_1} = \frac{\Delta Q_S}{\Delta p_1} + \frac{\Delta Q_N}{\Delta p_1} \qquad (4.10)$$

As a final step, we will use the last line of Equation 4.4, which was derived in Step 1 of this section. We will substitute it for Δp in the last term of Equation 4.10. This gives:

$$\frac{\Delta Q_1}{\Delta p_1} = \frac{\Delta Q_S}{\Delta p_1} - \frac{\Delta Q_M}{\Delta M}Q_1 \qquad (4.11)$$

What we have derived in Equation 4.11 is known as the **Slutsky equation**. Avoiding a double fraction, what we have done is to move the denominator of the last line of Equation 4.4 (which is Q_1 after we solve it for Δp_1) to become the numerator of the second term, while the numerator of the fraction in the denominator of the second term ΔM stays where it is. To emphasise Q_1, we do not actually write it as the numerator of the last term but pull it out to the right on the same level as the fraction bar.

The Negative Sign in the Equation
When we express the Slutsky equation in terms of the rate of change, it turns out to be convenient to define ΔQ_M to be the "negative of the income effect" or:

$$\Delta Q_M = -\Delta Q_N \qquad (4.12)$$

Recall that in Fig. 4.10, the shift of the budget line is achieved by a *reduction* in nominal income. However, the change in *quantity demanded* (and this is precisely what the Slutsky equation is here to help us with) resulting from the change in income (holding prices constant), is in actuality positive, i.e. pointing rightwards. For this reason, the sign of the last line of Equation 4.4 needs to be changed before it can be substituted in the third term of Equation 4.10.

The Relevance of the Slutsky Equation
You may have wondered what the point was of going through all the hard work above in the process of arriving at the Slutsky equation. First of all, it is useful to see that the formulae you are working with are actually true and can, if necessary, be derived at any point in time. It is a way of showing you that the equations we work with are not "magic" but logical derivations from knowledge attained by a set of assumptions. Secondly, the derivation of the Slutsky equation helps you understand each element of the final equation. For this reason let us discuss it in a bit more detail.

The Elements of the Slutsky Equation
Let us take a look at Fig. 4.11, which serves as a summary of some of the most vital points that we have learned in this chapter. We observe three

rows, each pertaining to one type of good (normal, inferior and Giffen), while each column shows us either a positive or a negative sign. A negative sign in a box means a change *opposite* to the change in price and a positive sign means a change *with* the change in price. Each column also belongs to each of the three elements of the Slutsky equation. The first column is the total change in quantity demanded following a change in price, the second column is the substitution effect and the third column is the income effect.

So for example, as we have already learned in principle, the substitution effect always moves in the opposite direction to the change in price, and so the sign in the second column is always negative.

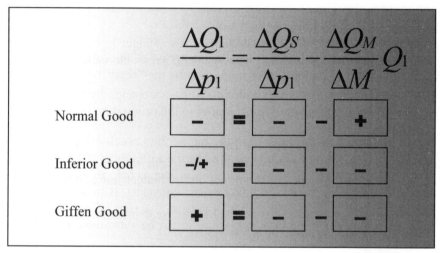

Fig. 4.11. The Slutsky equation and its application. We see in which direction the change in quantity demanded moves following a price change

Ambiguous Change in Quantity Demanded
As you know, the change in quantity demanded for an inferior good is ambiguous because the income effect moves in the same direction as the change in price. This is illustrated using both a positive and a negative sign in the first column of the second row. It means that when the price changes, the change in quantity demanded for an inferior good may either be against or with the change in price. In the latter case, the income effect overrides the substitution effect and we would be dealing with a Giffen good. The Giffen good is also an inferior good, but not all inferior goods are Giffen goods.

4.7 Chapter Summary

Change in Income

*   A normal good is a good for which the quantity demanded (at any price) increases when income rises.
*   An inferior good is a good for which the quantity demanded (at any price) decreases when income rises.
*   Whether a good is considered normal or inferior can change over certain income ranges and across different consumers.
*   Using the Engel curve, which graphs income against quantity demanded, one can show whether a good is considered normal or inferior.

Shift and Rotation of the Budget Line

*   When the price of one good changes, the budget line rotates around the intercept of the budget line with the axes belonging to the other good.
*   When income changes or both goods' prices change by the same proportion, the budget line shifts parallel to the original budget line.

Interconnectedness of Price and Income

*   When both goods' prices change by the same proportion, nominal income stays the same but the effect on the budget line is *as if* nominal income had changed.
*   If the price of only one good changes, real income changes while nominal income stays the same.

Income Consumption Curve

*   The income consumption curve ICC is the connection of all optimal bundles (i.e. points of tangency between indifference curves and budget lines) as income changes.
*   The bundles along the ICC can be used to make deductions about the kind of good we are dealing with. If the horizontal position of the optimal bundle moves rightwards as income increases, the good on the horizontal axis is normal; if it moves left, the good is inferior.

Income and Substitution Effects

*   The income effect is that change in quantity demanded of a good following a change in price of that good solely attributable to the change in real income.

- Real income is the purchasing power of income while nominal income is the £-amount of income.
- For a normal good, the income effect moves in the opposite way as the change in price (e.g. quantity demanded increases when price falls).
- For an inferior good, the income effect moves in the same direction as the change in price (e.g. quantity demanded decreases when price falls).
- The substitution effect is that change in quantity demanded of a good following a change in the price of that good that is solely attributable to a change in relative prices.
- The substitution effect always moves in the opposite direction to the change in price.
- Therefore, for a normal good income and substitution effect reinforce each other by moving in the opposite direction as the change in price.
- For an inferior good, the income effect moves in the same direction as the change in price and so the direction of the change in quantity demanded relative to the change in price is ambiguous.
- For a Giffen good, the income effect moves in the same direction as the change in price and overrides the substitution effect. This violates the "law" of demand and hence the Giffen good is considered to be a theoretical curiosity.

Graphical Representation of the Change in Quantity Demanded
- The Hicks decomposition shows the substitution effect by theoretically adjusting income so that the consumer is just as well off as before, i.e. the budget line is moved back to the original indifference curve.
- The Slutsky decomposition shows the substitution effect by theoretically adjusting income, i.e. moving the budget line back, so that the old consumption bundle is just affordable. The result is that we have to draw a third indifference curve.

The Slutsky Equation

$$\frac{\Delta Q_1}{\Delta p_1} = \frac{\Delta Q_S}{\Delta p_1} - \frac{\Delta Q_M}{\Delta M} Q_1 \qquad (4.11)$$

Part II – The Firm and Factor Input Markets

Part II switches our focus from the consumer to the firm. Rather than looking at individual firm behaviour, the aim of Part II is to provide methods and concepts as a contextual understanding for Part III. Chapter 5 serves as an introduction to the firm by familiarising ourselves with the production process encompassing both quantitative and graphical tools. Chapter 6 looks at the firm's inputs (or production factors) required for production a little closer; labour and capital. As these are inputs the firm needs to purchase, we talk about markets for factor inputs. Lastly, Chapter 7 comprises cost analysis.

5. The Firm and Production

Introduction

From this chapter onwards, our discussions will centre around the firm rather than the consumer. Here we introduce the concept of the firm by examining production processes. Important principles include the production function, the distinction between short and long run, and the optimal combination of factors of production to minimise cost given a certain level of output.

Required Knowledge

Prior to working through this chapter, it is vital that Chapter 3 has been read and understood. We frequently refer back to Chapter 3 as there is significant overlap between the firm's behaviour and rational consumer choice. This is especially with regards to the discussion of the firm's optimisation and the intuition preceding it in Sections 5.6 and 5.7.

Key Terms

firm, factor of production, labour (L), wage rate (w), capital (K) , rental rate (r), land, entrepreneurship, total product, total product curve, short run, long run, variable input, fixed input, law of diminishing returns, constant/increasing returns, marginal product of labour/capital $(MP_{L/K})$, average product of labour/capital $(AP_{L/K})$, increasing/constant/decreasing returns to scale, Cobb–Douglas production function, degree of homogeneity (D), isocost line, factor-input space, isoquant, isoquant map, marginal rate of technical substitution (MRTS), perfect complements, perfect substitutes.

5.1 Introducing the Process of Production

What Is a Firm?

Before we can learn about production, we have to give some thought to who engages in production in the first place. This is, of course, the firm. While the consumer's goal is to maximise her utility, the firm is defined as an economic agent whose interest it is to maximise profit, i.e. the difference between total revenue and total cost:

$$\Pi = TR - TC \qquad (5.1)$$

> A firm is an economic agent
> with the goal to maximise profits.

Outlook
Although we introduce the firm's objective with its definition, we leave the examination of profit maximisation until Chapter 9. In Section 5.8, however, we discuss the second element of the firm's profit — its cost. To be more precise, we explore how the firm can minimise this element of its profit function. This discussion, as you will see, is in its intuition very similar to the consumer's optimisation introduced in Chapter 3.

What Is Production?
Part of our discussion in consumer theory was about consumers making decisions regarding their optimal choice of consumption bundles. Of course, it is firms producing all these goods available for consumption. But firms may also produce for other firms. Pens, for example, are not only used by consumers but also by employees of firms for commercial rather than private use. In the latter case, the pen constitutes a **factor of production**[1].

The results of production are everywhere around us. The sandwich you eat in the morning, the train you ride to university, the notebook you buy at the shop, the clothes you are wearing and much, much more. These are all examples of the results of production, namely goods[2].

---

[1] As there are many different types of factors of production we revisit this concept in Section 5.2 in more detail.
[2] We recall from Chapter 1 that we employ a definition of "good" which also includes value-added activities that would in everyday terminology be considered "services".

Production Defined

Let us now define production. Production is any process by which present or future utility[3] is created. For this reason, we commonly refer to processes as "production" that would not be labelled as such in everyday language. While most people would only use the word "production" in their day-to-day language to refer to manufacturing processes, in economics a haircut, for example, yields utility (providing the hairdresser is doing a good job) and must therefore also be referred to as production.

> Production is a process whereby
> present or future utility is created.

The definition of production assumes that everything being produced must be a good and cannot be a bad, as from the latter one does not derive utility but disutility. We might be tempted to say that a pulp factory, for example, is "producing" pollution, but you now know that this phrasing is incorrect.

Lastly, the term "future" is included in the definition of production as some goods may not necessarily yield utility at the same time as they are being produced. While in many instances a good is used almost instantly following its production, as would be the case for a meal in a restaurant, for example, most goods produced would only be consumed following some delay. An example would be an ostentatious watch that spends years in a shop before it is sold.

5.2 Factors of Production

In order to produce *output* the firm requires *inputs*, and these inputs are known as **factors of production**. There are many examples of factors of production we can think of, such as the stationery mentioned above, and anything else that directly or indirectly aides the process of production. These inputs may include cars, hours worked by a lawyer, the rent for and utilities of an office building, oil as a raw material and much more. For

---

[3] The word "utility" implicitly assumes that production would take place for consumption only. We accept the definition of production although we know that in reality firms utilise goods as well.

convenience sake, economists group the abundance of factors of production in different categories which are elaborated on below.

Labour
When we speak of labour, we might possibly think of a person with a huge hammer in a noisy smelly steel mill full of dust and grime, but really, labour is any activity by a person that is part of the process of production. So, a labourer could of course be working in a steel mill but could also be a nurse, a professor or a postal clerk. A special type of labour is entrepreneurship, as we will see shortly. The price of labour is defined as the wage rate w. The concept of labour is dealt with in more detail in Chapter 6.

Capital
Upon hearing the term capital, many people may picture a bundle of cash in their minds. If we want "capital" to refer to cash, we use the term **money capital**. But this is not where the economic definition of capital ends, as it can also include items such as raw materials, machine hours or production premises. In fact, in this chapter we will focus on examples of the latter kind known as **real capital**. The cost of capital is defined as the rental rate r. Like labour, capital is also discussed in more detail in Chapter 6.

Land
The term "land" encompasses physical land on which we build a factory or office building for example. Land also includes any natural resource. It might seem strange, but any scarce natural resource such as copper, salt or oil is labelled land in economics.

Entrepreneurship
This category is slightly more abstract than those discussed thus far and has only been included in microeconomic study relatively recently. Entrepreneurship can be regarded as a special type of labour, as utility is created by the conception of ideas for business ventures. If you sit in your room and you have an idea to write a book, you have already engaged in production even if you have not written a single word yet (assuming, of course, the book will be written eventually).

Limitation to Capital and Labour
Although all of the named groups of inputs are equally valid, it is commonplace at this level of analysis to limit ourselves to labour and capital as the only factors of production. Moreover, we assume that there is only one

type of labour and only one type of capital for any one problem we discuss.

Of course, we know that this is an abstraction from real life as firms will have more than just two factors of production as well as a number of different inputs in each category. For example, a textbook publisher might use a writer, an editor and a manager in the production of a textbook, rather than relying on writers only.

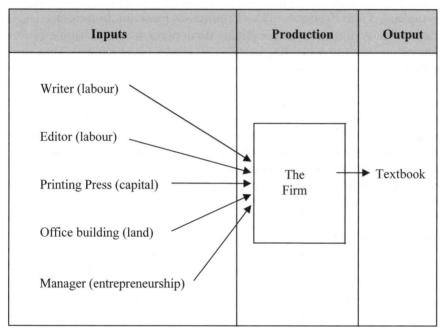

Fig. 5.1. The process of production illustrated with the example of a textbook. Inputs are transformed into outputs via the process of production

5.3 The Production Function

As we can see in Fig. 5.1, the firm is given inputs and then produces an output. In this section, we want to show the relation between output and input in more detail; to do so, we need the help of the production function. Just like the firm itself, any function can be viewed as a machine that is "fed" something — the independent variable — and then delivers something else — the dependent variable.

In production, we can show how output changes with an increase in one or both of its inputs. Naturally, if you hire a third and fourth writer for your publishing company, you will be able to produce more textbooks. The same holds true for capital. The more machine hours of the printing presses you use, the more books you will be able to produce. But we must be careful. Often matters are more complicated than initially meets the eye, and the output can behave in ways that are not necessarily intuitive at first sight, as we will see later in Section 5.4.2.

Graphing Total Product — The Production Function in Action
As you know, functions are frequently used to graphically illustrate the relationship between variables. Let us now introduce an example of a specific production function:

$$Q(K, L) = 3K \cdot L \qquad (5.2)$$

Here, output Q is related to the inputs of capital K and labour L in a linear way. In a two-dimensional graph, and we limit ourselves to these, it would be impossible to depict output against capital *and* labour at the same time. For this reason, Fig. 5.2 shows us how output changes with a change in labour input, *holding capital constant*[4]. The fact that capital is exogenous to the graph is signified by the presence of the square brackets. We arbitrarily pick an exogenous amount of capital $\bar{K} = 1$. The symbol $\bar{K}$ (pronounced "K bar" is used to signify the fact that capital is constant.

Assuming our production function of $Q(K, L) = 3K \cdot L$ and a constant K equal to 1, the production function can be rewritten as $Q(K, L) = 3L$, which makes the function simply a straight line with a gradient of 3. This is shown in Fig. 5.2. If the exogenous amount of capital changed, then the gradient of the function would be altered. If K was equal to 1/2 rather than 1, for example, the function would exhibit a gradient equal to 3/2 rather than 3[5].

Note that although we are talking about a production "function", it is correct not only to call the equation a function as we would normally do, but also to call the graphical representation thereof a function. Alternatively, to avoid confusion, you may call the graphical representation of the production function the **total product curve**. The total product is simply the amount of output Q the firm produces.

---

[4] Situations in which capital is fixed occur often, as we will see in Section 5.4 where we introduce the concept of the short run.

[5] As the function would become $Q(K, L) = 3 \cdot 0.5L = 1.5L$.

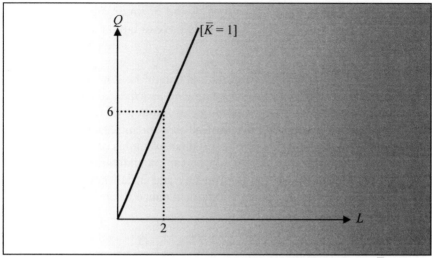

Fig. 5.2. A short run production function with an exogenous quantity of capital $\bar{K} = 1$

5.4 Changing the Quantity of One Input – The Short Run

As already implicitly assumed above, whether we alter one or both inputs has to do with the time frame under which we consider the production process. This section is focused on the short run while Section 5.5 concentrates on the long run. In addition, we will also consider the connection between average and marginal product at the end of this section.

5.4.1 The Distinction Between Short and Long Run

Variable and Fixed Inputs
Before we can commence our discussion of how output reacts to a change in inputs, we need to discuss four relatively simple concepts. To begin with, a variable input is an input the quantity of which can be altered whereas a fixed input is an input the quantity of which cannot be altered. This is intuitive and therefore not difficult to remember.

Short Run and Long Run
From the understanding of fixed and variable inputs arises the concept of short run and long run. The short run is defined as the *longest period of time during which at least one factor of production is fixed*. A factor of production that might be fixed in the short run is the number of printing presses your publishing house owns. To increase the maximum number of

books that you can produce in a given period of time, you might have to buy a second press and you might possibly have to build a larger manufacturing plant.

Things of this sort naturally take time and cannot be done overnight. The long run is hence that *shortest period of time in which all factors of production are variable*. The long run in our example is therefore the time it takes to install a second machine, to find new premises, or to rent more machine-hours from a service provider. Other examples of the long run include that shortest period of time it takes a car manufacturer to build a new plant, the launderette down the road to buy and install new washing machines, or the night club to open an additional dance floor.

The longest period of time during which at least one factor of production is fixed is known as the short run.

That shortest period of time it takes to vary all factors of production is known as the long run.

What is important to note is that the allocation of which input is fixed and which one is varied is not carved in stone. For example, you might find that there is no problem in hiring a second writer for the production of the textbook if you had six months to do so, but it turns out to be practically impossible if you only had one day. Hence, whether an input is fixed or varied always depends on what our time window is. *Almost any factor of production is variable if the time frame is long enough.*

Decreases in Production Quantity
Note that the definition of the long run also works the other way round. Sometimes firms may wish to *decrease* the amount of their factor(s) of production, perhaps due to an economic downturn. Here too, the firm needs time to alter the quantity of factors of production it employs in its production process. Say you own a production facility. While you may be able to fire your employees relatively quickly, selling the plant may take months or even years.

Variability of Labour in the Short Run
Theoretically, it is possible that capital is variable in the short run and labour is fixed, but this would be unusual. Therefore, unless otherwise stated, we assume that in the short run labour is *always* variable and capital is *always* fixed.

5.4.2 The "Law" of Diminishing Returns

Now that we know what the short run is, let us have a look at production within this time frame. We are interested to see what happens to output Q as we increase the variable input L while capital K is fixed.

A Non-linear Total Product Curve
Looking at Fig. 5.3, we observe that initially total product does indeed increase as labour input rises. This can be seen by the positive slope of the curve. However, as indicated earlier, the intuition that total product would keep increasing as we add more of the variable factor of production can fail us. This is seen by the eventual negative slope of the total product curve.

Increasing Returns
Let us look at the curve more closely. For inputs smaller than L_1, not only does total product increase with an increase in labour, it also increases at an *increasing rate*. Graphically this means that the gradient of the production function is increasing. This is known as increasing returns. In our example, increasing returns are present for all input quantities smaller than L_1.

Diminishing Returns
For inputs larger than L_1 and smaller than L_2, output is still increasing with an increase in labour, but now it is doing so at a *decreasing rate*. In other words, the slope is becoming less and less steep. Beyond input quantities of L_2, the gradient is even negative. So, we can say that for all quantities larger than L_1, the production function exhibits diminishing returns.

Constant Returns
Having talked about the areas of the total product curve where the gradient is increasing and those areas where the gradient is decreasing, let us focus on that one point in between. By definition, L_1 is the **point of inflection**. You can think of it as a turnaround point at which the rate of change momentarily stands still, and then goes in the other direction as we keep in-

creasing the variable input[6]. The first production function we looked in this chapter had constant returns — for a given level of capital, every additional unit of labour generated the same additional output.

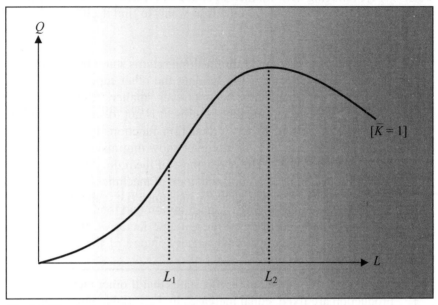

Fig. 5.3. The production function exhibits increasing returns for labour input smaller than L_1, shows constant returns at L_1 and diminishing returns beyond L_1

The Intuition

Let us briefly use our intuition for an example of a production process that would yield a total product curve such as the one shown in Fig. 5.3. As we hire a second and third writer for our book yields ever larger increases in total product up until a quantity of L_1 is reached. A reason for this may be that writers can now divide up tasks and can therefore make more efficient use of every labour hour. Every increase in total product from an increase in the variable input in this range is larger than the increase in total product from any previous addition of (equal chunks of) labour units (e.g. number of workers, labour hours, working day).

Beyond, L_1, further increases in labour still result in an increase in total product but at a decreasing rate, which means that upon hiring more writers bottle necks would occur. There may only be a fixed number of com-

---

[6] In Section 5.4.3 we will pick up the discussion of the rate of change (i.e. the marginal product) of the variable factor input.

puters that can be shared, for example, or maybe there is not enough room in the office for everyone to have their own desk. If you hire yet more writers, as L becomes larger than L_2 the labourers are likely to be in each other's way, reducing one another's productivity; hence, total product actually *decreases* — not a position the firm wants to find itself in.

Diminishing Returns — A Real Law?
The concept known as the law of diminishing returns states that as we keep increasing the variable input while holding the other input fixed, the increases in output will eventually become ever smaller. Although we are speaking of the "law" of diminishing returns, it is not to say that it will inevitably always be present in any production function. It is conceivable that some production functions do not ever show diminishing returns such as the one shown in Fig. 5.2. However, most of them do. After all, gathering more and more labour to a constant stock of machines will be less and less productive, just as an abundance of machines (i.e. capital) leaves the operators (i.e. labour) increasingly stretched.

> The law of diminishing returns states that if other factors of production are fixed, equal increases in the variable input will eventually lead to ever smaller increases in output.

5.4.3 Marginal Product — The Change in Total Product

As we have seen above, a total product curve may exhibit increasing, constant or diminishing returns depending on the overall quantity of the variable input employed. This is related to the rate of change of the total product curve. Let us look at Fig. 5.4. The top panel of this graph is a reproduction of Fig. 5.3, while the bottom panel depicts the derivative of the total product function. Before we will get into the meaning and relevance of this derivative, let us make sure we understand the underlying mechanics of Fig. 5.4.

The Intuition of the Top Panel
To indicate that one curve is the derivative of the other, we draw tangents to three points on the total product curve (as indicated by the blobs) and

transfer them downwards into the second panel. L_3 is a point for which output is increasing at an increasing rate, so we know that increasing returns are present. L_1 is a point of inflection for which the gradient is about to "turn around". For inputs larger than L_1, the gradient is decreasing or even negative, which means diminishing returns are present. At L_2 the tangent is flat as the gradient of the total product curve is zero.

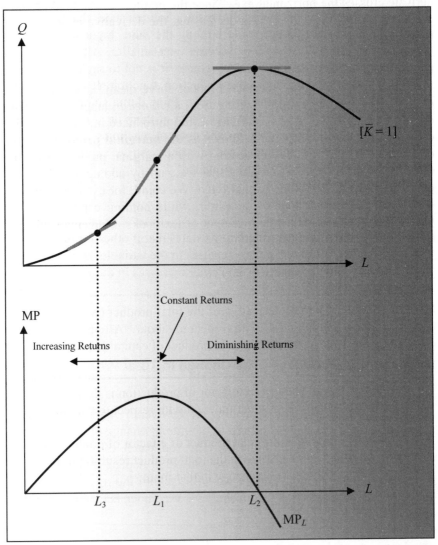

Fig. 5.4. A two-panel showcase depicting how the marginal product of labour curve is derived from the gradient of the total product curve

Translating Our Knowledge into the Bottom Panel
As a direct consequence of the three facts above, the slope of the derivative in the bottom panel is increasing for inputs lower than the point of inflection, reaches its maximum where the total product curve exhibits its point of inflection, and decreases for subsequent larger inputs. Moreover, where the total product curve is flat (i.e. where its gradient equals zero) its derivate crosses the horizontal axis. Since the gradient of the total product curve for inputs larger than L_3 is decreasing, the derivative is negative in that range.

Naming the Derivative
What does the derivate of the total product curve mean? It shows us the *rate of change* in the output resulting from a *change* in labour input. This definition is similar to that of marginal utility introduced in Chapter 3. The derivative of the total product is known as the **marginal product**. Within the context of Fig. 5.4, we are dealing with a marginal product of labour curve. It shows us the extra output that we gain by adding an additional unit of labour while holding capital fixed. We could, for example, say that one additional labour hour of an editor, while holding capital constant, yields an additional 0.01 units of output of textbooks. Mathematically denoted, the marginal product of labour is:

$$\text{MP}_L = \frac{\partial Q(K,L)}{\partial L} \qquad (5.3)$$

Equation 5.3 is the partial derivative of the total product (which is a function of capital K and labour L) with respect to labour.[7] All of the above discussion applies equally to the marginal product of capital MP_K.

The marginal product of a factor of production is the partial derivative of the total product function with respect to that input.

Alternatively, the marginal product of a factor of production can be defined is the change in the total product resulting from a one-unit change in that input.

---

[7] The marginal product of labour may be defined as the change in the total product resulting from a one-unit change in labour input. This is expressed as $\Delta Q/\Delta L$. This expression would be less precise as it shows the gradient of the total product curve over an area rather than a specific point on the curve.

5.4.4 Average Product

There is another concept related to the production of goods that needs to be considered: the average product. It is significant because it can tell us the overall productivity of a factor of production. For this, we do not need to know the gradient or the shape of the total product curve at any point. The average product is simply defined as the total product divided by the number of units of the variable input.

Taking the example of labour input, the average product of labour AP_L tells us how many units of output one unit of labour yields *on average*:

$$AP_L = \frac{Q}{L} \tag{5.4}$$

How can we analyse this graphically? Let us look at the total product curve one last time in the top panel of Fig. 5.5. As before, the MP_L curve is included in the bottom panel along with the AP_L curve. But how do we know how to draw the average product of labour curve in the first place?

The Use of Rays

Its connection with the total product curve can be understood by using rays, R_1 and R_2. Rays are straight lines branching out from the origin. Wherever the ray crosses or touches the total product curve, the gradient that this ray exhibits at that point will be the vertical position of the average product of labour curve in the second panel for this same quantity of labour.

Try changing the gradient of R_2 around and you will notice that you cannot draw a ray that still touches the total product curve and has a gradient steeper than that of R_2. Therefore, the amount of labour input at which R_2 is tangent to the total product curve is the same amount of input for which the average product curve reaches its maximum. This is L_5. Similarly, for inputs larger or smaller than L_5, the rays that would touch the total product curve must necessarily be of a lower gradient than R_2. R_1 is one such example which corresponds to a quantity of labour equal to L_4.

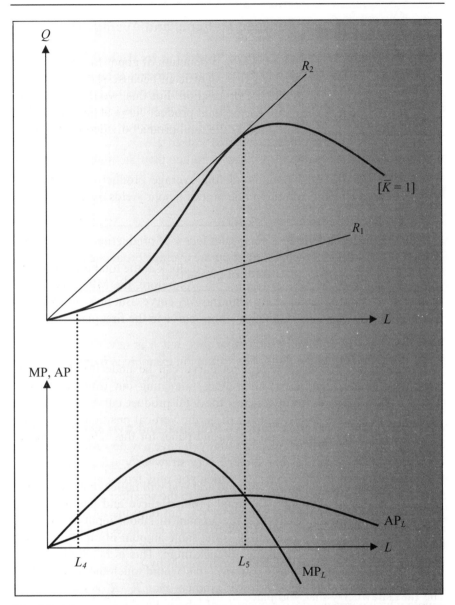

Fig. 5.5. A two-panel showcase depicting the connection of marginal and average products of labour with the total product. MP_L crosses AP_L where the latter reaches its maximum

5.4.5 The Connection Between Marginal and Average Products

Marginal Product Crosses Average Product at Its Highest Point

Looking at Fig. 5.5, we can see that: marginal product is higher than average product when the average product is rising; marginal product crosses average product at the maximum of the average product curve; and when marginal product is below average product, the marginal product is falling. These facts are no coincidence and will indeed always be true. However, the reason for this is purely arithmetic rather than stemming from economic intuition.

> The marginal product curve of a factor of production will always cut through the maximum of the average product curve of that factor of production.

You could of course simply remember this, but it is never a bad idea to know the logic behind the facts. The following example is included to help you understand the rationale of the connection between average and marginal products.

Illustrating the Connection Between Marginal and Average Product

Suppose you are a strawberry farmer and you have a wide variety of strawberry sizes, from small to very large. Every strawberry size exists exactly two times except the largest one, of which you only have one. You form a single line from smallest to largest and then to the smallest again. Now you place a bucket on a scale that can show you not only the total weight but also the average weight of all strawberries. (It can detect when a strawberry has been placed in the bucket and so always knows the total number of strawberries it needs to divide the total weight by.)

The first strawberry that you place in the bucket makes the scale read the same average weight as marginal weight (i.e. the weight of each individual strawberry). Every subsequent strawberry that is being placed in the bucket is larger than the preceding one and as long as this will be the case, the average weight will always be lower than the marginal weight. The average weight must be lower than the weight of each new strawberry because the weight of the *less* heavy strawberries still affects the average weight negatively.

Once you have reached the heaviest strawberry, every subsequent one is now *lighter* than the preceding one, but still larger than average weight. Hence, average weight keeps increasing at a decreasing rate. The increase in average weight becomes ever smaller the closer the weight of each new strawberry gets to it. Eventually average weight stops increasing, once that one strawberry which is equal in weight to the average weight is placed in the bucket.

From now on every strawberry that you add is of a lesser weight than the average weight because the weight of the heavy strawberries is influencing average weight. This analogy illustrates the rationale by which marginal and average products are connected.

The Mathematical Connection Between AP and MP

In case you are not a big fan of strawberries and understand things more easily in mathematical terms, the following discussion might be more to your liking. How can we mathematically prove that marginal product crosses average product where average product is at its maximum? The first step is to differentiate average product AP with respect to labour L and set the expression equal to zero. Remember, setting the derivative equal to zero gives us the critical point, here the maximum. Firstly, let us recall the average product function:

$$AP_L = \frac{Q}{L} \tag{5.5}$$

One may use the quotient rule for differentiating the above expression but it is easier to rewrite AP_L as a product:

$$AP_L = Q \cdot L^{-1} \tag{5.6}$$

Now we can use the **product rule** to differentiate the average product. The rule states: "Take the derivative of the first term and multiply it by the second term and add the derivative of the second term multiplied by the first term." Letting the derivative be equal to 0 we can therefore write:

$$0 = \frac{\partial AP_L}{\partial L} \tag{5.7}$$

$$0 = \frac{\partial Q}{\partial L} L^{-1} - QL^{-2}$$

Since we are not working with specific numbers, the derivative of Q is $\partial Q/\partial L$. In other words, the derivative of the average product includes another derivative, which may be a source of confusion. Think about it this way: if you had a simple function such as $y(x) = x^2$, then the derivative would be dy/dx. However, in the case of Equation 5.7, we have Q instead of y, and L instead of x. Therefore we take the derivative of Q with respect to L.

One final thing about Equation 5.7 before we move on: we see a negative sign in front of the second term. This is the result of the negative exponent of the second term L^{-1} which was brought in front of the term in the process of the differentiation. To simplify Equation 5.7 we can multiply each term by L, which gives:

$$0 = \frac{\partial Q}{\partial L} - QL^{-1} \tag{5.8}$$

As a final step, let us put the equation back into fraction form:

$$0 = \frac{\partial Q}{\partial L} - \frac{Q}{L} \tag{5.9}$$

What does our finding mean? Look at the two terms very closely. Do you notice anything? From Equations 5.4 and 5.5, we know that $\partial Q/\partial L$ is the marginal product of labour while Q/L is the average product of labour. Thus, we can put our equation into the final form:

$$0 = MP_L - AP_L \tag{5.10}$$

Recall that Equation 5.10 is the derivative of the average product. Therefore, the values of the individual terms correspond to the vertical position of the marginal and average product curves. Hence, when the derivative of average product is zero (i.e. the curve is flat as it has reached its maximum), the vertical positions of average and marginal products are the same. Putting it differently, the two curves cross each other when average product has reached its maximum. This is precisely what we wanted to show.

5.5 Introducing the Long Run

Recalling the Implications of the Long Run
In our discussion of the short run, we looked at the total product curve and how it changes with a change in the variable input whilst keeping all other inputs fixed. In the long run, however, all inputs are variable. This means that we can choose a variety of input *combinations*. For example, we would now not only be free to hire editors but we would also be flexible to change the size of the office building, the number of printing presses and

indeed any other factor of production that might have been fixed in the short run.

5.5.1 Returns to Scale — A Change in Both Inputs

Now that we are dealing with the long run, we are interested in what happens to output when we change not only one, but both inputs. If your factory doubles in size and you hire twice as many workers, how will output react to it? We would, of course, expect that output will increase, but by what proportion relative to the increase in the factor inputs?

We are dealing with **increasing returns to scale** when *an equal increase in both inputs yields a more than proportionate increase in output*. For example, if we equally increase labour and capital by 10% and the resulting rise in output is larger than 10%, then we are dealing with increasing returns to scale.

Similarly, when equal increases in inputs yield a *less* than proportionate increase in output, we are dealing with **decreasing returns to scale**. This would be the case if, for example, an increase of 10% in both inputs yields an increase in output of less than 10%. Finally, when equal increases in inputs yield an equal increase in output we are dealing with **constant returns to scale**. Here, 10% increase in both inputs would yield exactly 10% increase in output.

> The terms increasing, constant and decreasing returns to scale refer to situations in which equal increases in both factors of production result in more than proportional, proportional, and less than proportional increases in output, respectively.

Diminishing Returns vs. Decreasing Returns to Scale

While the terms are very similar, a common mistake is to confuse diminishing returns with decreasing returns to scale. Care must be applied in communication in order to ensure correctness of application.

You will not make a mistake of confusing the two concepts when you keep in mind that in the long run, the scale of the operations can be changed, (hence we speak of "returns to *scale*") while in the short run the scale of production is unchanged. You are simply piling up labourers on the shop floor rather than expanding the factory or buying new machines, so to speak.

As we can see in Fig. 5.6, in the short run, the amount of capital remains unchanged and only labour (the variable input) can be altered, while the size of the factory remains unchanged. In the long run, however, all inputs can be changed, including the size of the factory.

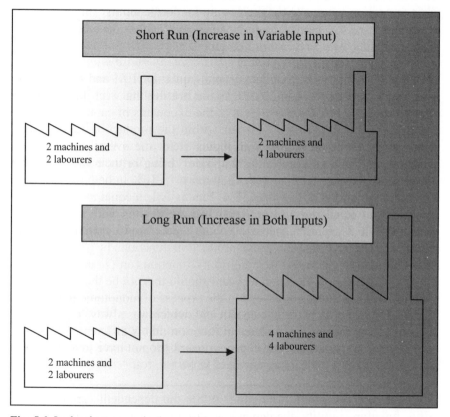

Fig. 5.6. In the short run only the variable factor of production can be increased, while in the long run both inputs (i.e. the scale) can be altered

Diminishing Returns and Increasing Returns to Scale Are not Mutually Exclusive

In distinguishing diminishing returns and decreasing returns to scale, we must understand that it is easily conceivable that a production function, whether it has increasing, constant or decreasing returns to scale, is likely to display diminishing returns when the variable input increases sufficiently.

5.5.2 The Cobb–Douglas Production Function

At the beginning of Section 5.3, we had a look at an example of a production function which was then also represented graphically in Fig. 5.2. Now we will again use a production function, but this time a specific type of function known as the Cobb–Douglas production function. This function is commonly used to quantify production processes and is denoted as:

$$Q(K, L) = A \cdot K^{\alpha} \cdot L^{\beta} \qquad (5.11)$$

This function tells us that output depends on capital K, and on labour L. Specific to each production process is the bearing that each factor has on the output. This is denoted by α and β, the exponents of capital and labour respectively. Finally, A is a constant within the production function that also influences the output. A is an indicator for the overall efficiency of production — higher values of A mean more "bang for the buck", i.e. more efficient production.

Making the Connection to the Utility Function
In Section 3.6.3 we initially learned about the Cobb–Douglas *utility* function, which is very similar to the production function. In Chapter 3, we stated that exponents α and β in the utility function (on Q_1 and Q_2, respectively) always have to be equal to 1 and should this not be the case, the exponents could always be adjusted via the process of monotonic transformation. The same held true for the coefficient, which was always equal to 1 in the utility function. In the production function this is different. We do not apply monotonic transformation, the exponents do not have to add up to 1, and the coefficient A also does not have to be 1.

The reason for this is the following. While the dependent variable of the utility function is utility, the dependent variable of the production function is output. We recall from Chapter 3 that the absolute value of utility is irrelevant, as the only important thing we were interested in was our ability to construct an ordinal ranking of different consumption bundles. In production, however, the absolute value of the dependent variable is objective and all important. 10 units of production are twice as many as 5. Hence, applying monotonic transformation in production would distort the firm's output level and must therefore never be applied in production.

Returns to Scale and the Cobb–Douglas Production Function
Now that we have conceptually understood returns to scale, we can relatively easily state mathematical conditions for the Cobb–Douglas production function that will hold true for the three possible cases of returns to scale. The concept that we introduce to our analysis now is the **degree of homogeneity**, which sounds more intimidating than it really is. The degree of homogeneity D tells us whether we are dealing with increasing, constant, or decreasing returns to scale. For this reason, consider the following equation in which we multiply both K and L by a constant C:

$$Q(C \cdot K, \, C \cdot L) = C^D \cdot Q(K, L) \tag{5.12}$$

If you recall the definition of increasing, decreasing and constant returns to scale, Equation 5.12 is very intuitive indeed. Multiplying capital K and labour L by the same constant $C > 1$ is the same as increasing both inputs by some percentage. Hence, we focus on the exponent D.

Suppose C is equal to 1.1. This would correspond to an increase in both inputs of 10%. If C^D was then larger than 1.1, the production function would exhibit increasing returns to scale; if it was less than 1.1, it would exhibit decreasing returns of scale; and if it was equal to 1.1, it would exhibit constant returns to scale. As a direct consequence, we can state the following generally applicable rule: *if* D *is smaller than 1, the production function exhibits decreasing returns to scale; if it is equal to 1, it exhibits constant returns to scale; and if it is larger than 1, it exhibits increasing returns to scale.*

Incorporating Our Knowledge into the Cobb–Douglas Function
While the above insight from Equation 5.12 is a good starting point, we would also like to be able to draw conclusions with regards to the Cobb–Douglas production function as shown in Equation 5.11. As we will see in the process of the following discussion, the sum of the exponents α and β on K and L, respectively, can tell us about the degree of homogeneity. We will prove that if:

$\alpha + \beta < 1$, then $D < 1$, and $C \cdot Q(K, L) < Q(C \cdot K, C \cdot L)$
which means that decreasing returns to scale are present,

$\alpha + \beta = 1$, $D = 1$, and $C \cdot Q(K, L) = Q(C \cdot K, C \cdot L)$
which means that constant returns to scale are present, and

$\alpha + \beta > 1$, $D > 1$, and $C \cdot Q(K, L) > Q(C \cdot K, C \cdot L)$
which means that increasing returns to scale are present.

Proving the Rule for Constant Returns to Scale

To prove that the analogy between the sum of exponents and the degree of homogeneity is correct, we start by picking a case in which $\alpha + \beta = 1$, which according to our assertion corresponds to a production process exhibiting constant returns. Let us translate the fact that the sum of the exponents is equal to 1 into the Cobb–Douglas production function by replacing β with $1 - \alpha$:

$$Q(C \cdot K, C \cdot L) = A \cdot (C \cdot K)^{\alpha} \cdot (C \cdot L)^{1-\alpha} \tag{5.13}$$

Equation 5.13 can be simplified in the following way:

$$Q(C \cdot K, C \cdot L) = A \cdot C^{\alpha} \cdot C^{1-\alpha} \cdot K^{\alpha} \cdot L^{1-\alpha} \tag{5.14}$$

Since C and K, and C and L each had their own bracket, the exponents of α and $1-\alpha$ are applied to C and K, and C and L, respectively. As a last step the two Cs can be multiplied, which results in the cancellation of the α in the exponent:

$$Q(C \cdot K, C \cdot L) = C \cdot A \cdot K^{\alpha} \cdot L^{1-\alpha} \tag{5.15}$$

Now, as a final step, we can replace $1 - \alpha$ with β again:

$$Q(C \cdot K, C \cdot L) = C \cdot A \cdot K^{\alpha} \cdot L^{\beta} \tag{5.16}$$

Equation 5.16 is all we need to prove our assertion of the connection between the sum of the exponents and the degree of homogeneity. Equation 5.16 says that when the exponents α and β add up to 1, some equal increase in both inputs results in exactly the same increase in the total product and the exponent D is equal to 1. This is what we wanted to prove. Let us verify what we found using a simple example of a production function in which $A = 5$ and $\alpha = \beta = 1/2$:

$$Q(K, L) = 5K^{1/2} \cdot L^{1/2} \tag{5.17}$$

This is a function that exhibits constant returns to scale. This means that if we increase both inputs by some equal percentage, output should change by that same percentage and D should be equal to 1. Let us see if this is the case, choosing arbitrary numbers for K and L:

$$Q(K, L) = 5 \cdot 1^{1/2} \cdot 1^{1/2} = 5 \tag{5.18}$$

Increasing both inputs by 10% to 1.1, total output increases to:

$$Q(K, L) = 5 \cdot 1.1^{1/2} \cdot 1.1^{1/2} = 5.5 \tag{5.19}$$

The increase in output from 5 to 5.5 is 10% — exactly equal to the percentage increase in inputs, and hence D is equal to 1.

Verifying the Rule for Decreasing and Increasing Returns to Scale
We can verify that our rule is not only correct for constant returns to scale by using our intuition. Let us now say that $\alpha + \beta$ is smaller than 1. Taking Equation 5.18 and picturing that either one of the exponents was smaller than 1/2, the total product would have to be smaller than 5.5. The result of this would be an increase smaller than proportional in output compared to input, which is synonymous to saying that decreasing returns to scale are present and that D would be smaller than 1. The intuition works the other way round too: If either one of the exponents was larger than 1/2, total product would have to be larger than 5.5. Increasing returns to scale and a D larger than 1 would be present.

5.6 Introducing Isocost Line and Isoquant

Sections 5.6 to 5.8 significantly overlap with Sections 3.5 to 3.9, and we therefore keep the following discussion short. The goal of Sections 5.6 to 5.8 is to introduce the concepts of the isocost line and the isoquant, which have their equivalents in consumer theory in the budget line and the indifference curve. Furthermore, we will reformulate the Cobb–Douglas production function so that we can use it to draw isoquants, and we will also have a closer look at the slope of the isoquant, which is called the marginal rate of *technical*[8] substitution MRTS. As a last step we show that when the slopes of the isoquant and the isocost line are equal, the input combinations of the firm are optimal so that cost is minimised for the given output level.

5.6.1 The Isocost Line

Factor Input Space
The isocost line is the firm's equivalent of the budget line. The critical difference is that the firm does not consume but produce. Therefore, while the consumer's budget line was drawn in commodity space, this is inevitably different for the firm. We therefore introduce factor–input space at this instance. The factor–input space is simply the area encompassed by a graph with capital and labour as its vertical and horizontal axes, respectively.

---

[8] "Technical" is in italics here because the slope of the indifference curve in consumer theory is the marginal rate of substitution MRS.

Stating an Equality
Next, let us state the firm's cost which (as we learned in Section 5.2) comprises the cost of labour w and the cost of capital r. Recalling the consumer's budget constraint, which was:

$$M = p_F \cdot Q_F + p_S \cdot Q_S \qquad (5.20)$$

we can slightly restate the formula for the process of production:

$$C = r \cdot K + w \cdot L \qquad (5.21)$$

Equation 5.21 states that combinations of capital and labour multiplied by their respective prices result in some cost C that the firm incurs. This is extremely intuitive.

Drawing the Isocost Line
Drawing an isocost line is very similar to drawing a budget line. We simply need to find the intercepts on the two axes and then connect these by a straight line. Any location on the vertical axis means that only capital is used and no labour, and hence the intercept can be found by dividing the entire cost C by the cost of capital, r. This gives us the total number of units of capital that can be purchased for any given C. Similarly, the horizontal intercept is the entire cost divided by the unit cost of labour, w. Now intercepts C/r and C/w have to be connected. By doing so we get a triangle that contains the feasible factor combinations, given a certain (maximum) cost.

Also note that the slope of the budget line is $-w/r$. Drawing a parallel to the consumer's problem, the logic of the derivation of the slope of the budget line is identical to the one shown in Equations 3.7 and 3.8.

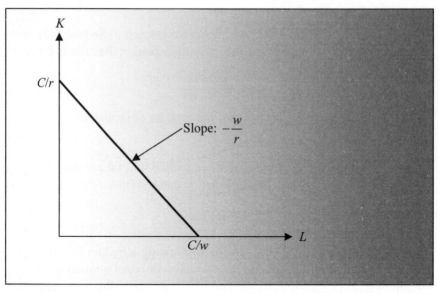

Fig. 5.7. An isocost line in factor input space with vertical and horizontal intercepts of C/r and C/w, respectively

5.6.2 The Isoquant

The isoquant is equivalent to the indifference curve in consumer theory. Rather than constituting a curve representing all consumption bundles that yield the same utility, the isoquant is a curve representing all possible input combinations giving the same output. Let us look at Fig 5.8.

> The isoquant is a curve representing all possible input combi-
> nations which yield the same level of output.

What we see is known as an isoquant map, also drawn in factor input space. Each isoquant represents an infinite collection of input combinations that all yield the same constant output $\bar{Q}$ (pronounced "Q bar") . The further an isoquant lies from the origin, the larger the output achieved by these input combinations.

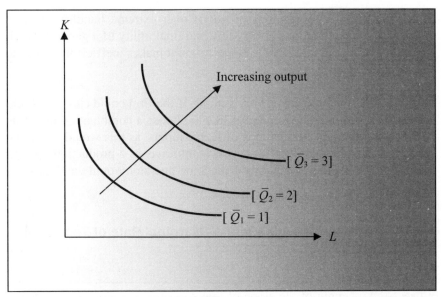

Fig. 5.8. An isoquant map in factor-input space depicting three isoquants with different exogenous total products. The further the isoquant lies from the origin, the larger the output level

A Vital Difference to Indifference Curves

The only marked difference of the concept of the isoquant to the indifference curve is the comparability of different curves by way of the value of quantity Q. The values of Q given by different isoquants have a meaning beyond their ordinal comparability. For example, not only can we say that some output $\bar{Q}_{10} = 10$ is larger than $\bar{Q}_8 = 8$ but we can also say that $\bar{Q}_{10}$ is 25% larger than $\bar{Q}_8$. Recall that such analogies were not possible when comparing different utility levels. In consumer theory, all we were able to say was that some utility was higher than another level of utility.

The More Output, the Further Away from the Origin

In factor input space one can draw infinitely many isoquants. Naturally, the more input (of both factors) we allocate to the production process, the more total product will be the result, and hence the further the isoquant will be from the origin. Hence, the higher each isoquant is, the more total product is associated with it. As with indifference curves, isoquants will never cross each other, are convex, and slope downwards.

Explaining the Shape of the Isoquant

As you may remember from Chapter 3, the slope of the indifference curve was the marginal rate of substitution MRS. We developed the intuition that consumers prefer combinations of goods over extreme bundles because, given their utility functions, a very low marginal utility of a good of which the consumer already possesses a large amount makes inefficient use of the "space" in a bundle.[9]

In production, the rationale is very similar. If the firm could choose a finite number of input units it would also like to choose a combination of inputs rather than extreme combinations of factor inputs, as this would cause the total product to be relatively low. This is intuitive, as a production process with, say, 100 machines and only 1 machine operator would yield very little output.

5.6.3 The Slope of the Isoquant — Marginal Rate of Technical Substitution MRTS

The Slope of the Isoquant
What is the meaning of the slope of the isoquant? The slope shows us the rate at which one input has to be given up for another input in order to keep output constant. We are interested in the slope of the isoquant because in Section 5.7 we will need it to determine the optimal input combinations of the firm so that it can produce a certain output at the lowest cost possible.

As the heading of this subsection reveals, the slope of the isoquant is known as the MRTS and is very similar to the MRS in consumer theory. Since the slope of any curve is its "rise over run", we can state that:

$$\text{MRTS} = \frac{\Delta K}{\Delta L} \tag{5.22}$$

Moreover, it should be noted that the MRTS is also the negative quotient of the marginal products of the two factors of production[10]:

$$\text{MRTS} = -\frac{\text{MP}_L}{\text{MP}_K} \tag{5.23}$$

---

[9] In other words, a finite number of units of goods can be consumed in a way as to increase total utility. We illustrated this in Table 3.1 by assuming that the consumer was only able to purchase 10 units in total.
[10] We can state $-\text{MP}_L\Delta L = \text{MP}_K\Delta K$ because the total product is the same anywhere on the isoquant. The expression can be cross-multiplied so that the marginal products form a fraction, and this is what we see in Equation 5.23.

Since the marginal products of the two inputs are the partial derivatives of the production function with respect to each of those inputs, we can write:

$$\text{MRTS} = -\frac{\partial Q(K,L)/\partial L}{\partial Q(K,L)/\partial K} \qquad (5.24)$$

5.7 Optimal Input Combinations — Cost Minimisation

Cost Minimisation Rather than Quantity Maximisation
The combination of indifference curve and budget line in consumer theory helped us find the combination of goods which maximises the consumer's utility. Therefore, it is tempting to think that the combination of isoquant and isocost line could help us find the combination of factor inputs that would yield the largest total product possible. However, with the production process we proceed somewhat differently. Let us explain:

In real life, the choice of the production process ("how to produce") is closely linked to the scale of production ("how much to produce"). Here, we take the quantity choice as given and simply ask for the cost-minimising combination of factor inputs to produce this quantity. In other words, we choose the optimal production process *conditional on* the quantity.

In summary, while it is theoretically not impossible to run the firm's optimisation in the same way as we did for the consumer, it would nonetheless be very unusual. Hence, for the firm, we are looking for the most cost efficient way of producing a given quantity of output Q.

The Theory of Finding Optimal Combinations
Having discussed the intuition behind the optimisation, we now want to derive a rule with which we can determine the producer's optimal input combinations to produce a given output Q while minimising cost C. Very similarly to the end of Section 3.9, we can state 2 conditions which must hold in order for this to be fulfilled. Firstly, we state:

$$\frac{\partial Q(K,L)/\partial L}{\partial Q(K,L)/\partial K} = \frac{w}{r} \qquad (5.25)$$

Equation 5.25 states that the slope of the isoquant (the left-hand side) needs to be equal to the slope of the isocost line (the right-hand side)[11]. When the two slopes are equal it means that the isocost line is tangent to the isoquant. Given some constant Q, this point of tangency represents a combination of labour L and capital K for which production can be accomplished at the lowest possible cost C. For this statement to hold true a second condition must also be satisfied:

$$C = w \cdot L + r \cdot K \qquad (5.26)$$

This is to ensure that the tangency actually occurs on an isocost line.

The Practice of Finding Optimal Combinations
Let us now try out the principles learned using a specific production function of:

$$Q(K, L) = 5K^{1/2} \cdot L^{3/2} \qquad (5.27)$$

and an isocost line of:

$$C = 3L + 4K \qquad (5.28)$$

Equation 5.28 entails that the cost of labour w and the cost of capital r is 3 and 4, respectively. Finally, let us say that we want to produce a level of output equal to 40 units. Therefore, we can restate Equation 5.27 as:

$$40 = 5K^{1/2} L^{3/2} \qquad (5.29)$$

It is now our goal to find the optimal quantities of labour L^* and capital K^* for which cost is minimised. Remember, the asterisk signs signify the fact that we are dealing with optimal quantities. Let us firstly only work on the left-hand side of Equation 5.25, using our specific production function 5.27:

$$\frac{\partial Q(K,L)/\partial L}{\partial Q(K,L)/\partial K} = \frac{7.5K^{1/2} \cdot L^{1/2}}{2.5K^{-1/2} \cdot L^{3/2}} \qquad (5.30)$$

Remembering that when we divide variables with specific exponents, the values of these exponents are simply subtracted in our equation:

$$\frac{\partial Q(K,L)/\partial K}{\partial Q(K,L)/\partial L} = 3\frac{K}{L} \qquad (5.31)$$

---

[11] Note that the minus signs on both sides have been removed.

Now we need to set the right-hand side of Equation 5.31 equal to the negative[12] slope of the isocost line (i.e. $w/r = 3/4$) which gives:

$$3K^* \cdot L^{*-1} = \frac{3}{4} \qquad (5.32)$$

Solving for K^* we get:

$$K^* = \frac{1}{4}L^* \qquad (5.33)$$

We can substitute this into Equation 5.29:

$$40 = 5 \cdot \frac{1}{4}L^{*1/2} \cdot L^{*3/2} \qquad (5.34)$$

Taking 1/4 to the power of 1/2 and multiplying out the right-hand side we get:

$$40 = 2.5L^{*1/2} \cdot L^{*3/2} \qquad (5.35)$$

Now the exponents on the Ls are simply added up. At the same time we divide both sides by 2.5, and so:

$$16 = L^{*2} \qquad (5.36)$$

Taking the square route of L^* we get:

$$L^* = 4 \qquad (5.37)$$

Finally the optimum amount of labour L^* can be substituted into Equation 5.29 so that we are also able to find the optimal amount of capital K^*:

$$40 = 5K^{*1/2} \cdot 4^{3/2} \qquad (5.38)$$

Multiplying the right-hand side out, dividing both sides by 40, and squaring both sides, we get:

$$K^* = 1 \qquad (5.39)$$

Hence, in this particular production process, the firm should use 4 units of labour and 1 unit of capital in order to produce optimally, i.e. to produce as cost efficiently as possible. Producing 40 units the firm will spend

$$C = 4L + 3K = 4 \cdot 4 + 3 \cdot 1 = 19 \qquad (5.40)$$

monetary units.

---

[12] As we have removed the minus signs in Equation 5.25.

5.8 Perfect Complements and Substitutes

Perfect Complements

Once again, perfect complements and substitutes are concepts that we are already familiar with from consumer theory. First, let us have a look at perfect complements. Two perfect complements, in the context of the theory of the firm, are inputs which can only be used together (at some fixed proportion) in the process production. An example for this is a crane and a crane operator or a lecture theatre and a lecturer.

If you had ten lecture theatres and only 2 lecturers, the excess theatres would be useless (at least for the purpose of teaching) as they would not yield an additional output. Similarly, if you had 10 lecturers and 2 theatres, the excess lecturers would not yield additional output. For this reason, perfect complements in the theory of the firm are also known as **fixed proportions**. This gives a characteristic L-shape of the isoquant that we can see in the left-hand panel of Fig. 5.9.

The firm's optimisation problem in a production process with two perfect complements, as factors of production is mathematically a little tricky. As it is not possible to find a point of tangency of an L-shaped isoquant to an isocost line, we simply state that the optimal bundle occurs where the isocost line just touches the corner of the isoquant.

Perfect Substitutes

Let us now look at perfect substitutes. The example that we used in consumer theory for perfect substitutes was gas from two different gas stations. If it was the case for your production process that each unit of labour and capital can produce the same amount of input, then these inputs would be considered perfect substitutes.

Say you provide a DVD copy service to help people put their old VHS recordings onto this newer medium. In order to produce some output Q it does not matter whether you use blank DVDs made by Sony or TDK. This case of perfect substitutes is shown in the right-hand panel of Fig. 5.9. The optimal combination of factor inputs occurs either on one of the axes or on any point on the isoquant depending on the respective prices of the inputs.

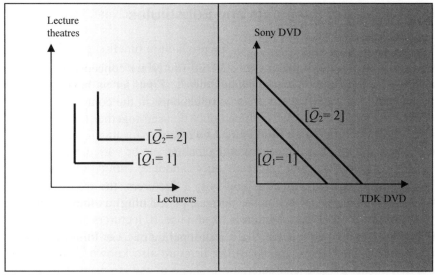

Fig. 5.9. Perfect complements and substitutes are shown in the left- and right-hand panels, respectively

5.9 Chapter Summary

The Process of Production
- A firm is an economic agent with the goal to maximise profits.
- The goods produced by firms are consumed by consumers and are also employed as factors of production by firms.
- A factor of production is some input with which the firm is able to produce output.
- Production is a process whereby present or future utility is created.

Factors of Production
- The most common factors of production are labour, capital, land and entrepreneurship.
- The cost of labour and capital are the wage rate w and the rental rate r, respectively.
- Beyond physical land, the factor of production of land also includes raw materials.

The Production Function
- In the process of production, inputs are transformed into outputs.

- The production function can show us how output changes with a change in inputs.
- The graphical representation of the production function goes by the same name but can alternatively be called "total product curve".
- When graphing output, we hold capital fixed and see how output changes with an increase in the variable input.

The Distinction between Short and Long Run

- A variable input is an input whose quantity can be varied, while a fixed input is an input whose quantity cannot be varied in the production process.
- The short run is defined as that longest period of time during which at least one factor of production is fixed.
- The long run is defined as that shortest period of time during which all factors of production are variable.

Increasing, Constant and Diminishing Returns

- Increasing, constant and diminishing returns refer to situations in which an increase in the variable input (holding the other input fixed) results in an increasing, constant or diminishing increase in total product. In the latter case, a total decrease may also be possible.
- These concepts apply to the short run only.
- The "law" of diminishing returns states that all production functions will eventually exhibit smaller and smaller increases (and feasibly decreases) in output when the variable input rises. We use quotation marks to signify the fact that, although rare in practice, there is at least a theoretical possibility that production functions do *not* ever exhibit diminishing returns.
- Graphically, that amount of the variable input that results in constant returns corresponds to the point of inflection on the total product curve.

Marginal and Average Products

- The marginal product is the derivative of the total product curve. The vertical position of the marginal product curve corresponds to the gradient of the total product curve for this same quantity.
- The marginal product curve increases when increasing returns are present, reaches its maximum for constant returns, falls for diminishing returns, and is negative when the total product curve falls.
- The average product is the total output Q divided by the quantity of the factor of production in question.

- The vertical position of the average product curve is the gradient on the ray on the total product curve for that quantity of the input.
- The marginal product curve cuts through the average product curve where the latter reaches its maximum.

Returns to Scale

- Returns to scale refers to a situation in which both inputs are increased by the same proportion. By definition, therefore, it is a long-run concept.
- Situations in which some equal increase in both inputs results in a more than equal, equal, or less than equal increase in output are known as increasing, constant and decreasing returns to scale, respectively.
- The degree of homogeneity D is a variable that can be used in a production function and whose value allows us to make deductions about returns to scale. When D is smaller, equal to, or larger than 1, decreasing, constant, or increasing returns to scale are present.
- When the sum of the exponents on capital and labour in the Cobb–Douglas function is smaller, equal to, or larger than 1, so is D. Hence decreasing, constant, or increasing returns to scale are present, respectively.
- Increasing, constant, and decreasing returns to scale must not be confused with increasing, constant, and diminishing returns, as they are short-run concepts.
- Production functions with increasing, constant, or decreasing returns to scale are all likely to exhibit diminishing returns at some level of the variable input.

Cobb–Douglas Production Function

- A commonly used production function is the Cobb–Douglas production function.
- An important difference compared to the Cobb–Douglas utility function is that the production function gives us a meaningful absolute value, the output quantity. Therefore the coefficient A and the sum of the exponents α and β do not each necessarily have to equal 1 and we must not use monotonic transformation.

Isocost Line

- The isocost line is the equivalent of the budget line of consumer theory.
- It is drawn in factor-input space, which is the area encompassed by a graph with labour and capital on its axis.

- Any point on the isocost line represents a combination of factor inputs which all cost the same.
- The vertical and horizontal intercepts of the isocost line are C/r and C/w, respectively.
- The slope of the isocost line is $-w/r$.

Isoquant
- The isoquant is the equivalent of the indifference curve of consumer theory.
- It represents an infinite collection of input combinations that all yield the same exogenous total product Q.
- The slope of the isoquant is the marginal rate of technical substitution MRTS, and shows us the rate at which one input has to be given up in order to add more of the other input.

Optimisation
- While in consumer theory the goal was to find the highest indifference curve for some level of income, for the firm the output quantity and hence the isoquant is regarded as given.
- Therefore it is our aim to find the lowest isocost line possible (i.e. that line that minimises cost).

Perfect Substitutes and Complements
- Perfect complements in the theory of the firm are inputs that can only be used together in some fixed proportion. Therefore perfect complements are also known as fixed proportions.
- Perfect substitutes are inputs that can be substituted for each other in the production process.

Marginal Product of Labour

$$MP_L = \frac{\partial Q(K,L)}{\partial L} \tag{5.3}$$

Average Product of Labour

$$AP_L = \frac{Q}{L} \tag{5.4}$$

Cobb–Douglas Production Function

$$Q(K, L) = A \cdot K^{\alpha} \cdot L^{\beta} \tag{5.11}$$

Isocost Function

$$C = r \cdot K + w \cdot L \tag{5.21}$$

The Firm's Optimisation Condition

$$\frac{\partial Q(K,L)/\partial L}{\partial Q(K,L)/\partial W} = \frac{w}{r} \tag{5.25}$$

6. Labour and Capital

Introduction

At the end of Chapter 5, we found out how to arrive at optimum combinations of labour and capital to minimise the cost of a production process. In this chapter we analyse the factor inputs of capital and labour in more detail. Specifically, we derive two separate optimality conditions for the use of labour and capital, weighing up their respective costs w and r against the benefits, where the latter depends on the market structure. Furthermore, we look at the backward bending labour supply curve and money capital.

Required Knowledge

To understand how this chapter fits into the wider context of this text, Chapter 5 should have been read and an understanding of the principles of supply and demand (Chapter 2) is beneficial. Moreover, a basic understanding of marginality (Chapter 1) will also be of use here. A detailed understanding of market structure is not necessary.

Key Terms

labour (L), marginal product of labour/capital (MP_L/MP_K), labour demand, short run, marginality, perfect competition, monopoly, value of marginal product of labour/capital (VMP_L/VMP_K), value of average product of labour/capital (VAP_L/VAP_K), wage rate (w), law of diminishing returns, long run, price elasticity of demand, marginal revenue (MR), marginal revenue product of labour/capital (MRP_L/MRP_K), backward bending supply curve, capital (K), real capital, money capital, rental rate (r), compounded interest, economic rent, capital growth, (net) present value / principal (P), loan, risk premium, bond, equity, weighted average cost of capital (WACC).

6.1 Choosing an Optimal Amount of Labour

Connection to Chapter 5

When dealing with production in the previous chapter, we looked at how output of the firm reacts to a change in the variable input, which, by convention, will most commonly be labour. We also looked at the marginal product of labour MP_L and showed it graphically in Fig. 5.4. The main finding was that, holding capital constant, the total product eventually increases at a decreasing rate the more units of labour we add (and potentially even decreases in absolute terms if the variable input rises even further).

Benefit and Cost of Labour
In this section, we will again look at the MP_L, although this time we do not analyse the output of the firm. We will ignore the fact that one may not necessarily want to produce as many units of output as can profitably be produced as, for example, the market might not support such a large output. Instead, we focus on the cost and benefit of labour and determine from this how much labour to utilise in our production process. This constitutes the demand for labour of the firm.

The Marginality Rationale
In order to solve this problem intuitively, we need to wear our "marginality thinking hat". We consider every additional unit of labour individually and ask ourselves: "Is the cost of this one unit less than what the benefit is?" If the answer is "yes", then we should employ this unit in the process of production. So, we would simply start with the first unit and keep asking the same question until cost and benefit are just equal. Once this has happened, we must not add any further units of labour to avoid making a loss on every additional unit.

6.1.1 Perfect Competitor's Labour Demand in the Short Run

The Influence of Market Structure on Output Price
Before we move on with our reasoning, it is important to be aware of the fact that the labour demand of the firm depends on the market structure in which it operates. The concept of market structure is introduced in Chapter 8, so we will keep the discussion very brief at this point.

As you will soon see, the output price for the good that is being produced is of relevance in choosing the correct number of labour units. While the price is independent of the firm's output in a perfectly competitive market, the price (of every unit) changes with each additional unit produced in an imperfectly competitive market, for example a monopolistic market. Thus, the important point to keep in mind is that the firm's problem of how much labour to choose depends on the market in which it operates, i.e. whether it is perfectly competitive or imperfectly competitive.

Coming Back to the Marginality Rationale

Let us now solve our problem using marginality. We said that we want to keep hiring units of labour until the cost and the benefit are equal. In order to solve this we need to be aware of both the cost and the benefit that belong to each unit of labour on the margin. While the cost of labour simply constitutes the wage rate w, stating the benefit of each unit of labour requires a little more thought.

As you know from Chapter 5, each unit of labour produces an additional quantity of output equal to the MP_L. The **value of marginal product** VMP is how much the additional unit of input is worth to the firm. In this context, this is simply the marginal product of labour multiplied by the market price of the good:

$$VMP_L = MP_L \cdot p \qquad (6.1)$$

Recalling what we said a minute ago, we want the benefit of each unit of labour to be equal to the cost at the optimum point. We do *not* want to increase labour any further beyond the point at which VMP is equal to the wage rate:

$$VMP_L = w \qquad (6.2)$$

Why Equation 6.2 is true in equilibrium is easy to grasp if we recall what the VMP_L means. It is the additional value that each unit of labour brings to the firm. And so long as this value exceeds the cost (i.e. the wage rate), we want to keep hiring labour. We should hire our last unit of labour when the benefit is equal to the cost (on the margin). When this happens, Equation 6.2 holds true. Working with this equation we can substitute the right-hand side of Equation 6.1 for VMP_L, which gives us:

$$MP_L \cdot p = w \qquad (6.3)$$

Therefore, at the optimum point the MP_L multiplied by the price (i.e. the extra revenue achieved from each additional unit of labour), must be equal to the wage rate w.

Showing Marginal Product Graphically

Let us now look at this problem graphically. We draw the MP_L and the VMP_L curves in the top and bottom panels of Fig. 6.1, respectively. What can we learn from the top panel? The MP_L curve that we see is not dissimilar to the second panel of Fig. 5.4. The difference is that we have simplified this curve to show a straight line with a constant downward slope. You may also recall that a downward slope of the MP_L curve means that **diminishing returns** are present. In other words, for every extra unit of labour we add, the increase in total product is less than what it was for the addition of the previous unit of labour.

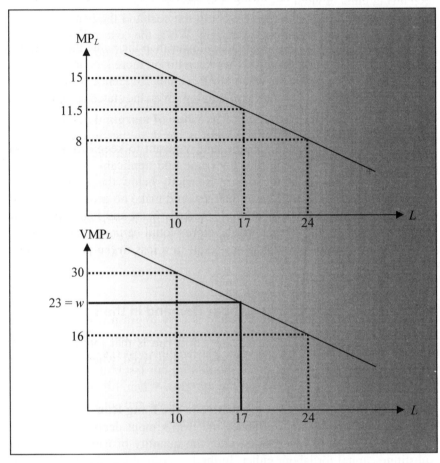

Fig. 6.1. Demand for labour of the perfectly competitive firm. An optimum amount of labour is employed where its benefit (i.e. the VMP) is equal to its cost w on the margin

For example, if 17 units of labour are already employed, hiring an additional unit will yield an extra 11.5 units of output. If, however, 24 units of labour are employed, hiring an additional unit will only yield an extra 8 units of output.

Showing Value Marginal Product Graphically
Moving to the second panel, everything is identical, except that now we are dealing with the VMP_L and so the figures on the vertical axis are multiplied by the price the product yields in the market. Suppose there is a price of $p = 2$ and a wage rate w of 23. When, for example, 10 units of labour are already employed, hiring an additional unit of labour yields 30 monetary units.

At this particular point, the wage rate is lower than the value the additional unit of labour achieves. Therefore, we keep hiring more labour until VMP_L is equal to w, which happens when VMP_L equals 23. Hence, 17 units of labour is the optimal input quantity to employ given the stated assumptions.

Hiring No Labour
The only instance in which the rule that we want to keep hiring until the VMP_L is equal to the wage rate does not find applicability is when the VAP_L (i.e. AP_L times output price p) is strictly below the wage rate w. If this were the case, it would mean that it would make no economic sense to even hire the first unit (as we would make a loss) and hence no labour would be hired at all. In other words, there would be no amount of labour that we could hire which would not result in a loss in the process of production.

6.1.2 Perfect Competitor's Labour Demand in the Long Run

To quickly recap from Chapter 5, the short run is that longest period of time in which at least one factor of production is fixed, whereas in the long run all factor inputs are variable.

Labour Demand Is Less Cost Sensitive in the Long Run
How does the time frame influence the firm's input decision for labour? Since in the short run we cannot alter the quantity of capital, we cannot substitute capital for labour either. In the long run, it may be useful to substitute capital for labour, for example when the wage rate increases. By contrast, in the short run we have to settle for labour as the only variable factor of production, and so during that time frame the demand of labour is less sensitive to price changes than in the long run.

From Chapter 2, we know that the responsiveness of the quantity demanded to a change in price is called **price elasticity of demand**. Analogously, *the demand for labour is less price elastic in the short run than it* *is in the long run.* We would therefore expect the demand curve of labour in the short run to be steeper than in the long run.

6.1.3 The Imperfect Competitor's Labour Demand

As already hinted at in Section 6.1.1, the demand for labour of the *im*perfect competitor is different than for the perfect competitor because the output price depends on the total number of units produced. This is due to the fact that unlike the perfect competitor, the imperfect competitor does not face a perfectly elastic demand curve but a downward sloping one.

The imperfect competitor's equivalent of the VMP_L is known as the **marginal revenue product of labour** MRP_L. This is marginal revenue MR multiplied by the marginal product of labour MP_L:

$$MRP_L = MP_L \cdot MR \qquad (6.4)$$

Before we go any further with this formula, let us discuss the rationale behind it: the right-hand side of Equation 6.4 is identical to that of Equation 6.1 with the difference that price p is replaced by marginal revenue MR. The reason for this is that the imperfect competitor's output price is dependent on total quantity produced and is not, as in the case of the perfect competitor, independent of output. In other words, the price the imperfect competitor receives for his product in the market is a *function of quantity produced*[1].

Working with the Equation
Now that we are clear about the intuition, let us rewrite Equation 6.4. The marginal product of labour MP_L is the additional output Q the firm achieves from an extra unit of labour, or $\Delta Q / \Delta L$. Similarly, the marginal *revenue* is the change in total revenue TR resulting from a change in quantity Q, or $\Delta TR / \Delta Q$. Therefore:

---

[1] Think about it this way: Suppose you were the only person in the world selling apples. As you determine world output, the price would be much higher if you offered 1 unit than if you offered 1 billion units. Conversely, taking a slightly more realistic example, if you were selling apples on a market with thousands of other producers, the price you could charge would be taken as given and your output would make no difference to this price. This intuition is discussed further in Chapter 10.

$$\text{MRP}_L = \frac{\Delta Q}{\Delta L} \frac{\Delta TR}{\Delta Q} \qquad (6.5)$$

As a final step, we cancel the ΔQs and we get:

$$\text{MRP}_L = \frac{\Delta TR}{\Delta L} \qquad (6.6)$$

Intuitively, Equation 6.6 is very satisfying. What it says is that in an imperfectly competitive market, the value of each additional unit of labour is simply the change in total revenue resulting from a change in the labour input. The same holds true for VMP_L except that MRP_L takes into account that a cut in price would be necessary for the imperfect competitor to sell more units.

Solving the problem of how many units of labour to employ here is identical to the case of the perfect competitor. We simply let the wage rate w be equal to the MRP_L, and so for the perfect competitor, at the optimum:

$$\text{MRP}_L = w \qquad (6.7)$$

Holds true. As was the case for the perfect competitor, when VAP_L is below the wage rate, no labour will be hired at all.

The perfect competitor hires the optimal amount of labour when $\text{VMP}_L = w$, whereas the imperfect competitor hires the optimal amount of labour when $\text{MRP}_L = w$.
An exception in both cases is when $\text{VAP}_L < w$, in which case no labour would be hired.

6.2 The Backward Bending Labour Supply Curve

Having discussed the demand for labour, we now move on to its supply. The supply of labour results simply from the decision made by labourers of how much to work in a given time period. We equate choosing not to work with consuming leisure, which by definition would then include any activity other than work.

A Problem of Consumer Choice

The problem the worker is faced with is how much she should work and how much leisure she should consume. This type of problem may sound familiar to you because it is, in essence, one of consumer choice similar to what we discussed in Chapters 3 and 4. The "goods" the worker is choosing from are income and leisure. We therefore draw a graph in commodity space and place these two goods on the vertical and horizontal axes. This can bee seen in Fig. 6.2.

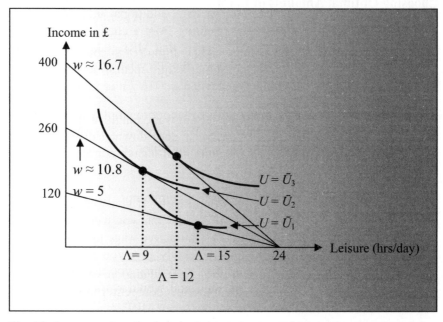

Fig. 6.2. A consumer's optimal choice between income and leisure Λ moves towards less leisure as the wage rate rises from £5 to £10.8, but reverts towards more leisure when the wage rate rises even further to £16.7

Explaining the Graph

Fig. 6.2 includes three budget lines and three indifference curves, each one of which exhibits one point of tangency with one of the budget lines. All of our budget lines meet at 24 on the horizontal axis, as it is it is not possible (even for the most comfortable person) to consume more than 24 hours of leisure a day[2]. The vertical intercept is also influenced by the constraint of time. The maximum amount that can be worked a day is also 24 hours.

---

[2] At the time of writing, there is nothing the authors would like more than a couple of these "24-hour leisure" days.

Since the "good" on the vertical axis is income, the intercepts are simply 24 hours times the hourly pay. This is what the worker would earn working non-stop all day. Now we know why there are three budget lines included: each budget line belongs to a different wage rate w. The intercepts of 120, 260 and 400 correspond to wages of 5, about 10.8 and about 16.7 monetary units respectively. This is analogous to a situation where the price of one good changes, which we have first observed in Chapter 3.

Choosing Optimal Amounts of Leisure

Lastly, the graph also includes three indifference curves of exogenous constant utilities $\bar{U}_1$, $\bar{U}_2$ and $\bar{U}_3$ whereby $\bar{U}_1 < \bar{U}_2 < \bar{U}_3$. Each of these indifference curves exhibits one point of tangency with one of the budget lines. As we can observe, when $w = 5$, the consumer's time spent in leisure Λ^3 is 15 hours, when $w \approx 10.8$ it is 9 hours, and when $w = 16.7$ it is 12 hours.

As you can see quite clearly, within a certain wage range, as the wage rate increases, the amount of leisure consumed goes down. However, as the wage rate increases even further, the amount of leisure consumed goes up again.

Why this is the case can be answered intuitively. If you were given a job that brings with it a good hourly pay, it is likely that you would work much more than if you had a job that pays a less attractive wage just about covering your expenses. Now imagine that somebody gave you a truly stunning hourly wage, so high that you could buy everything you need even if you didn't work all day. It is likely that then you would work relatively few hours.

Translating Our Findings to a Labour Supply Curve

So far, we have not actually arrived at the labour supply curve yet. In order to do so, we need to produce something similar to a mirror image of Fig. 6.2 as we want the supply of labour L rather than leisure Λ on the horizontal axis. The vertical axis needs to be changed as well. Here, rather than the income, we need the wage rate, which is the cost of labour. Doing this translates our findings of Fig. 6.2 into the labour supply curve shown in Fig. 6.3.

How did we derive the curve? When the wage rate is 5, the labour supply is 24 hours minus 15 hours of leisure, which is equal to 9 hours of work a day; when it is 10.8, the labour supply is 24 hours minus 9 hours of leisure,

---

[3] We use lambda for leisure as L is already reserved for labour.

which is equal to 15 hours of work a day; and when the wage rate is 16.7, the quantity supplied is 24 hours minus 12 hours of leisure, which equals 12 hours of work a day. Now we simply need to draw these coordinate pairs on our graph and connect the dots. This gives us the backward bending supply curve of labour.

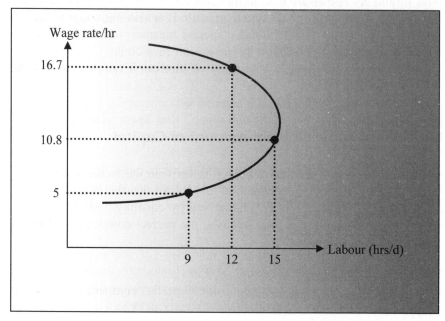

Fig. 6.3. The backward bending supply curve of labour shows that a change in the quantity supplied of labour following an increase in the wage is ambiguous: it may increase or decrease depending on the total amount of hours worked

This curve is interesting, as it is different from what we are used from Chapter 2 where all supply curves were strictly moving towards the northeast. While firms are always willing to supply more as price goes up, when the wage rate rises beyond a certain level, individuals are very likely to offer *less* of their time to the labour market.

6.3 What Is Capital?

Having discussed some important aspects of labour, let us now move on to capital. You may recall from Chapter 5 that capital can mean a number of different things. In the process of production, capital may refer to a physical factor of production such as machinery or buildings, but also cash. To avoid confusion, when we want capital to refer to money we use the term **money capital**, whereas physical inputs such as machine-hours are known as **real capital**.

You should also be aware that, in this chapter, we use the terms "money", "cash" and "(money) capital" synonymously. It is also important to bear in mind that the term "money" holds a special meaning in macroeconomics — i.e. the amount of currency in circulation in a country's economy — and therefore when there is possibility of confusion one should use the term "money capital".

6.4 Choosing the Optimal Amount of Capital

Choosing an optimal amount of capital is very similar to the exercise that we ran through with labour in Section 6.1. Recall that the perfect competitor's optimum usage of labour was derived by equating VMP_L to the cost of labour, the wage rate w. Analogously, the perfect competitor's demand for capital is given by:

$$VMP_K = MP_K \cdot p \qquad (6.8)$$

The similarity to labour also exists for the *im*perfect competitor's optimum use of capital:

$$MRP_K = MP_K \cdot MR \qquad (6.9)$$

It should be remembered that, by convention, choosing an optimal amount of capital is only possible in the long run. For example, a manufacturing business could, by definition, only change the size of its factory or the number of machines it used in the long run.

Analogous to labour, both the perfect and the imperfect competitor do not seek to employ any capital in their production process if the VAP_K is strictly below the rental rate of capital r.

> The perfect competitor hires the optimal amount of capital when $VMP_K = r$ whereas the imperfect competitor hires the optimal amount of capital when $MRP_K = r$.
> An exception in both cases is when $VAP_K < r$ in which case no capital would be hired.

Rental Rate
In Equations 6.8 and 6.9 we have used the cost of capital known as the rental rate r without explicitly referring to it. But what is this rental rate exactly? **Economic rent** does not necessarily have to be an actual rent that is paid by the firm although, of course, it can be. For example, if the firm uses a machine in its production that it borrowed from somebody else, then it would indeed be paying some sort of rental fee for it to whoever owns the machine.

Rent and Opportunity Cost
Many other production processes, however, use the firm's own equipment. What about the rental rate in such an instance? Where the firm owns its own equipment, *the economic rent is the opportunity cost of holding the capital*. The money that went into buying the equipment could have generated some revenue for the firm if used in a different way; at the very least it could have earned, say, 5% per annum in a bank account[4].

6.5 Capital Growth

An Example
In the context of money capital, capital growth is an important part of our discussion. Let us discuss one application of this: Most large firms somehow need to pay their employees' pensions when they retire. For this reason, these firms invest large amounts of capital in a number of ways. Let us take a simplified example in which a firm puts capital in a bank account and watches it grow over the years. How large will a sum invested today be in a number of years? In order to answer this question, we need to define a few variables and then for the sake of illustration we will pick specific values for these.

Defining Variables
Firstly, we need to know what the initial sum invested is, i.e. the principal P. Secondly, we are interested in the growth rate of our capital. This is the interest rate r. You can see why the same letter as for the rental rate is used. If somebody deposits money in the bank, it is in principle not that different from when a firm hires machinery from another firm for the pur-

---

[4] However, putting the cash in the bank is not likely to have been the second best option for the firm. By definition, the opportunity costs are the returns that could have been generated if the capital was allocated to the second best alternative. Such an alternative would probably have been another project.

pose of production. For the bank's process of production such as lending, it requires money capital which it borrows from the firm that has just deposited some cash. So the economic rent the bank pays for the usage of this factor input is known as the interest rate r.

Next, we need a variable for the time frame — N. N can be any time frame such as a day, week or a month, however, in the context of capital growth in most instances it is one year. Finally, C is the amount of capital available at the end of the time period during which the money was deposited. This usage of the variable C might be a source of confusion. Normally C is used for cost while K is reserved for capital. However, in the context of finance where we deal with money capital, by convention, the variable C stands for capital (or to be more specific, that amount of money capital available after some time of capital growth).

An Example of Capital Growth

Let us now pick specific numbers for the variables introduced. Let the principal be £10,000, the interest rate 5% (which we will write as 0.05), and the time frame 10 years.

We can find our C by considering the following logic: Putting money in the bank today, a year from now you will not only have the amount of cash that you deposited at the beginning (the principal) but also the interest on top of it. In our example, after one year, it would be £10,000 plus 5% of £10,000 (which is £500). After the second year, you will again get the same interest rate, not only on the initial £10,000 but also on the previous year's interest. You are left with £10,000, 5% of 10,000 and 5% of £500. Hence, after the second year, you will have 105% of £10,500 which is £11,025.

The concept of receiving interest on previous years' interest is known as **compounded interest**. What happens every period is that whatever cash is available is multiplied by $(1 + r)$ for however many time periods there are[5]. Therefore the following formula is used to compute C:

$$C = P \cdot (1 + r)^N \qquad (6.10)$$

Taking the numbers from our specific example, we can write:

---

[5] The number 1 in the brackets is to signify the fact that at the end of the day, we not only get interest on the principal but of course, the principal itself also remains in existence.

$$C = 10{,}000 \cdot 1.05^{10} \approx 16{,}288.95 \qquad (6.11)$$

What we have just found is that when £10,000 is deposited today, this will be (roughly) £16,288.95 in ten years' time given an interest rate of 5%.

Solving for N

Using Equation 6.10 as a starting point, we can, in principle, also find out how many years we would need to keep a sum of money, such as £10,000, in the bank to double it, assuming the interest rate is again 5%. Plugging the numbers in Equation 6.10 we get:

$$20{,}000 = 10{,}000 \cdot 1.05^{N} \qquad (6.12)$$

Solving for N is not quite as simple as standard rearranging, but can still be done. First, let us divide both sides by 10,000 so we get:

$$2 = 1.05^{N} \qquad (6.13)$$

In order to solve for N we now have to take the logarithm of both sides. This is:

$$\log(2) = N \cdot \log(1.05) \qquad (6.14)$$

Now, we can divide both sides by $\log(1.05)$:

$$\frac{\log(2)}{\log(1.05)} = N \approx 14.21 \qquad (6.15)$$

Hence, at an interest rate of 5%, £10,000 doubles after a time period of a little over 14 years.

6.6 Present Value

The (net) present value[6] of a payment is closely related to our previous calculations. In fact, when solving for C in the previous section we implicitly asked: "If we invest a certain sum today, how much will it be worth to us in the future?" The net present value asks the opposite: "If we are promised a certain sum in the future (or a series of payments over time), how much is this worth to us today?"

---

[6] "Present value" and "net present value" are used interchangeably in the study of economics.

The simple answer might be that £100 is £100, no matter when you get it. However, we need to factor in the opportunity costs and the uncertainty of a future payment. For example, if you could invest £100 today at a rate of return of 5%, you would want to get at least £105 in one year's time to agree to wait for you payment. Similarly, if a friend promises you a sum of money for your birthday "once he is rich", that sum had better be large, because one never knows if the payment will ever materialise — in fact, you might even prefer him taking you out for a drink right then and there rather than a vague promise a of future payment.

The Relevance of Present Value
But what exactly does present value mean and why should we care about it? Present value is a useful tool because it can help the firm make important decisions. For example, a manager may be asked to choose between two projects. Project 1 will pay a net gain of £8,000 in 3 years and project 2 will pay a net gain of £10,000 in 7 years. Which project should she choose?

As you might be able to guess, the answer depends on the interest rate r. The interest rate is important to know because there is a cost connected to holding cash. Let us stick to the 5% and assume that is the opportunity cost. To answer the question of which project should be chosen, we solve Equation 6.10 for P^7, which is the inverse of the capital growth function and is known as the present value function:

$$P = \frac{C}{(1+r)^N} \qquad (6.16)$$

Now the task of answering the question is only a matter of comparing two numbers. The present value of project 1 is:

$$P = \frac{8,000}{1.05^3} \approx 6,910.70 \qquad (6.17)$$

Project 2's worth, in today's money, is:

$$P = \frac{10,000}{1.05^7} \approx 7,106.61 \qquad (6.18)$$

It is close, but it turns out that project 2, which pays off £10,000 in 7 years, would be preferred to project 1, which pays off £8,000 in 3 years. Putting

---

[7] P is used for the net present value and for the principal because they are in essence the same thing.

it differently, the interest you would earn on £8,000 between years 3 and 7 would not be enough to make up the missing £2,000.

Assuming a Change in the Interest Rate

How would our project evaluation change if the interest rate was higher, let us say 8%? In today's money, project 1 would be worth

$$P = \frac{8,000}{1.08^3} \approx 6350.68 \qquad (6.19)$$

while project 2 would be worth:

$$P = \frac{10,000}{1.08^7} \approx 5834.90 \qquad (6.20)$$

As we can see, things have changed dramatically. The manager would no longer choose the project paying returns in 7 years. The higher the interest rate is, the more costly it is not to receive one's cash, and the project paying off sooner has become relatively more attractive.

6.7 How Firms Raise Capital — A High Level Overview

Economics vs. Finance

This section merely gives an overview of how firms finance their growth. If you are interested in a more detailed discussion of this you should look at finance textbooks, which deal with this topic in much more detail. Nevertheless, we mention it here because it puts our conceptual discussions above in context.

Different Ways of Raising Capital

Firms have three primary options to raise money capital. Firms can get a loan, issue debt, or issue equity. Getting a loan from a bank as a firm is in general very similar to the provision of loans to private individuals. Firms are expected to disclose their operations in detail and depending on how well the bank thinks the firm is run, it will apply an appropriate risk premium to its loan. Now what does this mean exactly?

Loans

Say Deutsche Bank provides a loan of £50m to a large international firm for 3 years so that this firm can finance a large project. Let us moreover say that, before it can do so, Deutsche Bank has to get a loan itself from the Bank of England for which it pays 5%. The **risk premium** is then the amount of interest on top of the 5% the firm is charged by Deutsche Bank. This could be 3% if the firm is well run, or more if the bank thinks there is a chance it might not get the money back. Even if a firm exhibited no risk at all, some mark-up would still be charged by the commercial bank in any case because it wants to derive a profit on its operations. Generally, the risk premium is defined as *the excess return of some investment beyond a risk free investment.*

Bonds

Secondly, a firm can issue debt in the form of bonds. This is similar to the loan provision from the bank, with the marked differences that the capital providers do not necessarily have to be banks and the size of the debt per bond tends to be relatively small. The bond issuer promises to repay the holder of the bond the principal at some agreed point in the future; the maturity. In the meantime, the bond issuer pays the holder a fixed amount of interest known as the coupon. Since coupons on bonds are of a fixed size, bonds are often also known as **fixed income securities**. Bonds issued by firms are also distinct from government bonds and are therefore often referred to as **corporate bonds** to avoid confusion.

Similar to bank loans, there are risk premiums attached to bonds. If a firm has risky operations, potential bond holders would expect a large premium to compensate them for the risk of not seeing the principal again. Rating agencies such as Standard & Poor's, Moody's, and Fitch regularly issue credit ratings for the largest companies in the world. The firm has to pay an appropriate risk premium to bond holders depending on these credit ratings.

Bonds can be traded freely and their value changes with interest rates. When interest rates are high, bonds are relatively less attractive than cash holdings and vice versa.

Equity

Another way for the firm to raise money is through issuing equity. This simply means giving out shares. If you hold a share of a company it means that you own a part of this firm. If the firm is very large, this ownership may, as a percentage, be very small, or if the firm is a small start-up, you may become a significant shareholder[8].

---

[8] Venture capitalists make a living from buying equity in small firms and selling it at a profit once the firm has grown.

It should also be noted that companies can have shares even if these are not traded on the stock exchange, although for most large companies their stock is traded. The price of the stock depends on what the firm is worth, i.e. what its expected earnings in all coming years of operation will be (in present value terms). But since markets do not function in a fully rational way, stock prices tend to not always reflect the true value of the firm. This may result in over- or undervaluation. Picking stocks that are undervalued is how stock brokers attempt to make large profits.

6.8 Weighted Average Cost of Capital

In this section, we can combine what we have learned in Sections 6.6 and 6.7. The concept of weighted average cost of capital (WACC) can be regarded as advanced in this context, as it is not ordinarily part of a first year course. Still, it is interesting to think about it now that we have come this far. Let us consider the following scenario. A firm is financed with £100m. Suppose this capital comes from 80% equity and 20% debt and that shareholders demand a 5% return on their equity in the form of dividends; this will cost the firm:

$$100m \cdot 0.8 \cdot 0.05 = 4m \qquad (6.21)$$

Moreover, let us say that the coupon on their corporate bonds is 8% so this will cost the firm another:

$$100m \cdot 0.2 \cdot 0.08 = 1.6m \qquad (6.22)$$

Thus, the firm pays a total of 5.6m a year or 5.6% to hold these funds. This 5.6m constitutes the WACC. It derives its name from the fact that the firm has two (or more) sources of capital. The cost attached to each source of capital has a different weight (here 80% and 20%).

Combining WACC and Present Value
In Section 6.6 we discussed one example in which a manager had to choose between two projects, one paying off a comparatively small amount of money in three years from today, the other paying off slightly more, 7 years from now. We found that the interest rate was vital in determining which present value was higher, and ultimately which project was more attractive. Now we can qualify this statement even further by utilising the WACC instead of the more generic interest rate r, and so we rewrite the present value Equation 6.15 to include the WACC:

$$P = \frac{C}{(1 + \text{WACC})^N} \qquad (6.23)$$

In our example this would be:

$$P = \frac{C}{(1 + 0.056)^N} \qquad (6.24)$$

Using the future payoff and the time it takes for this payoff to happen, we could use Equation 6.24 for project evaluation against different sorts of benchmarks or other projects.

6.9 Summary

Choosing an Optimal Amount of Labour/Capital
- In order to choose an optimal amount of labour/capital, the firm should add additional units of labour/capital to the production process as long as the benefit, on the margin, is greater than the wage/rental rate w/r which is the cost of labour/capital.
- The benefit of each unit of labour/capital depends on the market structure. For a firm operating in a perfectly competitive market, it is the marginal product of labour/capital $MP_{L/K}$ multiplied by the output price p. For a firm operating in an *im*perfectly competitive market, it is the marginal product of labour/capital $MP_{L/K}$ multiplied by the marginal revenue MR.
- At the point of optimality, the wage w needs to be equal to the value marginal product of labour/capital $VMP_{L/K}$ or marginal revenue product of labour/capital $MRP_{L?K}$ for a perfect and imperfect competitor respectively.
- No labour will be hired if the value average product of labour/capital $VAP_{L/K}$ is strictly smaller than w/r.
- The labour demand of the firm is more elastic in the long run than in the short run, as capital can then be substituted for labour.
- By convention, optimal amounts of capital can only be chosen in the long run.

Backward Bending Labour Supply Curve
- Labour supply constitutes the decisions of workers of how much to work during any given time frame.

- Choosing between work and leisure is a problem of consumer choice. For any given time frame, the number of hours worked as opposed to spent on leisure (which depends on the wage rate w) can be used as data points to draw the supply curve of labour.
- Typically, the supply curve of labour is backward bending, which means that the quantity supplied of labour is low for low wages, rises when wages rise, but declines again when wages rise even further.

Basics of Capital

- The term "money capital" is used when we refer to cash, while the term "real capital" is utilised when we talk about physical inputs such as machinery, raw materials and the like.
- The cost of capital is the rental rate r, which may either constitute rent of machinery etc. when the capital input is rented, or it may constitute the opportunity cost of holding the capital. This applies to both real and money capital.

Capital Growth

- The concept of receiving interest on the previous years' interest is known as compound interest.

Present Value

- The present value of money is used to show today's worth of some amount of money in the future.
- In order to calculate this, our capital growth function is simply solved for P.
- Present value calculations are frequently used for project evaluations.

How Firms Raise Capital

- Principally, there are three ways a firm can raise capital: through loans, bonds or equity.
- Loans are usually secured from commercial banks and have a risk premium attached to them.
- The risk premium is the excess of the interest rate beyond a risk-free investment, and so the larger the risk is, the larger the risk premium will be.
- Firms can issue corporate bonds that can be purchased by institutional or private investors. These bonds yield an interest known as the coupon, and have a principal that the issuer promises to repay at some point in the future known as the maturity.

- Since a fixed coupon is paid for every agreed time period, bonds are also known as fixed income securities.
- Firms can also raise capital by issuing equity, also known as stocks or shares. Every share constitutes ownership of part of the firm.
- The fair value of shares is determined by the present value of all future earnings. Since markets do not behave in a fully rational manner, the market price of a share does not always reflect its fair value.

WACC
- The weighted average cost of capital (WACC) is the cost of capital weighted by source and expressed as a percentage.
- While the interest rate can be used to arrive at the present value, using the WACC is an even more accurate way to measure this.

The Perfect Competitor's Optimality Condition for Labour

$$MP_L \cdot p = w \qquad (6.3)$$

The Imperfect Competitor's Optimality Condition for Labour

$$MRP_L = w \qquad (6.7)$$

Capital Growth

$$C = P(1 + r)^N \qquad (6.10)$$

Present Value of Money

$$P = \frac{C}{(1+r)^N} \qquad (6.16)$$

WACC

$$P = \frac{C}{(1 + WACC)^N} \qquad (6.23)$$

7. Cost Analysis

Introduction
This chapter is a logical continuation of the concepts taught in Chapter 5. While cost minimisation was discussed in Section 5.7 in the context of production, we did not deal with costs in much detail then. In this chapter we therefore concentrate on different types of costs, both in the short run and in the long run. This chapter is also an important foundation for Part III of this text.

Required Knowledge
You need a good knowledge of the principles of Chapter 5 to ensure an understanding of cost analysis. These concepts include the distinction between short and long run, a basic understanding of factor inputs, and the concepts of increasing, constant and diminishing returns.

Key Terms
fixed cost (FC), variable cost (VC), total cost (TC) , revenue (R), profit, average variable cost (AVC), average fixed cost (AFC), average total cost (ATC), increasing/constant/diminishing returns, (dis)economies of scale, marginal cost (MC), long-run total cost (LTC), long-run average cost (LAC), long-run marginal cost (LMC).

7.1 An Introduction to Cost Analysis

At first, the term "cost analysis" may seem complicated and boring. There are a total of 10 different costs, but however intimidating this may appear these concepts are all interlinked and that their names are very intuitive. Cost analysis is not only inextricably linked to the firm's production process, but it is also, by definition, an important part of the firm's profitability. At the end of the day, it is the cost which determines if firms can compete in a market, and therefore if the firm can exist in the first place.

7.2 Fixed Cost, Variable Cost, Total Cost

The Connection to Chapter 5

As discussed in Chapter 5, we typically assume that inputs to production processes are labour and capital. Moreover, when considering the short run, we usually assume that the amount of capital is fixed while labour is variable. This means the quantity of labour used in the production process can be altered whereas the quantity of capital cannot. As we will see in this section, this property of variability and invariability of the two inputs also translates to the costs associated with these inputs. Let us consider the following example.

An Example of a Production Process

The firm Poster-X-Press specialises in poster printing services for other firms and private individuals. Let us simplify the production process by saying that the firm owns one printing machine which requires the attention of one person during the time the machine is running. There are no other inputs.

Fixed Cost

If we deal with short-run production decisions, the quantity of capital K employed is fixed. Assuming the rental rate[1] r of the machine also remains unchanged, we conclude that the cost associated with the running of the machine has to be constant and independent of the output quantity. Such a cost is known as a fixed cost FC. In our example, it is given by:

$$FC = K \cdot r \tag{7.1}$$

Equation 7.1 states that the FC in our production process is the product of the amount of capital K used (i.e. one machine) and the rental rate r of the machine for the period of time that we define as the short run. Suppose the short run is defined as one day and the rental rate per machine is £50 per day. Since K is equal to 1, the FC is then simply equal to £50.

Variable Cost

As mentioned above, our production not only requires the utilisation of the machine but also of labour. The cost of this is the wage rate w per unit of labour employed. This may be one labour-hour or whatever time interval we choose. Hence, the entire cost of the variable input is the amount of la-

---

[1] From Chapter 5, we remember that the rental rate of capital can either be literally the money that is paid in rent to whoever owns the machine or, if the firm owns the machine itself, the opportunity cost of having money tied up in the machine.

bour L times the cost of labour, w. Conveniently, the cost arising from the variable input is termed variable cost VC. Here this is:

$$VC = L \cdot w \qquad (7.2)$$

Total Cost
The final type of cost discussed in this section is total cost TC. This is the sum of variable and fixed cost and represents the overall expenses the firm has to cover in the production process. TC can thus be expressed in two different ways:

$$TC = VC + FC = w \cdot L + r \cdot K \qquad (7.3)$$

> Fixed cost is a type of cost which remains
> unchanged irrespective of the quantity produced.
> Variable cost is dependent on the number of units of output.
> Total cost is the combination of variable and fixed cost.

7.3 Breakeven Analysis

The Relevance of Breakeven Analysis
Assume you are the person running the Poster-X-Press business. Your primary concern is to maximise profits. To do so, you first need to ensure that all your costs are covered. In practice, situations like this are often analysed via breakeven analysis. A firm is said to break even when profit is equal to zero. Since profit Π is equal to the difference between total revenue TR (which in turn is quantity Q multiplied by price p) and TC, we can state that at the breakeven point the following holds true:

$$\Pi = TR - TC = 0 \qquad (7.4)$$

Introducing the Top Panel of Fig. 7.1
Let us look at the top panel of Fig. 7.1. The first thing to note about this panel is that we now have a pair of axes that we have not seen so far. Quantity is located on the horizontal axis here, which differs from the graphs we were used (i.e. those showing total product curves) to from Chapter 5 in which quantity was located on the *vertical* axis.

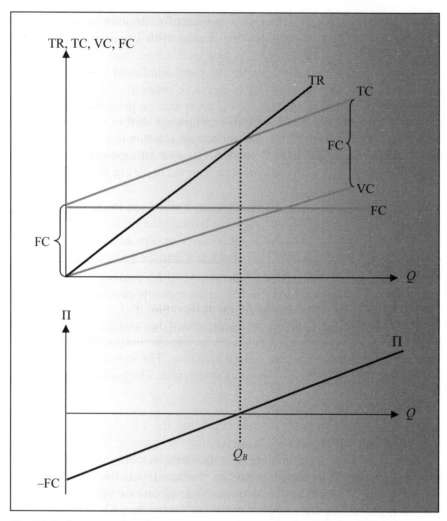

Fig. 7.1. In the top panel total revenue TR approaches and eventually exceeds total cost TC as the output increases. The bottom panel shows us the associated profit at different quantities. The break even point occurs at Q_B where the profit line intercepts the vertical axis at negative fixed cost FC

The Graphical Representation of VC, FC and TC

Having shown equations for VC, FC and TC in Section 7.2, their graphical representations can be found in the top panel of Fig. 7.1. This shows us the values of the three named costs for different output quantities Q. We notice that all cost "curves" are linear. But why is this?

FC is a horizontal line, as it remains constant for any output quantity. VC cuts through the origin and is upward sloping with a constant gradient because our underlying assumption is that each labour unit (holding capital fixed at $K^- = 1$) can produce exactly the same additional amount of output Q — one unit per minute[2], say. L is therefore proportional to Q. As VC is the product of L and a constant w, VC must also be proportional to Q. Finally, the TC curve simply constitutes an upward shift of the VC curve by an amount equal to the FC. At any quantity the difference between the TC and VC curves is equal to FC, which becomes evident from Equation 7.4. Moreover, this relationship is shown by the two braces in the top panel.

Variable Cost Goes Through the Origin, Total Cost Does Not
As a side note, the reason for VC going through the origin is that when the firm produces nothing, no cost is incurred — except, of course, the FC. In contrast to the VC curve, the TC curve intersects the vertical axis at a positive value due to the existence of FC.

The Graphical Representation of Total Revenue
The last element of panel 1 to be discussed is revenue. This too is a straight line. The reason for this is that we assume output price to be constant and independent of the output quantity. For example, selling 100 units rather than 1 gives 100 times as much TR[3]. Thus, TR is proportional to quantity.

There is one more thing of interest regarding the TR. As we can see, the lines representing TC and VC have a different gradient than the TR line. To be more precise, lines belonging to the costs have a lower gradient than the TR line. While for small quantities revenue lies below TC, it eventually overtakes TC as quantity increases and we find ourselves in a profit-making region. This happens for quantities larger than Q_B. Therefore, we know that if the gradient of the TR line was not steeper than that of the cost line(s), we would never be able to produce profitably[4]. Therefore in our example, if each unit of labour (i.e. one labour-minute) costs £0.25, for example, the total revenue TR associated with one minute's work by Poster-X-Press must exceed this for profitable production to be possible.

---

[2] As we learned is Chapter 5, this fact means that this particular production process exhibits constant returns for all output quantities.
[3] This is consistent with a market structure of perfect competition in which the firm takes the price as a given.
[4] In order to at least break even, in the case of non-linear cost curves, output price needs to be at least as large as the average total cost ATC.

Showing Profit — The Bottom Panel
The bottom panel in Fig. 7.1 shows us the profit. The reason for including this in the same showcase as the top panel is that profit is a function of revenue and cost, as we have seen in Equation 7.4. Revenue and cost in turn are dependent on the output quantity and, as a result, so is profit. We see that for quantities smaller than Q_B, the profit line is in the negative part of the graph, meaning that the firm is producing at a loss.

This follows from the fact that, for these quantities, the vertical position of revenue curve is lower than TC and so TC is larger than revenue. In turn, for quantities larger than Q_B, the profit line lies in the positive region of the graph which is a result of the fact that for these quantities, total revenue is larger than TC.

Finally, at quantity Q_B, the profit line intersects the horizontal axis so that profit is zero. This is a result of TR and TC being equal to each other, which becomes clear if we consider that TC and TR lines cross each other. By definition then, the output quantity Q_B is the breakeven point.

Negative Fixed Cost
There is one last thing to note about the profit line of the bottom panel. It intercepts the vertical axis at negative FC. The reason for this is simple when we keep in mind that at any point on the vertical axis Q is zero. Let us take the first two parts of Equation 7.4 and replace TC with VC + FC:

$$\Pi = TR - VC - FC \qquad (7.5)$$

If the firm produces nothing, both TR and VC disappear, and so we arrive at a profit of negative FC.[5]

Finding the Breakeven Point
Having looked at the breakeven analysis in a graphical framework, let us calculate it now. For this we simply set Equation 7.5 equal to 0:

$$TR - VC - FC = 0 \qquad (7.6)$$

Recalling that our FC was £50 and VC was £0.25 per minute (which is also the timeframe it takes to produce one unit of output), we can use Equation 7.6 to find the amount of output for which profit is zero.

---

[5] Unless it is equal to zero.

Now we need to fill in values for our variables. FC equals 50 while VC and TR are both functions of output Q. Let us pick a price of £0.40 per unit, and therefore at the breakeven point:

$$0.4Q_B - 0.25Q_B - 50 = 0 \qquad (7.7)$$

holds true. If we want to find the breakeven quantity Q_B, we subtract $0.25Q_B$ from $0.4Q_B$, add 50 on both sides of the equation and divide both sides by 0.15. Performing these operations gives:

$$Q_B \approx 333 \qquad (7.8)$$

This means that in order to break even (i.e. to attain a profit of zero) about 333 posters need to be printed. If the output is less, the firm loses money, if it is more, the firm's profit is positive. The topic of profitability will be discussed in detail in Part III of this book.

7.4 Introducing Average Cost

Having discussed VC and FC, we now move on to the concept of average cost. We already know that profit Π is given by total revenue TR minus TC. TR is the price p that the firm gets for each unit sold multiplied by the number of units sold Q. TC, as we learned above, is FC plus VC. Looking closer at the VC, this is the VC *per unit* multiplied by the number of units, and so:

$$\Pi = TR - TC \qquad (7.9)$$

$$\Pi = p \cdot Q - \frac{VC}{Q} \cdot Q - FC$$

Rather than using the term VC/Q which we named "variable cost per unit", we introduce the concept of average variable cost AVC, which means just that: the variable cost incurred by each unit, on average. We can therefore restate Equation 7.9 accordingly:

$$\Pi = p \cdot Q - AVC \cdot Q - FC \qquad (7.10)$$

The AVC is the entire variable cost incurred in the production process divided by the number of units produced.

AVC in Our Example
In the Poster-X-Press example, the variable cost per unit, i.e. the AVC, is constant — it is always £0.25, which is due to the assumption that every unit of labour produces exactly the same output. We know that VC is con-

stant because the VC curve is linear. When the VC item is not linear, however, the VC is potentially different for every unit produced.

Average Fixed Cost

Having found out about average *variable* cost, we can now look at other kinds of average costs — such as average fixed cost AFC. This is the entire FC incurred in the production process divided by the output quantity. Think of it as the "fixed cost per unit". There is an inverse relationship between AFC and the quantity produced. If you invested in buying many printing presses (rather than renting a single one), producing little would result in the AFC being very high.

However, if you used all of your presses every day for many hours, output would be relatively large and so the AFC would become very small. In other words, the burden of FC on each unit of output decreases the higher the total output is. In business, this process is often referred to as "spreading overheads", or "fixed cost digression".

Average Total Cost

Having looked at AVC and AFC, let us now examine average total cost ATC. Just as TC can be split up into VC and FC, *average* total cost can be split up into *average* variable and *average* fixed costs:

$$\text{ATC} = \text{AVC} + \text{AFC} = \frac{\text{VC} + \text{FC}}{Q} = \frac{\text{TC}}{Q} \qquad (7.11)$$

As you can see, ATC can be expressed in a number of different ways. Equation 7.11 can be computed using the first part of Equation 7.3 (i.e. TC = VC + FC). All we need to is to divide every term by Q.

No Need to Memorise *Everything*

Do not get intimidated by the abundance of expressions we have discussed thus far. There is no need to memorise all of them if you think about what each one *means*. When dealing with profit functions, for example, thinking about how *you* would make profit if you were running a business might turn out to be a useful "sense check". Depending on what the situation is and what the assumptions are, some formulae are more convenient than others and hence if you have an understanding of the concepts, the appropriate formula can easily be derived and the need for blind memorisation can be minimised.

A Different Naming Convention

There is something else to watch out for: cost analysis in managerial accounting is treated slightly differently from economics. Accountants may simply label what we understand to be the "average variable cost" (i.e. the variable cost per unit) as "variable cost". It is important that we know the difference between these two costs and that they are *not* interchangeable in microeconomics.

7.5 Introducing Non-linear Cost

Similarities of Fig. 7.2 to Fig. 7.1

Let us now look at another two-panel showcase in which we can see a number of different cost curves. The top panel of Fig. 7.2 is almost identical to the top panel of Fig. 7.1: in both instances the VC and TC curves are included. The major difference is that the shape of the cost curves is different from what we have seen earlier, as now the curves are actual curves and not straight lines.

For small quantities, the VC and TC curves rise steeply. Then, as Q becomes larger, the gradients decrease and eventually increase again as Q becomes still larger. What remains unchanged from the earlier linear case is the fact that the gradient of the TC curve is the same as the gradient of the VC curve for any one quantity.

The Need for Non-linear Cost Curves

The way the VC and TC curves are shaped in Fig. 7.2 is not arbitrary. While the straight-lined cost curves of Fig. 7.1 were a result of the assumption that each unit of labour would yield exactly the same constant output as the unit before or after, the curves in Fig. 7.2 are the result of a different assumption. Making the connection to Section 5.4.2, we recall that while holding capital fixed, an increase in the variable input will, for most production functions, have the following effect on output.

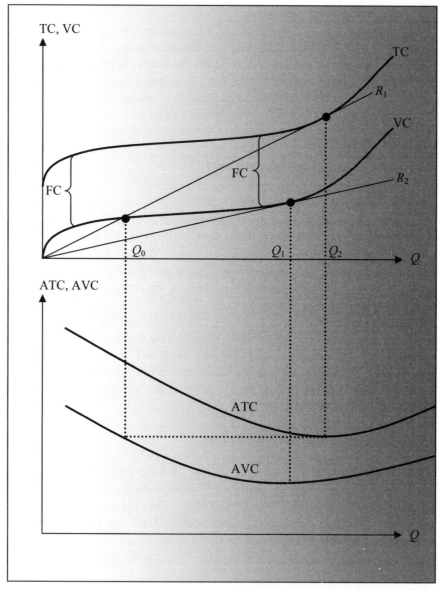

Fig. 7.2. In the top panel we see cost curves accounting for increasing, constant and decreasing returns of the variable input whereas the bottom panel displays the associated average cost curves. The vertical position of the average cost curves can be determined by using the gradient of the rays R_1 and R_2 on the VC and TC curves. Unlike in Fig. 7.1, here the Rs refer to ray rather than revenue

Looking at Fig. 7.3 (a reproduction of a total product curve from Chapter 5) for amounts of labour less than L_2, an increase in this input results in an increase in quantity at an increasing rate. We already know this property as increasing returns. At one point — the point of inflection — constant returns are present which means that the increase in total product from an increase in the variable input is constant. This occurs at L_2. Eventually, when the input exceeds L_2, further increases in the variable input result in an increase in the total product at a decreasing rate. This is known as diminishing returns.

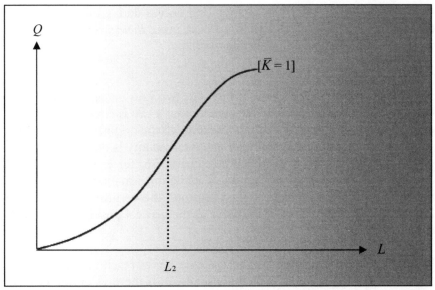

Fig. 7.3. Based on Fig. 5.3, this graph shows a total product curve exhibiting increasing returns for L values smaller than L_2, constant returns at L_2 and diminishing returns for L values larger than L_2

Connecting the Total Product and Variable Cost Curves

If we assume a production function such as that in Fig. 7.3, we can see how the properties of increasing, constant and diminishing returns can be directly translated into the cost curves of Fig. 7.2. With increasing returns for each unit of labour that we add, the increase in output is larger than the increase achieved by the previous unit of labour. Hence, producing an additional unit of output becomes less and less costly. This is represented graphically by the fact that the gradient of the VC curve decreases, as can be seen in the top panel in Fig. 7.2.

Similarly, with constant returns, for each unit of labour added, the increase in output is constant compared to the previous unit. This means that producing an additional unit of output is just as costly as the one before and hence the gradient of the VC curve is constant. Finally, when diminishing returns are present, an addition in the variable input results in less and less additional output. This means that the gradient of the VC curve will be increasing, as producing an additional unit becomes more and more costly. This is seen in Fig. 7.2 by the rising gradient of the VC and TC curves beyond their point of inflection.

The Shape of the Average Cost Curves
Moving to the bottom panel of Fig. 7.2, we see the graphical representations of AVC and ATC. The average cost curves derive their shape from the curves in the top panel, and as we have seen, *their* shape is a result of increasing, constant and diminishing returns.

The Use of Rays
As we can see in the top panel of Fig. 7.2, two rays named R_1 and R_2 are branching out from the origin. Remember that a ray is simply a geometrical concept: it is a straight line running through the origin. The vertical position of the average cost curves for any one quantity is determined by the gradient of the ray on the original cost curve. So, for example, ray R_1 is touching the VC curve at a quantity Q_0, while this same ray is just tangent to the TC curve for a quantity Q_2. Therefore, the vertical position of the AVC curve for quantity Q_0 is the same as the vertical position of the ATC curve for quantity Q_2.

It should also be noted that the average cost curves reach their minima for the respective quantities at which the gradient of the rays on the original cost curves is at its lowest. For example, looking at ray R_1 and the TC curve at Q_2, it is not possible to adjust the slope of the ray any further downwards while it is still touching the TC curve.

7.6 The Cost on the Margin

What Is Marginal Cost?
Marginal cost MC is the change in TC resulting from an infinitesimal change in output. For now, let us concentrate on the intuition; for the time being, we will define MC as "a change in TC resulting from a *one-unit* change in output."

An Example of Marginal Cost Calculation

Suppose you own a car factory that currently produces 1,000 cars per given time period at an associated total cost of:

$$TC_1 = 9,000,000 \qquad (7.12)$$

Increasing your output to 1,001 units, suppose that your total cost becomes:

$$TC_2 = 9,009,000 \qquad (7.13)$$

Hence, according to our definition, the MC is the change in TC from the one-unit change in output, or simply:

$$TC_2 - TC_1 = 9,009,000 - 9,000,000 = 9,000 \qquad (7.14)$$

As you can see, we found that the MC from increasing production from 1,000 to 1,001 units is 9,000.

Illustrating Marginal Cost Further

Since MC can be a bit tricky to understand, let us also illustrate it using a table. Before we do this, we will add to the above example. Having already stated that when the production increases from 1,000 to 1,001 units associated TC rises from 9,000,000 to 9,009,000, let us now also add a value of TC for a quantity of 1,002. We will say that this value is 9,017,990. Therefore, the MC of moving from 1,001 to 1,002 units of output is 8990.

These facts are summarised in Table 7.1. MC is shown on a separate line in between two discrete (i.e. integer) values of quantity. When defining marginal cost as the change in TC from a one-unit change in quantity, marginal cost cannot be attributed to any *one* quantity but only to a change from one value to another.

Table 7.1. The MC is the change in TC as output changes by one unit

Quantity	Total Cost	Marginal Cost
1,000	9,000,000	
		9,000
1,001	9,009,000	
		8,990
1,002	9,017,990	

Under the current definition employed, marginal cost can be expressed in the following way:

$$MC(Q) = \frac{\Delta TC}{\Delta Q} \qquad (7.15)$$

In words, Equation 7.15[6] means that the MC is the change in total cost ΔTC resulting from a one-unit change in quantity ΔQ. This is a more general way of calculating MC from what we set forth in Equation 7.14. Using the car example again and applying what we have just learned, the problem of the MC calculation can be expressed as follows:

$$MC(Q) = \frac{\Delta TC}{\Delta Q} = \frac{9,009,000 - 9,000,000}{1,001 - 1,000} = 9,000 \qquad (7.16)$$

Marginal Cost as a Derivative
The term "a change in one variable resulting from a change in another variable" should sound very familiar. Although the definition of MC as set forth in Equation 7.16 is correct, for certain applications it may simply turn out to be more beneficial to make use of the derivative. For this purpose, we switch back to the definition that we stated at the beginning of this section which defined MC as "the change in TC resulting from an *infinitesimal change* in TC". Under this original definition, Equation 7.16 can be slightly reformulated to become:

$$MC(Q) = \frac{dTC}{dQ} \qquad (7.17)$$

Equation 7.17 means that the MC can be calculated by taking the derivative of the TC function with respect to quantity. Another way of thinking about this is to assume that we can produce any quantity, i.e. 50 units, 50.5 units, 50.500001 units etc. If quantity is a continuous variable, taking the derivative makes sense.

> Marginal cost is the change in total cost brought about by a one-unit change in quantity. Alternatively, it can be defined as the derivative of total cost with respect to quantity.

---

[6] The notation $MC(Q)$ may be unfamiliar. The reason for us using this here is that previously we were not interested the MC with changing quantities. Now, however we explicitly consider a change in MC for different quantities produced.

Another Example of Marginal Cost Calculation
Having looked at the calculation of MC under the old definition in Equation 7.16, let us now also perform this calculation using Equation 7.17. For this purpose, consider the following TC function:[7]

$$TC = 500 + 2Q^2 \qquad (7.18)$$

Before we engage in any sort of calculation, let us first look at the above function a bit closer. The first part, 500, is the FC. It remains unchanged irrespective of the quantity of output produced. The second part, $2Q^2$, is the VC — it *does* change when output is altered. But there is more: the fact that we have placed 2 as the exponent on Q means that the further we raise output, the larger the extra cost of producing additional units will be. In other words, it is becoming more and more costly to increase output. Since Equation 7.18 is a short-run cost function (we know this from the existence of the FC portion), we can deduce that diminishing returns are present.

Moving on to what we initially set out to do and differentiating the TC function, we get:

$$\frac{d\mathrm{TC}}{dQ} = 4Q \qquad (7.19)$$

The FC element of 500 has disappeared in our differentiation[8], the exponent on Q has become 1 and the coefficient has doubled. Equation 7.19 tells us that the increase in TC is dependent on the number of units already produced. For example, if we move from 1 to 2 units, TC increases by 8. Moving from 2 to 3 units, TC increases by 12.

Graphing Marginal Cost
Since we know that a derivative is always a slope of the function that it is derived from, its follows that the MC curve tells us about the slope of the TC curve. The vertical position of the MC curve for any one quantity is determined by the gradient of the TC curve for that same quantity. In fact, the VC curve could also be used for this purpose, as we recall that the

---

[7] If you are interested, this is how we obtain a cost curve with these coefficients: A Cobb-Douglas production function with capital and labour can take the form: $Y(k, l) = (kl)^{1/2}$. If capital is fixed in the short run at, say $k=1$, the labour input l needed to produce Q units of output satisfies $y = 1 \cdot l^{1/2}$. Isolating l, we get $l = Q^2$. Assuming a cost of capital of $r = 500$ (because it is a big machine!) and a cost of labour of $w = 2$, the cost of producing y units of output is $C(Q) = r \cdot k + w \cdot l = 500 + 2 \cdot Q^2$.

[8] As we can see, FC has no bearing on MC whatsoever.

slope of the TC curve is always equal to the slope of the VC curve for any given quantity.

If we take a look at Fig. 7.4, we observe a TC curve similar to the one in the top panel of Fig. 7.2. In addition, the MC curve is included, which has been derived using this TC curve. For low quantities, the TC curve rises very steeply, which means that in order to produce an additional unit of output a lot of extra — or marginal — cost is associated with the addition of the variable input. Hence, the vertical position of the MC curve is very high for such low quantities.

Although the slope of the TC curve may be steep for low quantities, as quantity increases it becomes less and less steep. This means that as quantity increases, the additional amount of cost required to further increase output becomes smaller. We therefore observe a falling MC curve for such quantities. The MC curve keeps falling for as long as the slope of the TC curve decreases.

The point at which the slope of the TC curve no longer decreases, i.e. where the change in the slope momentarily stands still [9], is the point of inflection. This point is identified as Q_0 in Fig. 7.4 and coincides with the minimum of the MC curve.

As we keep increasing quantity, the slope of the TC curve starts increasing again. As a direct consequence, the slope of the MC curve is now positive again. This is how the characteristic U-shaped MC curve comes about. Remember, since we stated that most production processes exhibit diminishing returns, the associated TC curves will be shaped as shown in Fig. 7.4. Therefore, *U-shaped MC curves are common and are ultimately a result of diminishing returns to productive inputs.*

7.7 Long-Run Costs

Reviewing the Long-Run Concept
Since we now understand costs in the short run in some detail, there are only a few qualifications to the theory that we need to make in order to account for the long run as well. To begin with, the long run is defined as the *shortest period of time in which all factors production are variable.* As we

---

[9] This point also happens to coincide with the point in the production function with constant returns.

have learned in Section 5.4.1, the consequence of the long-run concept is that in this time frame, no distinction between variable and fixed inputs is made. As a consequence, there is also no distinction between variable and fixed *cost*. Indeed, in the long run all costs are variable.

Only Three Costs in the Long Run

Recalling the abundance of different types of costs we had in the short run, we know that there will now be fewer kinds of costs in the long run, namely long-run total cost LTC, long-run average cost LAC, and long-run marginal cost LMC. As mentioned, the distinction between fixed and variable cost and between average fixed and average variable cost becomes obsolete.

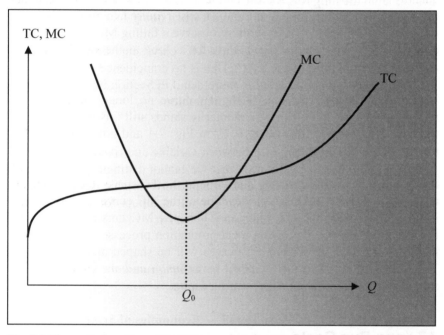

Fig. 7.4. The vertical position of the MC curve is derived from the gradient of the TC curve at that same quantity. This comes from the fact that MC is the derivative of TC with respect to Q. The lowest point on the MC curve is reached at Q_0, which is that quantity at which the TC curve exhibits its point of inflection

Introducing Fig. 7.5

Before we discuss each long-run cost in more detail, let us look at Fig. 7.5. We observe the LTC curve and ray R_1 in the top panel whereas the LMC and LAC curves are included in the bottom panel.

Explaining LTC, LAC and LMC Curves

To begin with, what is similar to the short run is the connection between the ray and the average cost curve. The slope of the ray as it touches or crosses the LTC curve at any point gives us the vertical position of the LAC curve. As we can see R_1 is the ray with the lowest gradient that still touches the LTC curve. This happens at Q_1, the quantity for which the average cost curve reaches its minimum. Secondly, similar to the short run, LMC is the derivative of LTC. The minimum of LMC is reached where the point of inflection occurs in the total cost curve.

Having discussed the similarities to the short run, an important *difference* is the fact that the total cost curve runs through the origin. The reason for this is that in the long run, the firm can decide not to produce anything, and other than in the short run, incurs no cost when doing so.

Moving on to the bottom panel, the LMC curve cuts through the LAC curve at the minimum of the LAC. This is no coincidence, and the rationale behind this fact is discussed in more detail in Section 9.4 when we deal with the market structure of perfect competition.

Looking at LTC in More Detail

Although we cannot distinguish between variable and fixed costs or inputs in the long run, this does not mean that we cannot distinguish between different types of inputs. The fact that all inputs are variable does not change the requirement of both labour *and* capital as inputs for our production process. Therefore, the LTC function is given by:

$$LTC = L \cdot w + K \cdot r \tag{7.20}$$

Equation 7.20 says that the total cost in the long run is the sum of the total cost from labour and the total cost from capital.

Looking at the LAC in More Detail — Economies of Scale

As we can see in Fig. 7.5, the shape of the average cost curve is very similar to what we have seen in the short run. Moreover, the connection to the total cost curve by the utilisation of rays is identical as well. But what is the intuition behind the U-shaped LAC curve?

By definition, a reduction in the average cost is a situation in which economies of scale are present. Let us explain this using an example. Suppose it is 1908 and you are Henry Ford. Since it is your goal to "put America on wheels", you invest heavily in your production plant where the Model T is assembled. By increasing the scale of production, you achieve a high degree of mechanisation and specialisation of tasks. As a result, the cost per vehicle drops from about \$3,000 to only \$800.

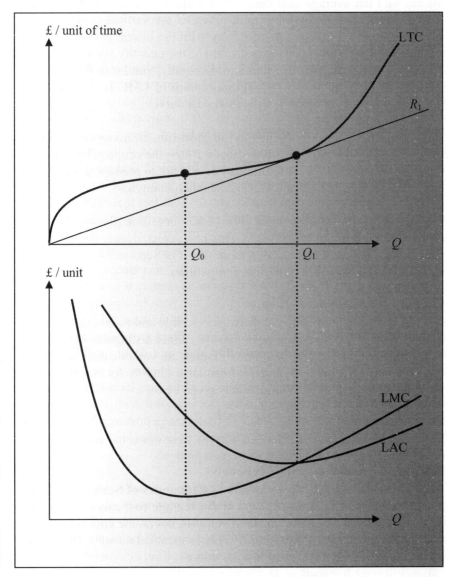

Fig. 7.5. For the quantity at which the LTC curve reaches its point of inflection, the LMC curve reaches its minimum. The quantity at which the ray with the lowest possible gradient touches the LTC is where the LAC curve reaches its minimum

This drop in average cost would be reflected by the falling portion of the long-run average cost curve in Fig. 7.5 for quantities up to Q_1. In other words, by increasing your output the average cost has fallen due to the presence of economies of scale.

Diseconomies of Scale
Using our intuition, how we can account for the rising portion of our average cost curve for quantities beyond Q_1? Fast forward about 100 years and take a modern car manufacturing plant. These facilities are truly huge, in some instances employing in excess of 5,000 individuals. A firm such as Ford produces an astounding number of vehicles every year, so why does the firm not simply concentrate all of its production within a single location to further exploit economies of scale? We might find many reasons for this, such as the availability of factor inputs, location of distributors and buyers — but a major reason is, undoubtedly, the fact that beyond a certain size, a production facility cannot further decrease its average cost significantly.

In other words, there is a limit as to how much "size matters"! While there certainly are lots of average cost savings to be exploited as a firm increases its scale, firms may also suffer from an *increase* in average cost as the scale of production grows *too large*. If this is the case, we speak of diseconomies of scale. How could this happen? Employees may take too long to get from one area of the plant to the other, additional facilities such as day care centres, a gym or on-site stores may become a necessity, or the communication among the many employees becomes increasingly difficult with the right hand not knowing what the left hand does. All of these examples have the effect of a growth in the average cost as output rises beyond a certain level and constitutes diseconomies of scale.

Making a Connection to the Monopoly
The discussion of the LAC curves find application in Section 10.6. There, we discuss that what is known as a **natural monopoly** occurs when it is more efficient for one firm to serve the entire market as opposed to many firms doing so. When economies of scale can still be exploited for very large quantities compared to overall market size (i.e. diseconomies of scale only set in once the scale of production becomes very large), it may make sense for only a single firm to serve the entire market[10]. Traditionally, many of the utilities networks like electricity or railroads have been con-

---

[10] Provided that some form of regulation prevents monopolistic pricing.

sidered natural monopolies, although this has been disputed in the last decades.

7.8 Seven Plus Three Costs

This section of the cost analysis chapter serves as a quick summary of all the costs that we have discussed. Since these were 10 in total, Table 7.2 and Table 7.3 can be used as a quick reference for short-run and long-run costs, respectively. Note that the formulae for variable and fixed costs in the short run are likely to hold true in most production processes but it is conceivable that they may be different (if labour were fixed and capital variable, for example). The formulae for all other costs always hold true.

Table 7.2. An overview of all short-run costs and their formulae

Name of Cost	Formula
Variable Cost (VC)	$L \cdot w$
Fixed Cost (FC)	$K \cdot r$
Total Cost (TC)	$TC = VC + FC$
Average Variable Cost (AVC)	$AVC = VC/Q$
Average Fixed Cost (AFC)	$AFC = FC/Q$
Average Total Cost (ATC)	$ATC = TC/Q = (VC + FC)/Q$
Marginal Cost (MC)	$\Delta TC/\Delta Q$

Table 7.3. An overview of all long-run costs and their formulae

Name of Cost	Formula
Long Run Total Cost (LTC)	$L \cdot w + K \cdot r$
Long Run Average Cost (LAC)	LTC/Q
Long Run Marginal Cost (LMC)	$\Delta ATC/\Delta Q$

7.9 Chapter Summary

Fixed Cost, Variable Cost, Total Cost
- In a production process, the fixed cost FC is that amount of total cost TC which does not change as a function of the quantity produced.
- By contrast, variable cost VC is that part of TC which is linked to the quantity produced.

- Since we used the convention that labour is variable and capital is fixed in the short run, VC is the product of the amount of labour L employed and the price w thereof, whereas the FC is the product of the amount of capital K employed and its price r.
- TC is simply the sum of VC and FC.

Breakeven Analysis
- A firm is said to break even when its profit equals zero, i.e. when the revenue TR is equal to TC.
- TR is the product of the output quantity Q and the price p.
- The VC curve always goes through the origin, as the firm incurs no cost (beyond the FC) when it produces nothing.
- When we assume that each unit of labour (while holding capital constant) is able to produce as much output as every other unit of labour (i.e. when the production function exhibits constant returns), the VC curve will be a straight line.
- At any positive value of FC, the TC curve will intersect the vertical axis at a value larger than 0.
- The total cost curve is an upward shift of the VC curve by an amount equal to FC.
- TR is a straight line, as we assume that price remains constant and does not change with the quantity produced.

Average Costs
- Average variable cost AVC is the "VC per unit", or simply VC divided by the number of units Q produced.
- Average fixed cost AFC is the "FC per unit", which is the FC divided by the number of units Q.
- Average total cost ATC is the "TC per unit", where this is the TC divided by output Q.

Non-linear Cost Curves
- Non-linear VC curves are a result of the presence of increasing, constant and diminishing returns in the production function. When increasing returns are present, increases in the variable input result in increases in quantity at an increasing rate, producing more output becomes relatively less costly, and the gradient of the VC curve decreases. This happens until constant returns are present. After this, increases in the variable input result in less and less increase in output and so the gradient of the variable cost curve starts increasing again.

- The graphical representation of AVC, the AVC curve, can be derived in the following way: the vertical position of the curve constitutes the gradient of a ray on the VC curve. The AVC curve reaches its minimum where a ray with the lowest possible gradient can still be drawn that just touches the VC curve. The same holds true for TC and its graphical representations.
- The AFC is inversely related to the output: the larger the output, the smaller the per unit burden attributable to the FC. This process is known as "spreading overheads".

Marginal Cost

- Marginal cost MC is the change in TC resulting from an infinitesimal change in output. If necessary, this definition can be adjusted slightly to "the change in TC resulting from a *one-unit* change in quantity"
- The vertical position of the MC curve is derived from the slope of the TC curve for any one quantity.
- For a typical TC curve, the MC curve will fall until that quantity at which the point of inflection occurs on the TC curve, after which the MC curve rises again.

Long-Run Costs

- Because all factors of production are variable in the long run, the only costs present in this time frame are long-run total cost LTC, long-run average cost LAC and long-run marginal cost LMC.
- The LTC curve passes through the origin as the firm can, for whatever reason, decide not to produce anything. When this happens, no cost will be incurred.
- When LAC cost is falling, the production process exhibits economies of scale, whereas in a situation in which LAC rises, we speak of diseconomies of scale. These two concepts can be used to intuitively explain the U-shaped LAC curves.
- In a situation in which LAC is falling for all relevant production quantities, a natural monopoly is likely to occur.

Breakeven Condition

$$\Pi = TR - TC = 0 \qquad (7.4)$$

Marginal Cost

$$MC = \frac{\Delta TC}{\Delta Q} \tag{7.15}$$

Marginal Cost as a Derivative

$$MC = \frac{d TC}{dQ} \tag{7.16}$$

Part III — Market Structure and Game Theory

Part II was an important building block for the understanding of the study of the firm. Until now, however, we have not analysed the firm's behaviour a great deal. Since the firm's actions depend to a large extent on the market structure in which it is operating, Part III introduces different types of market structure and how the firm behaves when operating in each one of these. Chapter 8 serves as an overview analysing the concept of market structure and comparing different types of it to each other. After that, we look in Chapter 9 at perfect competition. Chapter 10 introduces the monopoly, which in many ways can be regarded as the opposite of perfect competition.

In Chapter 11 we study the method of game theory as it finds applicability in the following chapter but also in a wider context in economics and beyond. The final chapter of this text, Chapter 12, discusses the market structure of oligopoly.

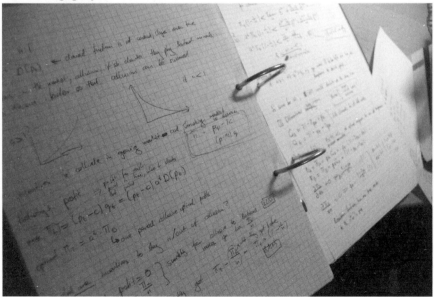

8. An Introduction to Market Structure

Introduction
In this chapter, we introduce the concept of market structure. Using real world examples, we examine what a market is, how to define it, and how this leads to the topic of market *structure*. The discussion at this point is rather "light", and the only bit of technical analysis is to be found in Section 8.4 in which we discuss market power using the Lerner index. Moreover, this chapter compares and contrasts the market structures of perfect competition, monopoly and oligopoly before they are separately examined in the coming chapters. This chapter is comparatively short because market structure is not typically part of an introductory micro course. Still, it helps knowing the basics of it for this part of the book.

Required Background Knowledge
A general understanding of the firm's production process as introduced in Chapter 5 is beneficial for this discussion.

Key Terms
market, industry, marketing, cross-price elasticity, product differentiation, market structure, perfect competition, monopoly, oligopoly, monopolistic competition, Lerner index.

8.1 Basic Terms

Before we can get started, it is important that we understand a few basic terms. You might have heard some of the following terms already, but be cautioned as their use in economics is distinct from everyday language.

8.1.1 Market

Introduced in Chapter 1 and elaborated upon in Chapter 2, the term "market" is the starting point of this chapter. Recall that the definition of a market in an economic sense comes close to the everyday meaning, which for many of us may include a fruit and vegetable market, for example. In economics, the definition of a market is a social arrangement in which buyers and sellers meet to take part in an economic transaction. As we will see, the definition of an industry is somewhat different.

> A market is a social arrangement in which buyers and sellers meet to take part in an economic transaction.

8.1.2 Industry

In the public understanding, "industry" is often synonymous with manufacturing or heavy industry. Indeed, many people may picture a Victorian factory in which labourers are slaving over noisy rattling machines that fill the air with dust and grime.

When we speak of an industry in an economic sense, however, we follow the definition of *Webster's New World Dictionary* and define it as "any large-scale business activity". Under this definition, we are not confined to manufacturing as the only type of industry; we may, for example, also refer to collections of firms located within one sector, such as financial services, telecommunications or consulting as industries. Large players in the financial services industry in London, for example, are Goldman Sachs and Merrill Lynch.

> An industry is any large-scale business activity consisting of at least one firm.

The difference between a market and an industry is most importantly that a market comprises buyers *and* sellers, whereas an industry only consists of sellers. Moreover, firms in one industry may be active in many markets at the same time. The financial services firms mentioned above participate in the markets of stocks, bonds and derivatives, for example.

8.2 Correctly Defining a Market

We are starting to build our understanding of an individual firm in the context of its surroundings — other firms in its "neighbourhood" with which it forms an industry. Every firm is part of an industry which operates in at least one market. If a firm invents a new product or service then it may, at least for a brief time, be the only firm in that newly established market, while under different circumstances there may be hundreds of firms in the same market.

How do firms compete with each other? This question is not only interesting in theory but also extremely relevant and exciting for anybody involved in running a business. Decisions a firm needs to make include the price it sets for its product(s), the quantity it produces, or the setting of budgets for advertising or research and development. All of these items on the firm's agenda are functions of the industry in which the firm operates, and ultimately what kind of competition it faces in the market place.

8.2.1 Important Variables for the Market Definition

How can a market be defined? There is no universally correct answer to this question, but we can give you food for thought by providing some variables which may be considered when a market is defined. These include, but are not limited to, the geography, price range of the product, time-frame, competing products, consumers, their lifestyles and any other consumer attributes. Which of these variables find application depends entirely on the circumstances.

Let us take the example of a geographical market definition. Including Iceland (the country, not the supermarket) as part of your market for air-conditioners, for example, may make only limited sense. In other instances, some markets would only be correctly defined when taking into account consumer characteristics. There is little doubt that the main market for Kinder surprise chocolates, for example, is indeed children[1], whereas *Green&Black's* dark chocolate (consisting of 70% or more cocoa) is likely to find its broadest customer base among a much older age group more concerned about sugar content and perceived quality.

---

[1] Although the purchase may often be made by somebody else, such as a parent.

Examples of Market Definitions

Showing the significance of the correct definition of a market, the following two subsections will discuss separate examples in which the market definition is suboptimal.

8.2.2 Defining the Market too Widely

Suppose you are a product manager at Coca Cola and you invented the new *Coke Zero*. During product design, you had to define the market for the new product.

If you had defined the market as "beverages in Europe", this would probably have been too wide a definition. After all, beverages include not only sodas such as cola and lemonade, but also milk, beer or even smoothies. There would have been several problems, both academic and practical, if such a wide market definition had indeed been adopted.

Firstly, this market definition gives a *distorted view of the actual size* of the market, which in turn throws up a whole host of further problems. Practically speaking, such a wide market definition would give unrealistic goals to management. Once a market is identified, it is usual to define a target percentage of that market that the firm would like to acquire for itself. But including milk drinkers in your market is erroneous. There is no way that anybody would consider *Coke* as a substitute for milk. Imagine how it would taste on your breakfast cereal!

Secondly, such a wide market definition would give us an *incorrect indication of consumers' price sensitivity*. Assume for a moment that *Coke* really was a substitute for milk, then a decrease in the price of *Coke* would see people switching away from milk. In reality, however, it is very likely that the quantity demanded of milk is completely independent of the price of *Coke*. In other words there is zero **cross-price elasticity**[2] between the two goods and hence defining the two as being in the same market (at least for our purposes) is incorrect.

---

[2] Discussed in Section 2.5.1 in the context of the degree of substitutability between different goods.

8.2.3 Defining a Market too Narrowly

Let us stick with our *Coke* example. Suppose that this time you define your market as beverages for teenage males in the UK. As you can tell from the title of this subsection, this definition is likely to be too narrow.

If this definition was believed, the firm might lose out on an opportunity here. Not including other counties may simply prove to be silly as there is no obvious reason why *Coke Zero* should not also be launched in Germany, for example. Secondly, only considering teenage males may ignore some customers who could have readily been added to this target market.

Lastly, by defining the market too narrowly you might also miss out some competitors to your product that you should be aware of. This point may not directly apply to our example in which we used customers to define the market, but it will be significant in other cases in which the ill-guided belief that you are the only firm in the market may lead you to set a price which is too high.

8.2.4 Getting it Right

Let us look at a specific solution. We are not claiming that the following definition is infallibly the right answer, but at least this should give you some idea as to which market definitions are better suited than others and why. For this reason, let us consider the relevant variables of the market definition. In this example, geography, gender and age of consumers happen to be vital variables.

Geography
Firstly, regarding the geographic focus, the drink could be launched almost anywhere around the world perhaps, adjusting for some differences in taste and/or culture in certain regions beforehand.

Gender of Consumers
Moreover, since it is unlikely that only males will drink *Coke Zero*, female consumers should be taken into account in the market definition as well. Having said that, this comment would need to be qualified further, as *Diet Coke* is targeting the female cola drinker market to a large extent[3]. For this

---

[3] Interestingly enough, the Diet Coke adverts from the 1990s showing hunky men carrying out physical labour while being watched by Coke-drinking female office

reason, a customer survey might give some insight as to what portion of females should be included in our *Coke Zero* market definition. A *mostly* male target group is likely to be the correct definition. In Britain, *Coke Zero* has been nicknamed "bloke *Coke*", referring to the fact that is mainly drunk by males.

Age of Consumers

Finally, since we have already identified the teenage market as too narrow, our guess would be that a product like *Coke Zero* would see most of its consumers lie between the ages of 6 and 30. It is likely that the primary focus would be on the mid- to upper spectrum of this age scale, as the average child prefers food articles high in sugar content and would therefore be likely to prefer regular *Coke* over the sugar-free *Coke Zero*. An upper boundary of around 30 appears reasonable, as after this age health consciousness might become prevalent in many consumers, perhaps causing them to switch to water or fruit juices.

An Entirely New Market?

An interesting side note: it appears that Pepsi has agreed with Coca Cola's discovery of this "new" market of male drinkers of sugar-free cola and slightly altered its image of Pepsi Max in response to the introduction of *Coke Zero*. Prior to the existence of *Coke Zero*, *Pepsi Max* appeared to have been only slightly geared towards male drinkers; Pepsi's advertising campaign in Britain launched in the autumn of 2006 is an indication of their change in target market.

The adverts we are referring to show a scale from "zero" to "Max", ranging from left to right across the billboard. In one example, pictured on the left-hand side, we see the wrapped feet of a ballerina, while on the right (where apparently the "Max" of this continuum of a yet to be identified variable is reached) we see attractive, long, naked legs connected to feet in high heels. Another example: a cute little bunny on the left, a playboy bunny on the right. Also notice that on the left-hand side, which is showing these stereotypically unmanly pictures or symbols, the scale reads "zero" rather than "0", unmistakably alluding to their competitor's product and hence leaving little doubt about the market Pepsi is aiming for.

---

workers have been brought back to British TV in early 2007 under the "Diet Coke break" slogan.

8.2.5 Product Differentiation and Marketing

Although implicitly discussed above, it is worth explicitly drawing our attention to the concept of **product differentiation** to round off the previous discussion. Let us take the example of Unilever, a firm which occupies a significant portion of the fast-moving consumer goods (FMCG) market in Britain and many other countries. Unilever offers a vast assortment of products including shampoos, soaps, razors and even food articles. Many of their products are very similar to each other but packaging and marketing differ considerably. The reason for this is to create as much perceived differentiation in the product as possible.

Deodorant Example — Mostly Real Differences
Let us look at a specific example here. The Lynx deodorant roll-on for men and the Sure deodorant roll-on for women comes in a packaging which is exactly the same shape, only the colour and print is different. Of course, the scent is different as well. Rather than offering one and the same product, Unilever has divided the market and offers a slightly different type of product. While doing so, it is also likely to exploit scale advantages in its production because certain parts of the production process and packing are interchangeable.

Washing Powder Example — Mostly Perceived Differences
While we would definitely suspect most manufacturers of deodorants to distinguish between male and female customers in designing their products, we can take another example in which the above point becomes even clearer. How can consumers tell differences in the effectiveness of washing powders? With many consumers unable to fairly assess such differences, variations in packaging and advertising serve an important purpose. Are you a student looking for "a cheap wash" or a caring mother wanting your kids' clothes to be 100% clean? No matter who you are, the right washing powder for you can be found. But what you may not know is that these products are much more similar than you really think.

What is important here is the *perceived* difference[4]. Firms selling washing powder have realised that it is not enough to offer a product differentiating itself in its objective attributes (such as perfume or production quality). Much of the differentiation is done through the packaging, advertising and

---

[4] Indeed, some philosophers would argue that when people believe something, it *is*.

brand-image creation. And surely, isn't it desirable to buy a product that was designed according to *your* needs[5]?

The Relevance of Product Differentiation

"Why is all this talk about product differentiation so important?", you may ask. Generally, a firm wants its product(s) to be differentiated as much as possible. As we will discuss in Chapter 10, when a product is unique (i.e. it is perfectly differentiated), the firm can achieve very high profits as it is a *de facto* monopolist. While it is unlikely that a firm can achieve complete differentiation — even if a large proportion of any degree of differentiation may only be in the heads of the potential customers — it is still possible to achieve higher profits with a partially differentiated product than with one that is just like any other. Product differentiation forms an important building block for both the study and the practical applications of marketing.

8.3 An Overview of Market Structures

Rather than going into detail at this point, this section gives you the most important cornerstones of information regarding the various market structures, whereas the detailed analysis is left to the remainder of Part III. At this stage, it is only important to get a feel for these different market structures and how they compare with each other. This is intended to enable you to understand each market structure in a wider context when working through the coming chapters.

Perfect Competition

This is the simplest of market structures. In perfect competition, as the name suggests, competition is maximised or "perfect" which, means there is a very large number of producers. These producers all sell a homogenous (i.e. the same) product, they make *no* profit in the long run and firms take the price in the industry as given[6]. The second point may make you shake your head and think: "nobody will be in an industry in which he cannot make any profit."

---

[5] This has been pointed out by Sally Dibb in her article "New millennium, New segment: Moving Towards the Segment of One", published in the *Journal of Strategic Marketing*, 1 September 2001, pp. 193–213.

[6] This is based on the assumption that individual output is too small to influence market price.

Firstly we are talking about economic profit and not accounting profit[7]. Secondly, the answer to the concern of the **zero profit condition** is that perfect competition is an approximation to real life rather than a case study. You would be hard pressed to find an industry in the real world that fulfilled all the conditions of perfect competition completely, but nonetheless it is a model that helps us understand more complicated market structures later on. In addition, the zero profit condition does not hold in the short run, during which at least one factor of production is fixed. This means that in the short run it is possible that firms in perfectly competitive industries do derive a positive economic profit. In any case, despite the zero profit condition in the long run, perfect competition is considered an efficient market structure as social welfare is maximised and resources are utilised efficiently.

Under perfect competition, there is free entry into the industry which means that any firm can produce in this market. This entails an absence of legal, technological or know-how-based barriers that would otherwise prevent a firm from entering the market. An example of an industry that satisfies the assumptions of perfect competition relatively closely is the farming of certain foodstuffs in large rural areas such as the Midwest of the United States.

Monopoly

The monopoly is often considered to be the opposite to perfect competition. In a monopoly, a single firm produces all the output in the market. By definition, there are no goods that are considered similar, let alone substitutes. The monopolist is free to choose any price she wishes and sets such a price as to maximise her own profit at the expense of society[8]. While this may sound very negative, in Chapter 10 we will see that in some instances the existence of monopolies may be a good thing, barring their complete pricing power.

Part of the definition of a monopoly entails that other firms find it impossible to enter the market. In contrast to perfect competition, there are legal, technological or other barriers preventing others from entering the market. Examples of monopolies include state-run postal and train services and pharmaceutical firms who by means of a patent gain a temporary monopoly position in the distribution of a new drug.

---

[7] The distinction of these two concepts is discussed in Chapter 1.
[8] In other words, monopolistic pricing entails a reduction in the welfare of society, as elaborated in Chapter 10.

Oligopoly

The term "oligopoly" is derived from the Greek word "oligos" which means "few". It is therefore a market structure consisting of few sellers. In the real world, most market structures lie somewhere between perfect competition and monopoly, and hence the oligopoly is perhaps the most realistic market structure that we will analyse.

The important difference compared to all other market structures we discuss is that firms in an oligopolistic market structure behave **strategically**[9]. This means they take into account each other's output and pricing decisions, since their own demand and therefore profit is a function of not only their own but also their competitors' decisions. Examples of oligopolistic market structures include the airline industry and the car industry.

As we will see in Chapter 12, there are different ways in which firms in an oligopolistic market structure compete with one another, and depending on the circumstances, profits range from zero, as in perfect competition, to the very high levels seen in monopolistic markets[10].

Monopolistic Competition

Although not discussed in the rest of this text, it is still worth briefly looking at monopolistic competition. As the name suggests, monopolistic competition has elements of monopolies, but the level of profits is the same as under perfect competition — zero.

Monopolistic competition is similar to perfect competition in that there is a large number of sellers in the market. Entry into the market is similarly unproblematic and costless as in perfect competition. The main difference to perfect competition is that products are differentiated rather than homogenous, i.e. every firm produces a unique product, similar to a monopolist. Another important assumption of models of monopolistic competition is that consumers are heterogeneous. That is, some consumers prefer one particular version of the product to another — this is what allows producers of these variants to charge prices above marginal cost, i.e. a mark-up.

The similarity of monopolistic competition to the monopoly is that firms under monopolistic competition set their own price to maximise their prof-

---

[9] This comment neglects situations in which the monopolist may behave strategically with regards to deterring the entry of potential competitors into the industry.

[10] At the end of Chapter 12, we include a table in which we see exactly what circumstances lead to the varying levels of price, output and profit.

its. Many types of retailers, such as outlets for branded clothing, operate in monopolistically competitive markets. That is, retailers within a certain geography are clearly in competition with each another, yet they generally charge relatively high mark-ups. Nonetheless profits are low, if not zero. In other words, the variable profits a firm makes just about cover the fixed cost of operating in the market.

8.4 Comparing the Market Structures

A Competition Continuum
Fig. 8.1 shows us a continuum of competition based on the assumptions of the different market structures discussed above. As can be seen, the monopoly is the market structure exhibiting the least amount of competition, whereas perfect competition is that market structure with the maximum amount of competition. The oligopoly exhibits an intermediate amount of competition whereas monopolistic competition is located relatively close to perfect competition in terms of the degree of competition exhibited under it. As we will see in Chapter 12, however, oligopoly is a catch-all term for a number of different forms of competition that can even result in a zero-profit (i.e. perfectly competitive) outcome with just two firms.

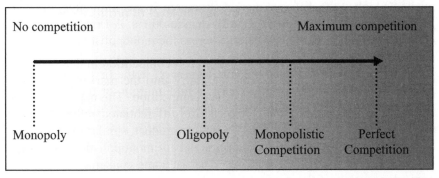

Fig. 8.1. A competition continuum in which we see that the largest amount of competition is present for the market structure of perfect competition, while the least amount of competition occurs at the market structure of monopoly

A Market Structure Matrix
Table 8.1 summarises the key assumptions of the different market structures we have discussed. The key variables we utilise to define a market structure are the degree of competition (which is a function of the size and

the number of sellers), barriers to entry and the influence of price on sellers (which is a determinant of profit)[11].

Table 8.1. A matrix showing the most important assumptions of the four market structures discussed using four variables

	Monopoly	Oligopoly	Monopolistic Competition	Perfect Competition
Degree of Competition	None	Some	Strong	Very strong
Barriers to Entry/Exit	Strong	Strong to None	Some to None	None
Product	Perfectly Differentiated	Differentiated	Differentiated	Homogenous
Profit	Maximum	Maximum to None	Some to None	None

8.5 Measuring Market Power — The Lerner Index

The last section of this chapter is not ordinarily part of a first-year syllabus, but it is nonetheless a very interesting part of microeconomics. Having had a look at the different market structures, it was implicit that players had more power in some market forms than in others. A firm in a perfectly competitive market has least power, whereas the monopolist has most.

But what exactly do we mean by "market power" in the first place? Market power is the ability of a firm to charge a high margin, or the lack thereof when competition is strong. Market power can be quantified using the Lerner index[12] which is denoted as:

$$L = \frac{(p - \mathrm{MC})}{p} \qquad (8.1)$$

Subtracting marginal cost from price $(p - \mathrm{MC})$ constitutes the mark-up that the firm charges. Intuitively, the higher the mark-up, the more market power the firm possesses. Hence, the larger the firm's ability to charge a

---

[11] Other valid variables that we do not discuss in this context in detail include the size and the number of buyers and the quality of information that buyers hold of alternative offerings.

[12] Named after American economist Abba Lerner (1903–1982). L in the context of Equation 8.1 must not be confused with labour.

high mark-up, the larger L will be and the larger the market power of the firm. You could also think about it the other way round: in perfect competition, profits are zero and hence the firm is not able to charge any mark-up, $p - MC = 0$ and so the Lerner index would be nil.

Generally, the index can take any value from 0 to 1, where 0 indicates no pricing power and therefore marginal cost pricing, and 1 (or a value close to 1), which implies that prices bear practically no relation to marginal cost, i.e. prices are much, much higher than marginal cost[13].

8.6 Chapter Summary

Basic Terms
- A market is a social arrangement in which buyers and sellers meet to take part in an economic exchange.
- An industry is any large-scale business activity consisting of at least one firm.

Correctly Defining a Market
- Variables that can be used in the definition of a market include, but are not limited to, consumers and their attributes, geography, price range of the product, time-frame and competing products.
- Markets need to be correctly defined in order to avoid academic and practical problems such as a distortion in the size of the market, incorrect identification of the consumers' price sensitivity, and ignorance of the existence of competitors.
- Many firms expend great efforts to differentiate their products as much as possible from those of their competitors, but also from some of their own products.
- Where products are very similar, product differentiation is achieved to alter the consumers' perceptions about the product's attribute by means of marketing.

---

[13] We should note that for a product with zero marginal cost, the Lerner index has no meaning: $(p - MC)/p = 1$ whenever MC equals zero. This is a special case, however, and unlikely to trouble us in real life.

An Overview of Market Structures

- Perfect competition is a market structure that includes a large number of sellers, all of whom are considered price takers. None of them derive any profit in the long run and there are no entry/exit barriers.
- A monopoly is an industry consisting of only one firm setting a price-maximising profit. This has the effect of reducing the welfare of society. There are strong entry barriers to monopolistic markets.
- An oligopoly is a market structure consisting of few sellers under which varying levels of profits are attained by the firms in it. Barriers to entry may range from very low to very high levels.
- Monopolistic competition is a market structure under which many sellers set a price (rather than taking it as given) to maximise their profit, which results in some level of profit for the participants. There are no entry barriers, and the producers each sell a differentiated product.

The Lerner Index

- The Lerner index is a measure of market power that helps us quantify a firm's ability to charge a mark-up and thus its market power.
- The index can range from 0 to 1, where 0 would mean no market power and 1 would mean complete market power.

$$L = \frac{(p - \text{MC})}{p} \qquad (8.1)$$

9. Perfect Competition

Introduction

Having had an overview of different market structures in Chapter 8, we examine one of them in more detail in this chapter. Firstly, we look at the assumptions of the model of perfect competition, and then we introduce the profit-maximising condition in the short and long run. We also analyse conditions for the firm to produce at all; the shutdown condition. Furthermore, we examine the connection to marginal and average cost curves, the firm's supply, and producer and consumer surplus.

Required Knowledge

A good working knowledge of cost analysis (Chapter 7) is a prerequisite for this chapter. Moreover, a basic understanding of the process of production (Chapter 5) as well as supply and demand (Chapter 2) is required. Although not absolutely necessary, the reader would benefit from the market structure overview in Chapter 8.

Key Terms

homogenous good, price taker, quantity demanded/supplied, price elasticity of demand, factor mobility, short run, long run, profit maximisation, marginal cost (MC), marginal revenue (MR), efficiency, average total cost (ATC), average variable cost (AVC), shutdown condition, zero profit condition, individual firm supply, industry supply, long-run average cost (LAC), breakeven point, (aggregated) consumer surplus (CS), (aggregated) producer surplus (PS).

9.1 Assumptions of Perfect Competition

From Chapter 8, you will already have some understanding of the characteristics of a perfectly competitive market. While some assumptions are very intuitive, others need to be discussed in more detail. Let us now have a look at each of the assumptions separately.

9.1.1 Firms Produce Homogenous Goods

The first assumption that is made under the model of perfect competition is that all producers within the industry sell **homogenous goods**, or perfect substitutes[1]. While this may appear far-fetched with regards to real-world situations, a closer look reveals that there are indeed industries for which this assumption applies. Perhaps most notably, farming, forestry, fishing and mining are all industries in which goods from different producers do not differ much, if at all.

9.1.2 Firms Are Price Takers as There Are Many Sellers

Overall Output too Large for Individual Output to Influence Price
The next assumption of perfect competition that we examine is that firms are price takers. This means there is only one price for the specific product in the market and no firm within the industry can influence this price. This assumption can only hold true when there is a sufficient number of sellers in the market (as is the case in perfect competition) so that each firm's output is too small compared to the industry output to influence the price[2]. This is in contrast to the monopoly, where output of one firm is so large that this firm has complete freedom to set any price it wishes for the product. This, however, entails that the product is perfectly differentiated, i.e. that there are no substitutes.

Intuition
So what does "being a price taker" mean? Don't firms in perfectly competitive markets set prices? Well, they do, but whatever they do as individual firms will not affect the overall market price and quantity. Say you run a small newsstand: whatever price you charge for a pack of chewing gum will not affect the overall market price for gum. Yes, you might sell more if you charge a lower price (you will not want to do this, as we will see shortly), but the market — i.e. all the other firms in the industry — will not react to such a change in prices.

---

[1] This concept is introduced in Section 5.8.
[2] As we examined in Chapter 2, the market clearing price in any industry occurs where quantity demanded and quantity supplied are equal to each other. If the quantity supplied in an industry changed, this would change the equilibrium and by doing so affect the market price.

Flat Firm-Specific Demand Curve
Another way of expressing the consumer's high responsiveness in quantity demanded following a change in price is the **price elasticity of demand**. In a perfectly competitive market all firms would sell their gum at, say, 50 pence. If one newsstand decided to sell their gum for 51 pence, they would not sell anything at all — at least in theory. Hence, *each firm's demand in a perfectly competitive industry is perfectly elastic*[3]. As shown in Fig. 2.6 in the context of the discussion of supply and demand, the demand curve for a perfectly elastic good is simply a horizontal line. It follows that all demand curves of perfectly competitive industries are flat. This can easily be remembered by keeping in mind the price-taking condition: there is only one price in the market and the flat demand curve is the way to account for this graphically.

9.1.3 No Barriers to Entry or Exit

Entry
Another important assumption of perfect competition is that firms are able to enter and exit the industry freely. Taking the example from before, there are no obstacles that would stop firms from entering the newsstand market. There are no laws against this, and the knowledge required to run such a stand is within the public domain.

Putting this assumption in perspective, entry barriers for the monopoly are significant. The airline industry, for example, is virtually impossible for firms to enter due to regulations (not to mention large, upfront investments). Similarly, opening a university is difficult because you need know-how and reputation to attract good faculty and students.

Exit
Although it may not seem perfectly intuitive, barriers to exiting an industry are as important as those determining the degree of ease of entry. So what is an exit barrier in the first place? As the name suggests, this is something that prevents a firm from leaving an industry should it wish to do so. Naturally, a firm will only want to do this if it cannot make positive economic

---

[3] "Each firm's" is vital in this sentence, because the industry demand is still downward sloping as consumers differ in their individual levels of willingness to pay.

profits[4]. Being prevented from exiting an industry may then prove to be very costly indeed. An exit barrier may be a factory that a firm cannot sell quickly, or a permit paid some time in advance. As we can see, most exit barriers manifest themselves as high fixed costs. Such fixed costs can, of course, also constitute an entry barrier at the same time. As we have stated, firms in perfectly competitive industries do not have to worry about either of these.

Perfect Factor Mobility
The non-existence of entry and exit barriers and the resulting ease of movement into and out of a perfectly competitive industry does in itself entail another assumption: that all factors of production are perfectly mobile. While this may seem perfectly plausible, it is still worth mentioning that we assume that factors of production can be freely added or reduced in this market structure. For example, we ignore any kind of job protection or capital shortage. It means that we can employ as little or as much labour and capital as we wish[5].

9.1.4 Perfect Information

In perfect competition, and indeed in any other market structure in this text unless otherwise specified, we assume that both producers and consumers have perfect information about all prices, costs and product characteristics in the market. Imperfect information is part of the explanation of why in real life, even if producers offer homogenous products, prices among competitors are hardly ever *exactly* the same. However, with the extremely widespread use of the Internet, some markets are moving towards a state of near-perfect information (at least with regard to pricing). Part of the perfect information assumption is that producers have knowledge about how to produce most efficiently and about the consumers' demand.

---

[4] The firm may be making an accounting profit yet incurring an economic loss due to the weighing of opportunity cost if, for example, a more attractive opportunity has presented itself elsewhere. The distinction between the two concepts is explained in Section 1.6.2.
[5] Provided that the time frame is long enough in the case of the fixed input.

9.2 Short-Run Profit Maximisation

Recalling the Short- and Long-Run Definitions
Before we start our analysis, let us make sure that we are clear on the basic terminology. As we know from Section 5.4.1, the short run is defined as the longest period of time during which at least one factor of production is fixed. Using the convention this means that we can alter the amount of labour used in the production process but not the amount of capital. By contrast, the long run is defined as that shortest period of time during which all factors of production are variable. This means that the firm can alter the amount of labour and capital as it sees fit.

The Graphical Representation of Profit
In Fig. 7.1 of the Chapter 7, we saw that the graphical representation of total cost TC and total revenue TR can be used to derive profit in a second, interconnected panel within the same diagram. Let us redraw Fig. 7.1 only now using non-linear total cost[6], as shown in Fig. 9.1. This graph shows us how TR and TC change with quantity. The TC curve intersects the vertical axis at the value of fixed cost FC. The curve rises steeply but at a decreasing rate as Q increases. Eventually the slope stops decreasing and starts picking up again. By contrast, TR is simply a straight line crossing the origin, as every unit of output gives the firm the same increase in TR, i.e. the unit price.

As the TC curve is above TR, the firm makes a loss until cost and revenue curves cross each other at the breakeven quantity, and when TR is above TC, the firm earns a positive profit. Hence, the firm is making a loss for quantities smaller than Q_{MIN}, breaks even for quantities Q_{MIN} and Q_{MAX} and derives profits for quantities between Q_{MIN} and Q_{MAX}. The highest profit is achieved where the (positive) vertical difference between the TR and TC curves is highest — this is Q^*. The asterisk indicates that this quantity is optimal. The firm will always want to produce at this quantity.

---

[6] As discussed in Section 7.5, this is required to account for increasing, constant and diminishing returns of the variable input which is exhibited by most production functions.

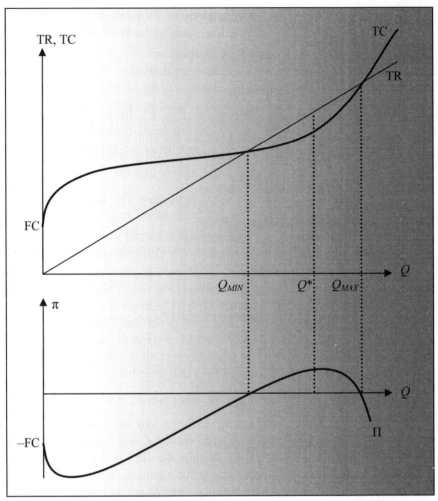

Fig. 9.1. Showing total cost TC and total revenue TR in the top panel, the vertical difference between the two represents profit which is shown in the bottom panel. Where the TC curve and the TR curves cross, the firm breaks even, whereas the largest profit is achieved at $Q*$

The Bottom Panel

The above facts about profit Π are all exhibited in the bottom panel of Fig. 9.1, which shows us how profit changes with quantity. The Π curve crosses the horizontal axis at Q_{MIN} and Q_{MAX}, and reaches its maximum at $Q*$. The intercept with the vertical axis is negative FC[7], as the firm will in-

---

[7] Care must be taken with the signs. Although costs are *subtracted* in the profit function, their values are still positive. E.g. VC = $10Q$ and FC = 100.

cur no variable cost VC and earn no revenue by producing a quantity of zero. Therefore FC is the only remaining item in the profit function:

$$\Pi = TR - VC - FC \qquad (9.1)$$

$$\Pi = 0 - 0 - FC$$

As a final note about the bottom panel of Fig. 9.1, for small quantities, Π falls even below negative FC, as producing small quantities is comparatively inefficient[8]. This holds true for all quantities at which $MC > p$.

The Profit-Maximising Condition
Although in the previous example we showed how TR, TC, and Π behave as quantity changes, we have not yet determined how we can find the profit maximising quantity Q^* in the absence of such a graphical display. The condition that must hold at the profit-maximising point is that marginal revenue MR equals marginal cost MC:

$$MR = MC \qquad (9.2)$$

But what is marginal revenue in the first place?

Marginal Revenue
Marginal revenue is a new term. Very similar to the intuition behind marginal *cost*, marginal *revenue* is the change in total *revenue* resulting from an infinitesimal change in quantity[9]. In other words, it is the derivative of TR with respect to Q:

$$MR = \frac{d TR}{dQ} \qquad (9.3)$$

In our example MR is calculated easily. As we know from the straight-lined graphical representation of revenue in Fig. 9.1, the change in TR resulting from an increase in Q is constant. And this is very intuitive: the more the firm sells, the more total revenue it will get, and the increase in total revenue — or MR — for each additional unit sold is simply the (exogenously given) market price of the product. Hence, for the perfectly com-

---

[8] The reason for this is that marginal cost MC is very high for low quantities. This, in turn, is the result of the property of increasing returns exhibited by most production functions. This is explained in Section 5.4.2.
[9] An alternative definition of "the change in TR resulting from a one-unit change in quantity" can also be employed.

petitive firm, price is equal to MR[10]. We can therefore refine the profit-maximising condition set forth in Equation 9.2 to become:

$$p = MC \qquad (9.4)$$

Proving the Profit-Maximising Formula

Before talking about the intuition behind the profit-maximising formula, let us firstly prove it mathematically. To begin with, let us state the firm's general profit function:

$$\Pi = TR - TC \qquad (9.5)$$

Which, for our purpose, we can change slightly to:

$$\Pi = p \cdot Q - TC \qquad (9.6)$$

Let us now set the profit function's derivative equal to zero, which helps us to find its maximum:

$$\frac{\partial \Pi}{\partial Q} = 0 \qquad (9.7)$$

$$p - \frac{dTC}{dQ} = 0$$

Rearranging, we get:

$$p = \frac{dTC}{dQ} \qquad (9.8)$$

From Section 7.6, we know that the derivative of TC, i.e. the right-hand side of Equation 9.8, is MC. This is so because MC is defined as the derivative of TC with respect to quantity[11]. Thus, we can write:

$$p = MC \qquad (9.9)$$

This is precisely the profit-maximising formula that we proposed in Equation 9.4. By taking the derivative of the profit function to find its maximum, we found that, at this maximum, price must equal MC.

---

[10] It should be noted that in the market structure of monopoly, MR is *not* equal to price, due to a changing market price as the monopolist alters output levels. Although Equation 9.2 holds true for the perfect competitor and monopolist alike, Equation 9.4 only holds true for the perfect competitor.

[11] An alternative definition of MC is "the change in TC resulting from a one-unit change in output". However, this alternative definition is not useful here.

The Intuition

But why should Equation 9.9 necessarily be true? Let us focus on MC to answer this question. Assume you are operating a flour business (which is part of a perfectly competitive industry) and you wish to maximise your profit. Suppose you have not commenced production and so your output is currently zero, while profit is equal to negative FC.

As you add your first unit, MC is extremely high compared to the price the good fetches in the market, and your loss becomes even greater. This can be seen in Fig. 9.2, as MC is markedly above price for small quantities. As we increase production, however, MC falls rapidly and eventually it will be below price for some number of output quantities. This means that while on the first few units you may not be able to produce at a "marginal profit", there are other units, namely those for which MC is smaller than price, for which marginal profit is positive.

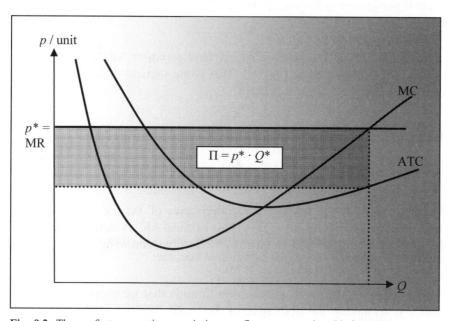

Fig. 9.2. The perfect competitor maximises profits at a quantity Q^* for which price p^* (which is also equal to marginal revenue MR) equals marginal cost MC under the condition that the MC curve is rising. This profit Π is shown by the dark grey area. This is the difference between price and average total cost ATC at the optimum quantity Q^*, multiplied by this same quantity

As long as MC is below price, producing more makes sense. You would therefore keep adding units to your production schedule and would not stop until MC is equal to price, because every additional unit below that quantity yields more than it costs. At the last unit, you produce at zero marginal profit. Every subsequent unit you produce would give a "marginal loss", and so you produce no more than that quantity at which MC is equal to price.

The Rising Portion of the Marginal Cost Curve

If we represent this finding graphically, the optimum output quantity Q^* can be found where the MC curve cuts through the (perfectly elastic) firm-specific demand curve equal to p^*. But be careful; the intercept must be where the MC curve is rising[12]. Taking the quantity at which MC equals price where the MC curve is *falling* would cause the firm to incur a loss on every unit produced, as it would not take advantage of *any* of the units that it could sell at a marginal profit, i.e. the units for which price exceeds MC. As we can see, the intuition behind the mathematics is sound and we can trust Equation 9.9 to help us find a profit-maximising quantity.

Calculating Profit in Fig. 9.2

Taking the correct intersection of MC and p (where MC is rising), Π is given by the grey area in Fig. 9.2. This is the vertical difference between price and average total cost ATC or:

$$p^* - \text{ATC} \tag{9.10}$$

multiplied by the number of units Q^* produced. Therefore Π is given by:

$$\Pi = (p^* - \text{ATC}) \cdot Q^* \tag{9.11}$$

We can show that Equation 9.11 is true by expanding it:

$$\Pi = p^* \cdot Q^* - \text{ATC} \cdot Q^* \tag{9.12}$$

Since price times quantity is defined as TR, and ATC times quantity is TC, we can reformulate the above equation to become:

$$\Pi = \text{TR} - \text{TC} \tag{9.13}$$

This is the general profit function that we are used to. Hence, we know Equation 9.10 is correct.

---

[12] One could also take the second derivative (i.e. taking the derivative of the derivative) to see if the point in question is a maximum or a minimum. After all, the first derivative is zero in both cases. The second derivative would then indicate if the first derivative goes from positive to negative and the point is a maximum (second derivative is negative) or vice versa. In this text, however, we approach the problem of finding maxima or minima graphically.

9.3 The Short-Run Shutdown Condition

Let us now qualify our above analysis by introducing the shutdown condition. As you can tell from its name, it is a condition for which the perfectly competitive firm will not want to produce, or in other words, will want to shut its production down.

Price Should Exceed ATC
Implicit in our discussion at the end of Section 9.2 was an important fact which must hold for the perfect competitor to be able to derive a positive profit. Looking at Fig. 9.2 again, it is conceivable that the cost curves are shaped in such a way that ATC is *never* below price. In this instance, profit would be negative even if we picked the point at which MC is equal to price.

If Price Is Between ATC and AVC the Firm Still Produces
Ideally, setting price equal to MC yields an optimal Q at which price exceeds ATC and the firm is making a profit. But what happens when price is above *average variable cost* AVC but *below* ATC? Clearly then, the firm is not making a profit.

The seemingly intuitive answer to this problem would be to shut down and to leave the industry. While this is certainly what would happen in the long run (as we will soon see), in the short run, capital is fixed and we incur an FC element which does not vanish by shutting down the business. When price is between ATC and AVC, not producing anything would in fact be even worse than producing at a loss.

How could this be? In such an instance, the firm is (on average) covering the variable cost element of production. It is, however, not covering the entire FC element. But as long as it covers *some* amount of FC, the firm will want to engage in production in the short run by setting price equal to MC. Not doing so would result in an even greater loss.

Loss Minimisation
It may seem absurd to speak of a profit maximising quantity in such a situation, as clearly profits are not positive! While the optimum condition of setting price equal to MC is still the same, we label it differently in this instance and refer to it as the "loss-minimising condition". Remember, this is still optimal because the firm would make an even greater loss in the short run by not producing at all.

> The perfectly competitive firm maximises profits at a quantity
> at which MC = MR = p holds. This must be:
>
> 1) In the rising part of the MC curve
> 2) When price exceeds AVC. If the last condition does not
> hold, the firm is better off shutting down.

9.4 Perfect Competition in the Long Run

In this section, we look at how market supply changes depending on initial profits by incumbents, how the behaviour of the perfectly competitive firm can be understood using a game theoretic approach and how the theory connects to the real world.

9.4.1 Shifting Supply

Industry Entry
Having spent some time on short-run profit maximisation, let us now see how things differ when we take a long-term view. Let us say that a new industry has emerged in which profits are initially very high. In response to this, many new firms are now entering this industry, as they anticipate a "piece of this pie". After, say, one year, which in this example we assume to be the time frame equal to the long run, so many new businesses have entered the industry that price has dropped in response to the outward shift in supply, as seen in Fig. 9.3.

Zero-Profit Condition
In perfect competition, we assume that, in the long run, prices drop so much that no firm is earning economic profit anymore. This is known as the zero-profit condition.

> In a perfectly competitive industry, profits are "competed
> away" in the long run. This is known as the zero-profit condition.

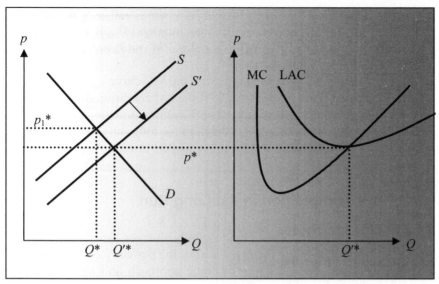

Fig. 9.3. In the long run, there is an absence of profits under perfect competition in the industry as potential producers are lured into the market by high profits. This results in an outward shift of industry supply and a subsequent reduction in equilibrium price from p_1^* to p^*

As we can see in the left-hand panel of Fig. 9.3, as supply increases (indicated by the outward shift of the supply curve from S to S'), price drops from p_1^* to p^*. This long-run equilibrium is associated with an increase in optimum quantity from Q^* to Q'^*. At this new quantity, price and MC are equal to the long-run average cost LAC, as we can see in the right-hand panel of Fig. 9.3. In other words, in the long run the perfectly competitive firm is not making any profit.

Industry Exit / Shutdown Condition
The idea of movement within an industry can also be looked at in a different way — namely exit from the industry rather than entry into it. As we saw at the end of Section 9.3, a perfect competitor will produce in the short run even if he is not making a positive profit, as long as the price is above AVC.

As we have already indicated, since this is a loss-making process of production, the firm would exit as soon as possible, i.e. in the long run. Fig. 9.3 could be adjusted slightly to account for a scenario of this kind. While the right-hand panel would be unchanged, the left-hand panel would merely need one change. The initial supply S would be located to the right rather than to the left of the final supply S' (which is itself unchanged).

Hence, the movement of supply would be inwards rather than outwards, when firms are making an initial loss in the industry. In any case, the result in the long run would still be the same: none of the firms in the industry make any profit (but no losses either).

> The perfect competitor shuts down in the long run if the LAC curve is strictly above market price.

9.4.2 Reality vs. Theory

Approximation of the Real World
You might think that the assumption that the perfectly competitive firm makes no profits in the long run is a little bit far fetched. Why would any-one want to operate a business if there is nothing to be gained? Your con-cern is justified. First of all, it must be said that perfect competition, just like all the other market structures, has some more or less realistic assump-tions that are rarely entirely satisfied in the real world. However, it still serves as a useful benchmark with which to compare real markets.

That is, some industries are considered more competitive than others. By making some (admittedly extreme) assumptions about a market, we are able to make predictions that are relevant to the real world. The alternative of using thousands of variables to account for all the characteristics of real firms seems unattractive in comparison.

Choosing an Example: Electronics Industries
Let us look at a real world example illustrating the theory of industry entry discussed in Section 9.4.1. In many industries, fading profits in the long run are a fact of life. Taking the example of virtually any electronics prod-uct, prices are usually very high with the introduction of the product. Then, as more firms enter the industry with the desire to share some of the profit, competition increases and as a result there is pressure on the margins. Eventually, firms in the industry produce without any economic profit. Today, many electronics products such as certain computer chips and DVD players are consumer staples. Once a luxury produced by very few firms and offered at an extraordinary price, DVD players are now available for as little as £20.

Efficiency of Perfect Competition
As we can see, the theory does predict some aspects of the real world. Perfect competition in the long run serves society most efficiently as consumers pay no more than the cost of production to the firm[13]. Moreover, firms are forced to allocate resources to their production process efficiently to avoid making losses. We explain the concept of efficiency in more detail in the next chapter, where we will see that in contrast to the perfectly competitive market place, the monopoly is an inefficient market structure.

> In perfect competition, consumers pay no more than what it costs the firm to produce the good, and firms produce at the cost optimum; hence, all welfare-creating trades are realised.

9.5 The Connection Between Marginal and Average Costs

This section is slightly more technical than the rest of this chapter. The subject of our analysis at this point is the connection between different cost curves. To be more precise, we investigate how the MC curve cuts through the average cost curves at their respective minima. This is shown in Fig. 9.4.

Shutdown and Breakeven Points
Before we commence with our analysis, let us link the graph back to some of the discussion above. Looking at Fig. 9.4 you may have noticed that the two quantities for the intersection of MC with AVC and MC with ATC are labelled Q_S and Q_B. These are the shutdown and breakeven points, respectively.

> The MC curve crosses the AVC and ATC curves at their respective minima.

---

[13] The result of this is that all welfare-enhancing gains from trade are realised.

As we discussed previously, when employing the profit-maximising condition and when AVC is equal to MC, we would be just about indifferent between shutting down or producing in the short run. Secondly, when we set price equal to MC and when at this point MC is also equal to ATC, the firm is just breaking even.

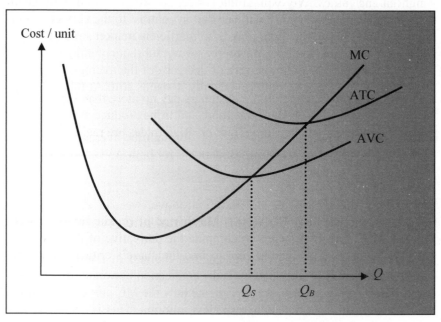

Fig. 9.4. The marginal cost MC curve cuts through average variable cost AVC and average total cost ATC curves at their respective minima. These points are the shutdown and break-even points, respectively

Marginal and Average Strawberries — An Analogy to the Arithmetic Connection Between Marginal and Average Costs

Beyond the discussion above there is no further economic meaning between the intersections of the cost curves as seen in Fig. 9.4. The connection is purely arithmetic, as we shall see using the example of strawberries previously used in Section 5.4.5, when we explained the connection between marginal and average products. The intuition is identical.

Suppose you have all sizes of strawberries, from very large to very small. Each size of strawberry exists twice except for the smallest, of which you only have one. Let us also say that you line these strawberries up from very large to very small, then to very large again. This is analogous to the U-shaped MC curve.

You take one strawberry after another and place them on a scale that tells you the average weight of all strawberries. The first strawberry that you place in the bucket is very large, while every subsequent one will be smaller (until you reach the smallest one). Because of the literal "weight" of the heavier ones, average weight is larger than marginal weight (i.e. the weight of each strawberry you handle). Average weight still decreases, although less steeply than marginal weight.

Once you reach the smallest strawberry, every subsequent strawberry will be larger, which means that the rate of decrease of the average weight becomes smaller and smaller until eventually it stands still. At this point, the marginal weight is just equal to the average weight.

This logic is an analogy of why MC cuts through the average cost curves at their minimums. The reasoning is identical for both AVC and ATC.

Mathematical Proof
Rather than blindly trusting the intuition above, we can also prove our analysis mathematically. Let us perform this proof for the intersection of MC and ATC. Our first step is to compute the derivative of ATC with respect to Q and set this equal to zero to find the curve's critical point, here the minimum:

$$\frac{d\text{ATC}}{dQ} = 0 \qquad (9.14)$$

In order to make Equation 9.14 usable, let us substitute TC/Q for ATC. Therefore, we get:

$$\frac{d(\frac{\text{TC}}{Q})}{dQ} = 0 \qquad (9.15)$$

To avoid complicated calculus, let us reformulate the numerator as a product:

$$\frac{d(\text{TC} \cdot Q^{-1})}{dQ} = 0 \qquad (9.16)$$

Remembering the **product rule**, we differentiate $\text{TC} \cdot Q^{-1}$ with respect to Q by taking the derivative of the first term and multiplying it by the second, and adding the derivative of the second term and multiplying it by the first. This gives us:

$$\frac{d\text{TC}}{dQ} Q^{-1} - \text{TC} \cdot Q^{-2} = 0 \tag{9.17}$$

Notice the negative sign between the terms, which is a result of the -1 "brought down" from Q^{-1} of Equation 9.16 in the process of differentiation. When looking at Equation 9.17, we notice that the very first term is MC and so we can write:

$$\text{MC} \cdot Q^{-1} - \text{TC} \cdot Q^{-2} = 0 \tag{9.18}$$

As a final step we multiply both sides by Q and write the second term as a fraction:

$$\text{MC} - \frac{\text{TC}}{Q} = 0 \tag{9.19}$$

Since, by definition, TC/Q is equal to ATC, we finalise our equation to become:

$$\text{MC} - \text{ATC} = 0 \tag{9.20}$$

Now our task of proving that ATC is equal to MC when ATC is at its minimum is easy. Having taken the derivative of ATC in Equation 9.14 to show its minimum, we have worked all the way to Equation 9.20. This last Equation will hold true, i.e. will correspond to a minimum of the ATC curve when we set MC and ATC equal to each other. Hence, when MC is equal to ATC, ATC is at its minimum. The same mathematical steps can be followed to prove the intersection of AVC and MC at the minimum of AVC.

9.6 More About the Firm's Supply

Having talked about the perfectly elastic demand in perfectly competitive industries at the beginning of this chapter, let us now also analyse the characteristics of supply in this market structure in more detail.

Price Elasticity of Supply Depends on the Time Frame
We recall that in the long run, the firm's capacity to alter its quantity produced is much greater than in the short run because of its ability to adjust the quantity of all inputs, including the ones that are fixed in the short run. The important implication of this is that while firms have some leeway in changing the quantity they produce, the price elasticity of supply is not as high in the short run as it is during the long run. The effect of a reduction

in price would not see all firms leaving the industry instantly, and if the market price increased, new firms would not enter the market straight away.

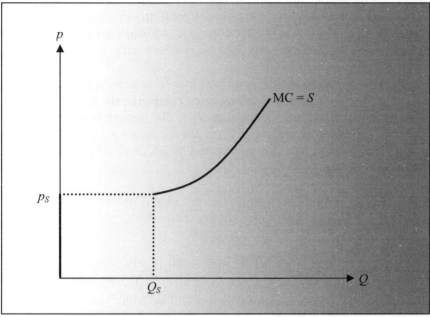

Fig. 9.5. The perfect competitor's output is zero until the shutdown quantity Q_S is reached. For quantities larger than Q_S the firm's output (i.e. its supply) is equal to its marginal cost curve MC

Graphing the Firms Supply
We recall that the firm produces the quantity where MC is equal to price. Therefore, the individual firm's supply is simply given by its MC function. The higher the (exogenously given) price, the more units it can produce profitably and the larger the optimum output quantity. We need to qualify this statement further by taking into account the shutdown condition. In some instances, the price is below average cost and so the firm will not want to produce anything. If this is the case, the firm's supply is zero instead of MC, as shown in Fig. 9.5.

9.7 Producer and Consumer Surplus

Producer Surplus
When talking about the benefit the producer receives from a transaction, we first think of profits. But there is a different way to account for the producer's benefit. This is the producer surplus. Although profit and producer surplus can be the same, usually they are not. So what is producer surplus?

It is the compensation the firm receives from producing a profit maximising output over and above the (negative) compensation that it would receive from not producing anything at all[14]. The benefit from engaging in production is hence the difference between the actual gain (the profit) and the loss that the firm would have incurred by not producing anything at all (negative FC).

It follows that the producer surplus is not merely the profit from setting price equal to MC but the addition of profit *and* FC[15]:

$$PS = \Pi + FC \qquad (9.21)$$

Note that cost is always positive, so the surplus increases with the addition of FC. When price is between AVC and ATC in the short run, profit will be negative, but producer surplus would still be larger than zero as negative FC is larger than profit.

> The producer surplus is the amount of money the firm gains
> from producing a profit-maximising output over the
> compensation that it would get from producing nothing.
> This is the sum of profit and FC.

Showing Producer Surplus Graphically
We can also now show producer surplus graphically with ease . From Fig. 9.2, we recall that the firm's profit can be shown graphically by the product of Q^* and the vertical difference between price and the ATC curve.

---

[14] The implication of this is that the firm wants to produce as long as price exceeds AVC (at least in the short run).
[15] Alternatively, we could also express producer surplus as PS = TR - VC.

Since profit is part of producer surplus, this clearly needs to be one part of its graphical representation.

In addition, as we recall from Chapter 7, when drawing the AVC and ATC curves for any one quantity, ATC will always be larger than AVC by the amount of AFC[16]. In other words, the ATC curve is simply an upward shift of the AVC curve by an amount equal to AFC.

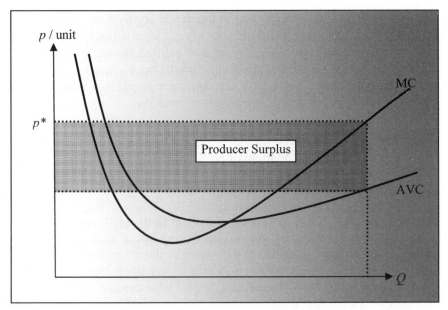

Fig. 9.6. The firm individual producer surplus is the area encompassed by the vertical distance of price and the AVC curve at the optimum quantity Q^* multiplied by Q^*, as represented by the grey area

Therefore, to add FC to our graphical representation of producer surplus, we simply take the rectangle as shown in Fig. 9.2 and extend it downwards by an amount equal to AFC. We do so by extending the vertical side of the rectangle downwards from price, beyond ATC all the way down to AVC. The result is that we can show profit plus FC in Fig. 9.6., which is the producer surplus[17]. Analogously, the benefit a consumer derives from a transaction is measured as consumer surplus.

---

[16] This arises from the simple rule ATC = AVC + AFC

[17] Recall the rectangle is the multiplication of the vertical distance times the quantity. The increase in vertical distance compared to Fig. 9.2 is AFC. Multiplied by Q, AFC becomes simply FC, and this is the missing element we sought to add to

Consumer Surplus

Similar to what we have done for the producer, when looking at the consumer we can also make statements about the benefit that she derives from an economic transaction, i.e. from purchasing a good. The consumer surplus is the monetary equivalent of utility that the consumer derives over and above the monetary equivalent of utility she would have had not engaging in the transaction.

Suppose you return from a day trip to the desert and you are thirstier than you have ever been in your life. If you were offered a bottle of water for £10 you might gladly pay this amount *and* gain additional utility, so that you retain a consumer surplus from this transaction. Generally, if the consumer surplus is not at least zero, the consumer would not engage in the transaction. We will resume this example in a minute.

Aggregated Producer and Consumer Surplus

Now that we have understood both consumer and producer surplus on an individual agent basis, let us extend this understanding to an industry-wide framework that encompasses all producers and consumers.

We can now use demand and supply curves to show what is known as *aggregated* consumer and producer surplus on a graph, as done in Fig. 9.7[18]. Let us start with the consumer. In the example above we assumed that the first bottle of water offered to you exhibited a very large consumer surplus. How about the surplus of the second bottle? Chances are that while you may still be thirsty, the utility that you derive from this additional unit is less than from the previous one. As we keep offering you additional bottles, eventually your thirst is satisfied and the monetary equivalent of the utility that you would derive from the consumption of an additional bottle is no longer larger than its price.

Alternatively, we may look at the demand curve as the amalgamation of a number of different consumers' maximum willingness to pay. So, for example, while you might pay up to £15 for a bottle of water, a camel, if it could buy water, may only want to pay £3, as they can survive for up to two weeks without drinking any water. If we combine all consumers' individual demands for water, we end up with a downward sloping industry

show producer surplus graphically. Producer surplus can also be shown graphically in a different way using MC, as we shall see in Section 10.7.

[18] While the demand curve every individual firm faces is perfectly elastic, industry supply is still downward sloping.

demand curve as seen in Fig. 9.7. Moving on to industry supply, the supply curve is upward sloping, as seen in Fig. 9.5.

Two Triangles

Combining demand and supply, the market clearing price is p^* and the quantity produced is equal to the quantity consumed at Q^*. Since both producers and consumers are taking part in the transactions, they must gain something from it. And this "gain" is their individual surplus. As the market price is already determined, the consumers who value the product very highly derive the highest consumer surplus. Take a point on the demand curve very close to the vertical axis where Q is equal to 1. This quantity is associated with a very high price.

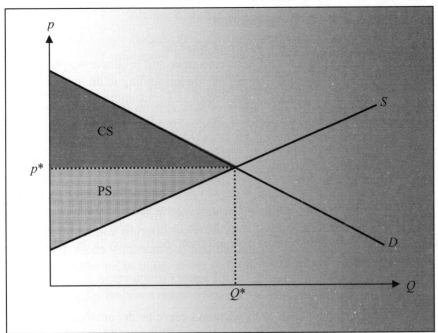

Fig. 9.7. The aggregated consumer surplus CS as shown by the dark grey triangle is the area encompassed by the supply curve S and the equilibrium price p^* up to the market clearing quantity Q^*. The aggregated producer surplus PS as shown by the light grey triangle is the area encompassed by the demand curve D and p^* up to Q^*

It means that this one person "sitting" at the top of the demand curve is willing to pay this very high price if need be. The good news to him is that he does not need to pay that much. Instead, every consumer in the industry is charged the same price p^*, and the individual consumer's surplus is the difference between the market price and their maximum willingness to pay. Taking all consumers together, their surplus is represented by the entire area encompassed by the demand curve and the market clearing price p^* up until Q^*, shown by the dark grey area in Fig. 9.7.

Similarly, the producer surplus is the triangle encompassed by price and the supply curve up until Q^*, shown by the light grey area. Implicit in this is the assumption that the firm does not incur FC[19]. Hence, the aggregated producer surplus is the addition of each individual firm's price that it receives minus the cost of production, here the MC.

9.8 Chapter Summary

Assumptions of Perfect Competition

- Under perfect competition, all firms in the industry produce a homogenous product, also known as perfect substitute.
- Moreover, firms in perfectly competitive market structures are said to be price takers. This is a function of the fact that there are so many sellers that the individual output of each of them is so small compared to the industry output, that no individual firm has any influence on price. As a result the demand curve facing each perfect competitor is simply a horizontal line, which is synonymous to saying that the firm faces a perfectly elastic demand curve.
- Under perfect competition, firms can enter and exit the industry freely. Entry barriers include regulation and technological know-how, while most exit barriers constitute high levels of FC. Underlying the assumption of ease of entry and exit to and from the industry is the assumption of perfect factor mobility.
- In the context of the analysis of all market structures in this text, both producers and consumers are assumed to have perfect information about pricing.

Short-Run Profit Maximisation

- At the profit-maximising quantity for the perfect competitor, MR is equal to MC. For the perfect competitor, MR is always equal to price.

---

[19] The upward-sloping supply curve shown in Fig. 9.7 assumes ordering the firms by their efficiency. That is, the most efficient firm would start producing at the lowest price, the second lowest at a slightly higher price and so on.

- As long as price exceeds AVC, the firm wants to keep adding units to its production schedule, as long as MC is below price. This means that the firm is making a profit on the margin for each unit. Once MC reaches price, the firm should no longer produce additional units.
- Graphically, the perfectly competitive firm should produce at a quantity at which price is equal to MC while the MC curve is rising (provided that price is above AVC at the optimum quantity).

Short-Run Shutdown Condition
- At that point at which price is equal to MC and is below AVC, the firm should shut its production down, i.e. it should not produce anything at all.
- If the price at the point where the optimum condition holds is between AVC and AFC, the firm produces but only in the short run. Although at this point the firm would produce at a loss, it can still cover some part of the FC, and hence producing nothing would be even more costly than producing at this loss-making quantity.

Perfect Competition in the Long Run
- While in the short run the perfect competitor earns a positive profit, in the long run new firms are lured into the industry until supply shifts outwards, up to a point at which the equilibrium price is equal to LAC. As a result, no firm in the market earns profit anymore. This is known as the zero-profit condition of perfect competition, which occurs in the long run.
- The perfect competitor shuts down in the long run if price is above ATC at the point at which price is equal to MC.

The Connection Between Marginal Cost and Average Costs
- MC always cuts through AVC and ATC at their respective minima.
- These intersections are the shutdown and breakeven points, respectively.

More About the Firm's Supply
- Since certain factors of production are fixed in the short run, the price elasticity of supply of the firm is less elastic in the short run than it is in the long run.
- The firm's supply is given by its MC function for prices above the shutdown point. For prices below the shutdown point, the firm does not produce at all and so the supply function for those quantities is simply part of the vertical axis up until the shutdown price.

Producer and Consumer Surplus

- The producer surplus is that amount of money the firm gains from producing a profit-maximising output over the compensation that it would get from producing nothing.
- This is the sum of profit and FC.
- Producer surplus can be shown graphically as a rectangle with sides Q^* and $p - AVC$.
- Consumer surplus is the monetary equivalent of the utility the consumer derives from taking part in an economic transaction, minus that monetary equivalent of utility that she would have derived without engaging in the transaction.

Aggregated Producer and Consumer Surplus

- Aggregated producer and consumer surpluses are the compensations to all producers and consumers in the market.
- Aggregated consumer surplus is the triangle encompassed by price and the demand curve up to the market clearing quantity on a traditional supply and demand graph.
- On the same graph, producer surplus can be shown as the triangle encompassed by price and the supply curve up to the market clearing quantity.

The Profit Maximising Condition

$$p = MC \qquad (9.4)$$

Producer Surplus

$$PS = \Pi + FC \qquad (9.21)$$

10. The Monopoly

Introduction

An important part of this chapter is the profit maximisation of the monopoly. We also examine the notion of lost welfare from monopoly pricing compared with competitive pricing. This is then qualified as we find that a regulated natural monopoly may in fact be the most preferred way of serving the market under certain conditions. In addition we discuss price discrimination, which is a way for the monopolist to inflate profits further. We finish the chapter by analysing factors contributing to the sustainability of the monopoly.

Required Knowledge

You should have a good understanding of cost analysis (Chapter 7) and demand theory (Chapter 2). Having an understanding of perfect competition (Chapter 9) is also a prerequisite, as the analysis in this chapter builds on previous principles.

Key Terms

entry/exit barriers, natural monopoly, government monopoly, geographic monopoly, patent-based monopoly, total revenue (TR), marginal revenue (MR), marginal cost (MC), short run, long run, average total cost (ATC), shutdown condition, price elasticity of demand, deadweight loss, efficiency, producer surplus, consumer surplus, long-run average cost (LAC), minimum efficient scale (MES), (dis)economies of scale, first-/second-/third-degree price discrimination, arbitrage, economies of scope, network effects, product proliferation.

10.1 Making the Connection to Perfect Competition

After having discussed the market structure of perfect competition in detail in the preceding chapter, we now turn our attention to the monopoly which, in many ways, can be regarded as the polar opposite of perfect competition. Although the structure of this chapter is slightly different to that of perfect competition, as we explain many of the relevant principles using fictitious case studies (based on real firms[1]), we set forth the assumptions of the monopoly at the beginning for consistency. We keep this discussion brief, since an understanding of the assumptions of the model of perfect competition as discussed in Chapter 9 is assumed.

Monopoly Assumptions — A Comparison to Perfect Competition
Whereas under perfect competition there are many sellers in the market, in monopoly only one firm supplies the entire market. Secondly, the monopolist has the freedom to pick any price for his product, which is in stark contrast to the perfect competitor whose individual demand curve is flat. A monopolistic market structure also exhibits significant entry barriers[2] (such as technical know-how) that are not present for the perfect competitor. Lastly, we assume that a monopolist and its consumers have perfect knowledge about the market parameters.

10.2 Good Monopoly, Bad Monopoly?

Back to Intuition
Let us now take a step back from the theory and focus our attention on intuition. The layman would possibly think of the board game when they hear the term "monopoly" outside of the study of economics. The idea of the game is basically trying to bankrupt the other players by possessing all the properties and charging outrageous prices when they are forced to stay in your seven star hotel suites. We are not suggesting that this is what monopolies do in the real world, but one thing is for sure: the monopolist does have a bad reputation. We will find out whether this reputation is justified by examining how "bad" monopolies really are and whether they are necessarily bad all of the time. First, however, we define what a monopoly actually is.

A monopoly is a market structure
consisting of only one firm.

---

[1] While it is difficult finding a convincing example of perfect competition, monopolies do exist!

[2] Entry barriers are discussed in more detail in Section 10.10.

The following examples should challenge your thinking about possible preconceived ideas of the monopolist.

10.2.1 National Rail Transport

Case
Imagine if the government had no say in the structure of the rail transport industry. Anyone with sufficient capabilities could start a rail network and compete with existing firms. Wastage would be horrendous as tracks, stations and wagons would have to be duplicated, or consumers might have to change frequently during their journey. Given the large initial investments, and the division of the market across different firms, average costs per consumer would probably be inefficiently high.

To avoid these problems of **inefficiency**, the federal government in many countries appoints *one* company that will take care of all rail traffic. By doing so, one avoids duplication of resources, and therefore the output price is likely to be much lower as a result of the reduction in average cost. In order for the monopoly not to exploit its position, it agrees to be regulated by the government upon its appointment. Do you think it is bad that the rail transport industries in many countries are monopolists, despite their many (potential) inefficiency problems?

Assessment
In an industry in which a single firm can serve the market most efficiently, the firm is called a **natural monopoly**. It is a favourable way of serving the market because we can avoid wastage of resources and thereby keep prices low by passing the savings on to the consumer. Of course, some kind of regulation is required for the monopoly not to exploit its dominant position. Section 10.8 deals with the natural monopoly in more detail.

A Similar Type of Monopoly
Rather than appointing a firm that takes care of an entire market, the government could operate such a firm itself. In this instance we would be dealing with a **government monopoly**. An often cited example of a government monopoly is the postal service.

10.2.2 Luigi's Pizza in Barnville

Case

Barnville is a small town of 500 people at least 1 hour's drive from the nearest large city. Joe decided to open Luigi's Pizza in 1973, as he was annoyed by the fact that there was no restaurant in his town. People liked Joe's idea and especially the younger "folks" enjoy the food. Since the early 1970s no one else has opened a restaurant in Barnville. Do you think this monopoly is bad?

Assessment

In this example, we are dealing with a **geographic monopoly**. Luigi's pizza is not the only place in the world that that serves food, but if you live in Barnville it might well be! If Luigi's pizza was doing very well, others might, consider "sharing the wealth" with Joe by opening further restaurants, in which case he would no longer be a monopolist.

10.2.3 StayAwake

Case

The pharmaceutical giant Prinz has recently developed a new drug called *StayAwake*, which helps pump blood into your brain. It is a top seller, as this concentration-enhancing pill makes students study-hungry beasts, able to pull all-nighters five times a week to expand their horizons. The components of the pill have been newly developed after a team of dozens of top scientists at Prinz spent almost a decade on research. The pill's active substances are protected by a patent granted by the US government and can therefore not be used by other companies without the permission of Prinz. Do you think it is bad that Prinz has a monopoly position (for a certain period of time) for supplying *StayAwake*?

Assessment

In this case we are confronted with a **patent-based monopoly**, a firm that has gained exclusive rights to produce a type of product, based on the ownership of a patent. In the chemical industry, it is common that a company develops a new way of producing a substance and thus gains a patent for the *means of producing* rather than the product itself.

10.3 Marginal Revenue Revisited

Introducing Ju-Nique

As we have seen in the preceding section, there are a number of examples in which the presence of a monopoly is not necessarily a bad thing. How come monopolies have such a bad reputation then? Let us look at the example of Ju-Nique and find out in what circumstances the presence of a monopolistic firm might not be ideal. Let us explore here what will happen when a monopolist is not regulated by the government. What will she do, and is our intuition to think of the unregulated monopoly as undesirable justified?

The Price Setter

Ju-Nique, as the monopolist, can theoretically pick any price for its product. Or, alternatively, it could produce a certain level of output and then let the market determine the price. It can do this because it is the only firm supplying this specific type of product. A monopolist is thus known as the **price setter** rather than a price taker, as discussed in Section 10.1. Although convention has it that we speak of the monopolist as a price setter, we will treat her as a quantity setter in this example for the sake of convenience.

Choosing The Optimal Output

Back to the problem: let's say you are Ju-Nique's CEO. How will you choose your optimum output level to maximise your profit? From Chapter 9, we recall that at the optimum output level marginal cost MC must equal marginal revenue MR. This is as true for the monopolist as for the perfect competitor. Hence, at the optimum:

$$MR = MC \qquad (10.1)$$

must hold.

The Connection to the Perfect Competitor

When the concept of MR was introduced in Chapter 9, we recall that it was simply equal to the market price, as the demand curve facing each individual firm under perfect competition is perfectly elastic. The demand curve facing the monopolist is simply the industry demand curve, which is downward sloping. It follows from this that MR cannot simply be equal to the market price any longer. But if it is not equal to price, what will it be equal to?

Calculating Marginal Revenue
In the first instance, we can calculate MR based on its definition. Since MR is that change in total revenue TR resulting from an infinitesimal change in output Q, we know that it is simply the derivative of TR with respect to Q:

$$MR = \frac{\partial TR}{\partial Q} \qquad (10.2)$$

Let us take an example of a downward sloping demand function:

$$Q = 20 - 0.8p \qquad (10.3)$$

By definition TR is equal to:

$$TR = p \cdot Q \qquad (10.4)$$

In our example, this can be reformulated to:

$$TR = p \cdot (20 - 0.8p) = 20p - 0.8p^2 \qquad (10.5)$$

by substituting Equation 10.3 into Equation 10.4. Taking the derivative of MR as set forth in Equation 10.2 we get:

$$\frac{\partial TR}{\partial Q} = 20 - 1.6p \qquad (10.6)$$

By looking at the negative sign in Equation 10.6, we know immediately that the MR for the monopolist is downward sloping.

Marginal Revenue Is Twice the Slope of Demand
Equation 10.6 tells us even more. When comparing it with Equation 10.3, something should catch your eye immediately: the coefficient on p is twice as large for the MR curve as for the demand curve. What this amounts to is that the slope of the MR curve is twice as steep as that of the demand curve. This holds true as long as the demand curve is linear. Moreover, since the constants for both the MR function and the demand function are identical, we can deduce that the intercept on the vertical axis for both the demand curve and the MR curve are the same.

> For a linear demand curve, the marginal revenue curve has a gradient twice as steep as the demand function but has the same vertical intercept.

Changes in Revenue on a Graph

Let us now have a look at how TR changes with a change in quantity by directing our attention to Fig. 10.1. Producing at a quantity of Q_1 yields a level of TR that is represented by the combined areas A and C. This is found as we multiply Q_1 with p_1.

Suppose the firm is now increasing its production from Q_1 to Q_2. TR is now equal to Q_2 times p_2, which is represented by areas B and C on the graph. Thus, from changing the output from Q_1 to Q_2 we lost an amount of revenue represented by area A, but at the same time we gained an amount of revenue represented by area B. Since B is larger than A, we have gained more than we have lost. Therefore, from a pure revenue perspective, increasing output made sense.

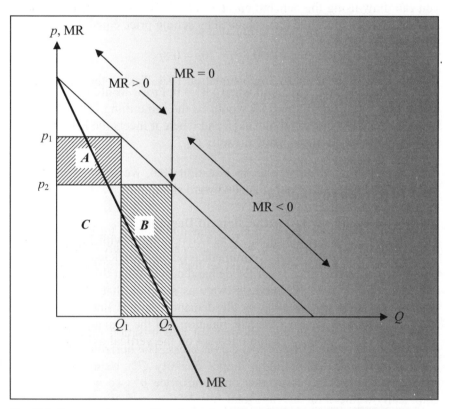

Fig. 10.1. Revenue changes with a change in output and reaches its maximum at Q_2

The MR Curve
Rather than awkwardly saying that we "gained more than we lost", we could simply say that "MR is positive". Our TR has increased as a consequence of our change from Q_1 to Q_2. As indicated in Fig. 10.1, at the upper part of the demand curve MR is positive, in the lower part it is negative, and at the mid-point it is zero. You can see why this is by looking at the MR curve (thickly drawn). For small values of Q, MR > 0, for larger values of Q, MR < 0, and for Q_2, MR = 0.

So, why do we care about the sign of MR? While we are in the region of positive MR, increasing output will *always increase* TR. This is the case until we hit MR = 0, at which point TR is maximised. Increasing output further would *decrease* TR. Any combination of price and quantity that you can draw using the demand curve in Fig. 10.1 will necessarily yield a revenue area smaller than that achieved by setting price equal to p_2 and setting quantity equal to Q_2.

If MC Were Zero
The condition of MR = MC still when MC = 0. Profit would be maximised where MR = 0, as profit and TR would be the same thing. The MC curve would be equal to the horizontal axis, and where it meets the MR curve we would get the profit-maximising quantity Q_2.

10.4 Profit Maximisation

At the end of the preceding section, we stated that profit for the monopolist is maximised when MR is zero, as long as cost is also zero. Since the non-existence of MC is not realistic[3], let us now discuss profit maximisation with positive MC.

MC = MR
Using Fig. 10.2, we can now show profit maximisation graphically. We draw a dot where the MR and MC curves cross. The horizontal location of the dot represents the optimum output quantity Q^*. Using the demand curve, we can see the associated optimum price p^*. To show the profit graphically we need the average total cost ATC curve[4]. We show the verti-

---

[3] Apart from certain services, for example Internet applications, where marginal cost comes close to being zero.
[4] If no fixed cost is present, this is equivalent to the average variable cost AVC curve.

cal difference between ATC and the optimum price at Q^* as one side of a rectangle, the area of which represents the firm's profit. The other side of the rectangle is the optimum quantity Q^*. Profit is therefore represented by area A in Fig. 10.2 and can be stated as:

$$\Pi = (p^* - \text{ATC}) \cdot Q^* \tag{10.7}$$

Avoiding Errors
There are two common errors when showing profit maximisation on a graph. Firstly, since you need to draw the MC curve in any case when you want to find out the optimal output and price, it is possible to forget to include the ATC curve when showing profit[5].

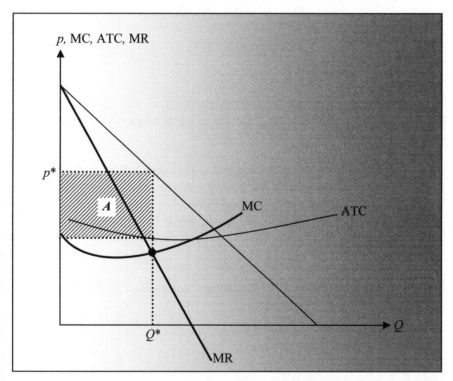

Fig. 10.2. The monopolist maximises profit at the quantity at which MR and MC are equal to each other. The profit at this quantity is shown by the difference between price p^* and ATC multiplied by the output quantity Q^*

---

[5] We can only use marginal cost for the calculation of profit when it is linear and when fixed cost is zero.

Secondly, it is tempting to believe that the profit is given by the area that lies strictly above the ATC curve. This would give a non-rectangular shape. We will not make a mistake in drawing profit if we bear in mind that profit is given by Equation 10.7. Since there are no exponents on the variables in this equation, the area that can be drawn from it must have linear sides.

Calculating Profit — The Principle

Having shown profit graphically, let us round our analysis off by also calculating it. When MC is constant and fixed cost FC is zero, calculating the profit for the monopoly is straight forward. It is simply the profit gained from each unit (which is price minus MC) multiplied by the quantity sold:

$$\Pi = (p - \text{MC}) \cdot Q \qquad (10.8)$$

$$\Pi = p \cdot Q - \text{MC} \cdot Q$$

$$\Pi = \text{TR} - \text{TC}$$

We can verify this formula by multiplying it out, as you can see. In the final line we get TR minus total cost TC is equal to profit Π, which is the definition of profit.

Calculating Profit — Using a Demand Curve and a Cost Function

Looking at a specific example, let us now calculate the monopolist's profit by using a cost function and a demand curve. For this, we need to find the optimum quantity and price by setting MC equal to MR. But before we do this, let us introduce a specific cost function for a monopolist:

$$\text{TC} = 15 + 2Q \qquad (10.9)$$

From this, we can calculate MC by taking the derivative of the above function with respect to Q:

$$\text{MC} = \frac{\partial \text{TC}}{\partial Q} = 2 \qquad (10.10)$$

Moreover, let us use a demand function of:

$$Q = 20 - 4p \qquad (10.11)$$

For arriving at the profit maximising quantity, we also require MR of the demand function (calculated as shown in Equations 10.2 to 10.6), which is:

$$\frac{\partial \text{TR}}{\partial Q} = 20 - 8p \tag{10.12}$$

Setting MC equal to MR, we get:

$$20 - 8p^* = 2 \tag{10.13}$$

and so:

$$p^* = 2.25 \tag{10.14}$$

Thus, the optimal price will be 2.25. To find the corresponding quantity we substitute p^* into Equation 10.11:

$$Q^* = 20 - 4 \cdot 2.25 = 11 \tag{10.15}$$

Hence, the profit-maximising output is 11, with an associated price of 2.25. As a final step let us calculate the profit, which we know to be:

$$\Pi = \text{TR} - \text{TC} \tag{10.16}$$

Using the definition of profit and Equation 10.9, we can reformulate Equation 10.16 to:

$$\Pi = p \cdot Q - (15 + 2Q) \tag{10.17}$$

Now we can simply substitute the optimum output and quantity levels in Equation 10.17, which gives:

$$\Pi = 2.25 \cdot 11 - (15 + 2 \cdot 11) \tag{10.18}$$

$$\Pi = -12.25$$

As we have just found out, given the firm's TC function and its demand function, we were able to calculate its profit by finding the optimal quantity and price. We were able to do this by equating MR and MC. It actually turns out that the firm's profit function is such that even in optimality its profit is negative[6]. Clearly this is not a satisfactory situation, and this brings us to the next point of discussion: the monopolist's shutdown condition.

---

[6] Should you feel dissatisfied with the above conclusion of negative profits, try a cost function of $TC = 2Q$ instead, which basically means that we take out the FC element. By repeating exactly the same steps as outlined above, you should find that now the monopolist's profit would be 2.75.

10.5 Shutdown Conditions in Short and Long Run

The Short Run — Perfect Competitor

Drawing the parallel to the perfect competitor, we remember that under certain circumstances the firm will want to shut its production down. For the perfect competitor this condition was "if AVC is above price, at that point at which MC is equal to MR shut down". If price is above AVC but below ATC, production will commence at least in the short run, as some part of FC can be covered. This is better than incurring the loss of the entire negative FC portion.

The Short Run — Monopolist

The logic behind the monopolist's shutdown condition is no different from the perfect competitor's — only the mechanics are. Since one major difference of the monopolist compared with the perfect competitor is the fact that the monopolist is facing a downward sloping demand curve as opposed to a perfectly elastic demand curve, the rule of the shutdown condition needs to be changed in that regard. We can therefore say that the monopolist will want to shut down production if at that point at which MR is equal to MC, AVC lies above the demand curve[7]. We can even take this one step further and say that if the AVC curve *lies above the demand curve at the optimal quantity*, then the monopolist will want to shut down. In the profit calculation at the end the preceding section, the monopolist would therefore not shut down in the short run as some part of the FC (i.e. 2.75) is covered[8]. However, as we will see now, in the long run things are different.

The monopoly shuts down in the short run if
the AVC curve lies above the demand curve
at the optimal quantity.

---

[7] This means that $AVC > p$.

[8] We assumed an FC equal to 15 above, and from our calculations we found that profit was 12.25. Hence, the firm incurs a loss of 2.75 units smaller than it would have incurred if it had not produced at all.

The Long Run – Adjusting the Condition
The alteration of our condition from the short run to the long run is very minor, as the difference from short to long run is exactly the same as it was for the perfect competitor. We only need to adjust this condition by replacing "AVC" with "LAC", and so we can say that the monopolist will want to shut down production in the long run if the LAC *curve lies above the demand curve at the optimal quantity*. And this is precisely what happened in the numeric example in the previous section. Therefore, in the long run the monopolist would want to shut down given the specific demand curve and cost function used in our example.

> The monopoly shuts down in the long run if
> the LAC curve lies above the demand curve
> at the optimal quantity.

10.6 Elasticity of Demand and Marginal Revenue

In Section 10.3, we stated that MR is positive for the upper half of the demand curve and negative for the lower half. Let us now examine this a bit more closely. As we can see in Fig. 10.3, MR is positive in the elastic region of the demand curve ($|\eta| > 1$), negative in the inelastic region of the demand curve ($|\eta| < 1$), and equal to zero where the elasticity of demand is unitary ($|\eta| = 1$).

> Marginal revenue is positive for quantities corresponding to
> the elastic region of the demand curve, it is negative where the
> demand curve is inelastic, and equals zero where the demand
> curve is unit elastic.

$|\eta| > 1$ Where MC = MR

From these facts it follows that for any positive MC curve that one can draw, this curve will *always* intersect the MR curve in the elastic part of the demand curve. Look at Fig. 10.3, and you will be able to see straight away that MC would have to be negative to intersect MR anywhere else than in the elastic region of the demand curve.

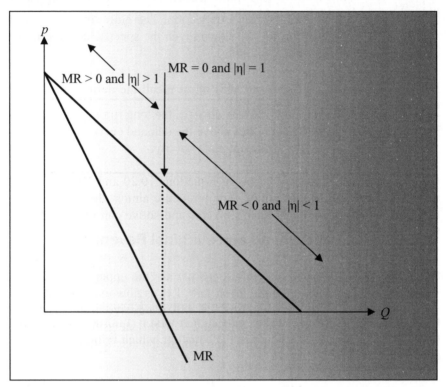

Fig. 10.3. For quantities at which MR is positive, the demand curve is elastic, whereas for quantities at which MR is negative, demand is inelastic. When MR is zero, demand is unitary elastic

Proving the Assertion

Rather than simply stating facts, let us also prove that they are correct. We can show the relationship between MR and the elasticity of demand analytically. Therefore, let us first express MR as the (partial) derivative of TR with respect to Q by using the product rule[9]:

$$MR = p + \frac{\partial p}{\partial Q} Q \qquad (10.19)$$

We can now take Equation 10.19 and bracket out p. For the equation to hold, the right-hand term must be divided by p:

$$MR = p \cdot (1 + \frac{\partial p}{\partial Q} \frac{Q}{p}) \qquad (10.20)$$

Before we move any further with MR, let us recall the definition of price elasticity of demand from Chapter 2[10]:

$$\eta = \frac{\partial Q}{\partial p} \frac{p}{Q} \qquad (10.21)$$

By looking at the right-hand terms of Equations 10.20 and 10.21, there is something that you should notice. The terms are almost the same. To be more precise, they are each other's inverse and so we can redefine Equation 10.21 to become:

$$MR = p \cdot (1 + \frac{1}{\eta}) \qquad (10.22)$$

As a final step, we recall that the price elasticity of demand is always negative, and so we use the absolute value sign around η. In order to adjust for this we need to use a minus sign in the equation, which brings us to the final equation:

$$MR = p \cdot (1 - \frac{1}{|\eta|}) \qquad (10.23)$$

Let us see what Equation 10.23 means. As we recall from Chapter 2, very large $|\eta|$s (i.e. elastic demand) correspond to points on the demand curve close to the vertical axis while points on the demand curve close to the horizontal axis are those at which $|\eta|$s are close to zero (i.e. inelastic demand).

---

[9] The product rule tells us to take the derivative of the first term and multiply it by the second term, and then to add the product of the first term and the derivative of the second term.

[10] This equation differs from Equation 2.5 in that the absolute value signs have been removed. It will soon become apparent why this is necessary.

Hence, if $|\eta|$ is very large, $1/|\eta|$ becomes very small and MR approaches p in Equation 10.23. This means that the MR curve intersects the vertical axis at the same point as the demand curve does[11]. Next, if $|\eta|$ is equal to 1, MR is zero (as the inside of the bracket in Equation 10.23 becomes zero). Finally, if $|\eta|$ is very small, $1/|\eta|$ is very large and hence $1 - (1/|\eta|)$ is negative, which makes the entire expression of MR negative.

As we can see, using the definition of the elasticity of demand and the derivative of TR, we illustrated the connection between MR and the price elasticity of demand as shown in Fig. 10.3.

10.7 Deadweight Loss

Thinking Back to the Beginning
Let us backtrack to the very beginning of this chapter. We briefly discussed the intuition that monopolies are somehow "bad". Until now we haven't specified what we actually mean by this. We know that monopolies set prices to maximise their own profits and not the utility of their consumers, or society as a whole for that matter. Therefore, we might think that the consumer surplus[12] that we would have had in a competitive situation has now all gone to the monopoly as producer surplus, or profits. It turns out, however, that this is not entirely true as there is a so-called deadweight loss to society.

> The loss in surplus as a consequence of monopolistic pricing compared to competitive pricing is known as deadweight loss to society.

A Shrinking Pie
Not just the consumers are worse off compared with the competitive case, but consumers and producers would have had more *combined* surplus had the situation been competitive and not monopolistic. In other words, the "pie" to be distributed between the monopolist and the consumers has

---

[11] In Section 10.3, we have already shown mathematically that this is true.
[12] This concept is introduced in Chapter 9.

shrunk. You can put it yet another way, and say that not all value-creating or welfare-enhancing trades have been realised.

Showing Deadweight Loss
In Fig. 10.4 we show deadweight loss to society, which includes the monopolist's profit-maximising price p_M and quantity Q_M (as already shown in previous graphs in this chapter), as well as the competitive price p_C and quantity Q_C. Table 10.1 shows us surplus areas in the graph and how they change when the situation is monopolistic rather than competitive.

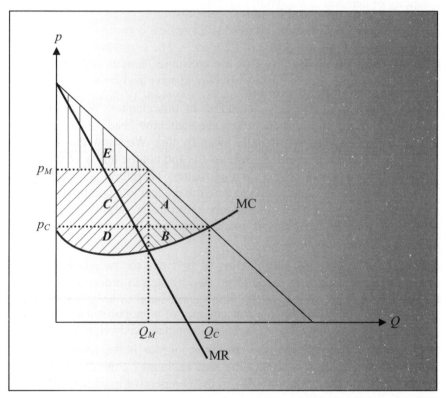

Fig. 10.4. The deadweight loss to society from the monopoly is shown by the combination of the areas A and B

Table 10.1. Comparing competitive output and price with those of the monopolist, we see that the surplus represented by areas A and B is lost entirely, while the consumer surplus represented by area C moves to the monopolist as producer surplus

Area	Competitive	Monopolistic
A	Consumer Surplus	Deadweight Loss
B	Producer Surplus	Deadweight Loss
C	Consumer Surplus	Producer Surplus
D	Producer Surplus	Producer Surplus
E	Consumer Surplus	Consumer Surplus

Review of Consumer and Producer Surplus

For the sake of convenience, let us quickly review consumer and producer surplus, which were introduced in Chapter 9. The consumer surplus is the monetary equivalent of utility that the consumer derives over and above the monetary equivalent of utility she would have had from not engaging in the transaction. The *aggregate* consumer surplus is the sum of all individual consumers' surpluses.

The producer surplus is the amount of money the firm gains from producing output, less the compensation that it would get from producing nothing in this market. This is the sum of profit and FC. It is not necessary to use *aggregated* producer surplus in this context, as there is only one firm in the market.

Surpluses in Fig. 10.4

As Fig. 10.4 might look intimidating at first due to the relatively large amount of information, we need to go step by step in order to understand it. The letters that you see on the graph correspond to areas representing surpluses.

In the competitive situation, the consumer surplus is the combination of areas A, C and E. This is simply the area enclosed by the demand curve, vertical axis and the optimum price in the competitive market p_C. By contrast, when a monopolistic price is set, the consumer surplus is represented by area E only. Therefore, the consumer surplus reduced by an amount equal to areas A and C. Table 10.1 is a quick reference framework that tells us how surpluses are different for monopoly and perfect competition.

Now let us look at the less obvious implications. As consumer surplus has decreased, you might wonder where it has gone. The part of consumer surplus represented by area C is now producer surplus. This means that part of the benefit that consumers would have derived from the transaction in a competitive situation now goes to the producer. Perhaps more interestingly, some proportion of consumer surplus vanishes into nothingness. We call this lost part of surplus a deadweight loss to society. But consumer surplus is not all that vanishes. Indeed, even area B[13], which represents producer surplus under competitive pricing, forms part of the deadweight loss under monopolistic pricing.

An Inefficient Market Structure

Finally, we know why monopolies are regarded as undesirable. The monopolist produces less ($Q_M < Q_C$) and charges more ($p_M > p_C$) than firms in a perfectly competitive market. The result of this is that the combined surplus of consumers and producers would be larger in a competitive situation than in a monopolistic situation. In other words, there is a deadweight loss to society which can be seen in Fig. 10.4.

There is another reason why the monopoly is an inefficient market structure. While in theory the monopolist has an incentive to produce efficiently to maximise profits, in practice situations without competition lead to complacency and inefficient means of production. As a result, monopolists such as national post services have a (justified or unjustified) reputation for bad service.

> Monopolies are inefficient due to the deadweight loss to society and their inefficient means of production.

10.8 The Good Kind — Natural Monopoly

In the preceding section we have done our best to give the monopoly a bad name, but as you know from the beginning of this chapter, we have to fur-

---

[13] The way producer surplus is shown warrants further explanation. From Fig. 9.6 discussed in the context of perfect competition, we recall that producer surplus was shown as a rectangular area encompassed by the difference between MC, AVC and the optimal quantity Q^*, where MC is equal to price. It is equally correct to show producer surplus as the area between MC and price, because the variable cost of producing an output Q is simply the sum of the marginal costs of all units produced to that point.

ther qualify some of our earlier statements. As you might remember, the national railroad industry was a type of a monopoly that we did not consider harmful as long as it was regulated.

In addition to our intuition, we can verify graphically that in some instances the most efficient way of going about things may be to have only one firm to produce the entire output in an industry. Because of the massive investments that each company would have to undergo in the example of railroads, it makes sense that only one firm provides all the output in that market.

Minimum Efficient Scale

Fig. 10.5 depicts the case of a market in which the long-run average cost LAC curve reaches its minimum point at a quantity that is not sufficient to cover the entire demand of that market at a price of p_1. This means that it is likely that more than one firm will serve this market, each producing at its minimum efficient scale MES — graphically this is the minimum of the LAC curve, represented by the dots in the left- and right-hand panels[14]. Producing at the MES means that you have already exploited your economies of scale, and further increasing output would throw you into *diseconomies* of scale as average cost rises again beyond this point.

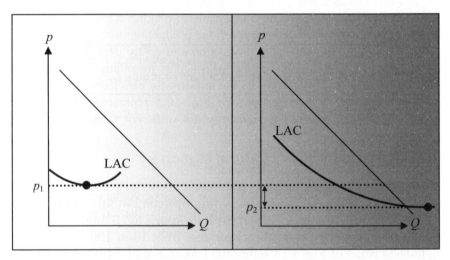

Fig. 10.5. Competition is more likely in the left-hand scenario than on the right, as the MES is reached for a quantity closer to the demand curve

---

[14] It should be noted that it is possible for there to be more than one MES, as it is conceivable that when the LAC reaches a very low point, it stays constant for further increases in output.

> The minimum efficient scale is the output at which the firm faces the lowest LAC.

MES for Low Quantities — Example: Welding Business
Let us now look at an example where the MES is reached for low quantities. Sir Weld-a-Lot specialises in car chassis repairs. If he has one garage with 10 employees, he can handle a certain number of jobs per year. Now assume that he opens a second garage of equal size with the same number of employees. He now decides, however, to specialise each garage according to chassis type and he is therefore able to handle individual jobs more quickly. As a result, the total number of jobs that can be handled a year is more than double what it was with only one garage. This results in a decrease of average cost and so we can say that the production process exhibits **economies of scale**. The point at which a further increase in the scale would no longer lower the average cost is the MES.

Beyond the MES, LAC will rise again and we will be dealing with **diseconomies of scale**. Such diseconomies may present themselves if Sir-Weld-a-lot expanded into all kinds of related and unrelated businesses. The head office would become large, incapable of making correct decisions in time, and it would be out of touch with the production process and the employees, resulting in inefficient production and costly delays. For a business such as this, it is likely that the MES occurs for relatively low quantities. This is one of the reasons why the industry for car chassis repair is not monopolistic. The left-hand panel of Fig. 10.5 represents such a case where the MES is reached at a quantity not sufficient to cover the entire industry demand.

MES for High Quantities — Railroads
An industry such as rail transport is different. Here, scale advantages operate for a large range of quantities. A firm operating in this industry may find its average cost falling when it expands from 5 to 10 train stations, for example, just as it is falling for an increase from 10 to 100 stations. The right-hand panel of Fig. 10.5 shows the LAC curve of a firm in which the MES is reached for very high quantities, as is likely to be the case for the rail transport industry. As indicated by the double-headed arrow in this panel, the LAC curve is formed in such a way that the price at which the MES occurs is lower (i.e. p_2) than it was in the left-hand panel (i.e. p_1).

Making the Monopoly Efficient
Where scale advantages are present, a firm may be allowed to serve the market exclusively for the sake of exploiting efficiency. What does this mean for the consumer? Since average cost is decreasing for the entire relevant range of quantities, the monopoly is an *efficient market* structure. In this particular example, the cost of producing a certain output is lowest when only one firm serves the entire market.

If this monopoly is regulated then its cost advantage can be passed on to the consumers. For example, if a firm buys a high-speed train worth £20m, it needs lots of consumers over many years to use it for the investment to be worthwhile. Of course, nobody would use the train if the ticket was, say, £1,000. However, if many people demand train rides, the average cost per ride sinks dramatically, and tickets can be sold for a more reasonable price if the reduction in average cost is passed on to the consumer.

> A natural monopoly is likely to occur when LAC is decreasing over the entire relevant range of outputs.

Entirely Good?
In this section, we have seen that it is not fair to say that monopolies are always bad, as there are situations in which we *want* only one firm in an industry. Nonetheless, state-run monopolies are not without problems either — postal services being an excellent example. Royal Mail in the UK has long been accused of being inefficient, too expensive and out of touch with its consumers. While it would be unfair to generalise, these are problems that are very often associated with state-endorsed monopolies. In a market with (real or potentially) inefficient firms, these would be replaced by more efficient ones, expensive firms would not make any sales and products that do not appeal to consumers would simply disappear from the market.

In a state-owned or state-endorsed monopoly, this discipline is hard to maintain. Royal Mail reacted to its criticism by bringing in management consultants to look at their cost structure, processes and marketing strategy. The end result was that Royal Mail was rebranded Consignia — a move that was reversed 15 months later and still features high on the list of rebranding disasters. But let's not stray; the problem with state-endorsed monopolies is that they do not have the same discipline imposed on them as other monopolies when it comes to cutting costs, reaching consumers and the like. An inefficient natural monopoly could still be replaced by a more efficient one, but a state-imposed one much less so.

10.9 Price Discrimination — Turning Consumer Surplus into Profit

Connection to Section 10.7
Let us recall our first discussion about profit maximisation of the monopoly in Section 10.7. We found that the monopolist managed to turn consumer surplus into producer surplus and thereby earned higher profits than would have been possible under competitive pricing. Despite the fact that some amount of consumer surplus was lost, it did not vanish entirely (area E in Fig. 10.4 was retained).

Reducing Consumer Surplus Further
This section of the chapter is called "the quest for turning consumer surplus into profit" because ideally this is what the monopolist would like to do to maximise profit. Previously, we have assumed that the monopolist will charge one price to all her consumers and hence every consumer-derived consumer surplus from the transaction. Implicit in the existence of consumer surplus is that consumers would theoretically be willing to pay an amount in excess of the price that they are already charged. Knowing this, the monopolist would like to have this surplus to herself and now charges different prices to different consumers — a regime known as price discrimination.

Assumptions
Before we start our quest, we must be clear about the assumptions that we make. In showing profit in our graphs, we earlier used ATC. For simplicity's sake, from here on we assume that MC is constant and that fixed cost is zero. We can thus use MC instead of ATC in calculating profit, which makes our graphs more "tidy" and gives us the ability to focus on what interests us right at this moment.

10.9.1 First-Degree Price Discrimination

Further Assumptions
Ideally, the monopolist would like to charge every consumer a different price equal to their individual maximum willingness to pay. The monopolist makes every person a take-it-or-leave-it offer, and we assume that a person accepts if the price is equal to his maximum willingness to pay. Alternatively, if you are not comfortable with the idea of consumers agreeing to transactions they do not get anything out of, simply assume the monopolist charges a price slightly lower than the maximum willingness to pay, say one pence.

No More Consumer Surplus
The fact that the monopolist charges a different price to each consumer results in a complete eradication of consumer surplus. If this is the case we are dealing with perfect or first-degree price discrimination. It is often called "perfect" price discrimination because the monopolist earns the highest profit possible, as we can see in Fig. 10.6.

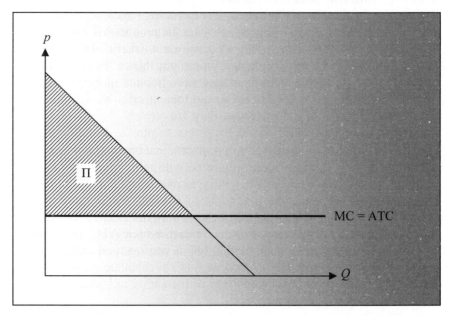

Fig. 10.6. Under first-degree price discrimination, the monopolist earns the highest profit possible (as shown by the shaded area) as consumer surplus is entirely eradicated

In reality, this type of price discrimination is rare at best because it requires perfect information about consumers' willingness to pay. Moreover, it is likely that such a monopoly would already be regulated before it can engage in such price discrimination.

10.9.2 Second-Degree Price Discrimination

Let us now look at another type of price discrimination. As you may be able to guess from the fact that first-degree price discrimination was "perfect", second- and third-degree price discrimination are "less than perfect". To be more specific, second-degree price discrimination is a case in which price changes according to the quantity purchased. Here, the monopolist does not require perfect information about consumers, and consumers self-select the deal that they like best, i.e. the one that gives them the highest consumer surplus.

Bundling in Action

A case of different prices for different quantities is something that we come across everyday. If you go to a supermarket such as Tesco[15] you might find a ready meal that sells for £1.99 with a red sticker on it displaying: "Any two for £3.50". Why does Tesco find it beneficial to make such an offer? If you are anything like us, you might think: "I really am quite broke, so I should get the offer, and save myself some money." So Tesco has sold *two* ready meals instead of one, and the profit of the bundle is still larger than if only one meal had been sold[16].

You can see that second-degree price discrimination makes sense when you think about it this way: John might be willing to pay a maximum of £1.80 for a ready meal, but Jane is willing to pay as much as £2.50. John is an energetic young man who plays lots of football and is hungry pretty much all of the time, so that his maximum willingness to pay for a second meal is as high as for the first. For this reason, he buys the bundle that is on offer. Jane, on the other hand, will only buy one ready meal because she

---

[15] You might think to yourself that Tesco is not a monopolist. You are correct, but this does not negate our arguments here. Moreover, we can reasonably assume that Tesco is taking the role of a quasi-monopolist for consumers who live in a certain area, as was the case for Luigi's Pizza in Barnville.

[16] Assuming that the marginal cost is less than the price difference between single and bundle price.

is very small and she cannot eat more than one meal a day. Her willingness to pay for the second meal in one day is zero[17].

The offering of the bundle has therefore allowed the firm to make a sale where it would not have been possible otherwise. While John is only willing to pay £1.80 for each ready meal, the firm has sold two units to him, whereas he would not even have bought one unit under regular pricing.

Showing it Graphically

Fig. 10.7 is an example of second-degree price discrimination with two different quantities, Q_1 and Q_2. The region that encompasses the profit is the same area as in first-degree price discrimination minus areas A, B and C. A and B are now consumer surplus. It was beneficial for the monopolist to introduce the bundle offer as she is now able to exploit previously unrealised gains from trade.

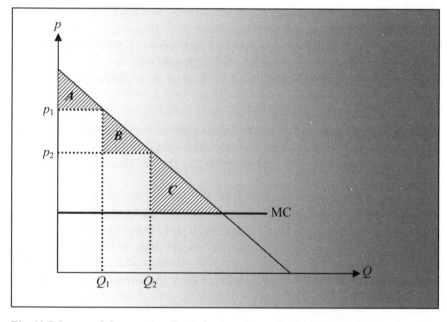

Fig. 10.7. In second-degree price discrimination, the profit of the monopolist is reduced because two bundles of quantities Q_1 and Q_2 are offered

---

[17] We assume that Jane cannot keep the second meal overnight.

10.9.3 Third-Degree Price Discrimination

Different Prices for Different Groups

This type of price discrimination entails charging different prices to different groups of people. You benefit from it everyday: tube passes are cheaper, you get discounts in cinemas, 2 for 1 deals and much more. And it is all due that that magical student card of yours. So why are students given discounts? Getting less out of someone is better than getting nothing at all. Since students do not have as much money on their hands as professionals do, the student's willingness (or ability) to pay is considerably lower than it is for the professional. So, charging students less can make sense if it was previously unaffordable for students to engage in the transaction.

An Example

If the student's reservation price for a movie in a cinema was as low as £1, then the theatre is able to increase its profits by lowering the price for student admission as long as the MC is covered[18]. Importantly, this assumes that there are always seats available and that there is hence no opportunity cost. If every viewing of a movie would sell out, with or without students, then the movie theatre should *not* make student discounts available as this would decrease its profit.

Other groups that are often offered discounts are seniors and small children, although the latter group, one could argue, gets a discount because they usually come with their parents who pay the full price.

Arbitrage

With price discrimination[19] we need to consider the problem of arbitrage. Arbitrage is a case in which a product is cheaply purchased by one person and then sold on to others to whom the market price is higher. For example, if BMW is selling their cars for a price £3,000 lower in Belgium than in Germany, these cars could be imported back to Germany for use of German consumers.

This is clearly not in the best interest of BMW. To avoid arbitrage, laws can be passed that forbid re-import, or BMW might threaten dealers to re-

---

[18] In a movie theatre, it is reasonable to assume that the marginal cost is negligible, as maybe apart from cleaning expenses, there is no additional cost for extra viewers.

[19] In practical terms, this will mostly be third degree price discrimination.

voke their franchise if they sell to the "grey market" for re-imports. Arbitrage is not possible for products or services that cannot be resold. Examples of this include hair cuts, consulting, or any commodity that is expensive to ship such as concrete. In addition, the firm can simply introduce a rule that one person can only buy one unit of a good at a time. This way, the movie theatre can avoid students buying 100 tickets and selling them in front of the box office just below the regular market price.

10.10 Sustaining a Monopoly

In our discussion about monopolies we implicitly dealt with some factors that allow the existence of a monopoly. We already explicitly referred to certain assumptions of the monopoly in Section 10.1, of which barriers to entry were an important one. Let us now discuss factors falling under barriers to entry that allow the monopoly to maintain its existence.

Various Examples of Entry Barriers
Firstly, a monopolist may have **absolute cost advantages** over the potential entrant. Industry incumbents are likely to benefit from learning curves, which refer to the situation of falling MC over time. The first DVD player ever produced cost thousands of pounds in shops, whereas now producers have become so much better at assembling these appliances that the price of a DVD player today is little more than meal for one in a regular restaurant.

While the industry of DVD producers is more oligopolistic than monopolistic, one thing still holds true. If you or we attempted to enter this industry, it would be next to impossible for us to produce at a cost allowing us to charge a competitive price. Our knowledge of electronics is simply not good enough — or, to be more precise, non-existent. With higher MC, the entrant's chances of making a positive profit are smaller, and thus absolute cost advantages may deter entry into an industry.

Moreover, entry can also be deterred if an incumbent holds **control over essential resources**. In 1980, a soap manufacturing called Minnetonka introduced the first modern liquid soap dispenser. In order to stay ahead in this market, the firm then bought the whole supply of the plastic pumps that were necessary for the functioning of the dispenser. This was an effective way of preventing other firms from competing with Minnetonka in this market, at least for some time.

The monopolist may also benefit from **marketing advantages**. There are two points to be made here. Firstly, if you imagine any firm with large brand equity, it comes as no surprise that a potential entrant will have problems getting the attention from consumers who already know and have preferences for an existing brand. Secondly, the marketing advantages can also be seen in the light of vertical relations. A firm that is heavily engaged in advertising, such as Coca Cola, is likely to have excellent vertical relations in the media and may be offered entirely different conditions (e.g. more visible or cheaper advertising space) for marketing than a potential entrant would. The same argument about preferential treatment applies to distribution and shelf-spaces.

Another important factor that may deter entrance to an industry is **economies of scale/scope**. As you are well aware, average cost falls over certain ranges in production. Since the dominant player in the industry will, by definition, be much bigger than an entrant, he will greatly benefit from economies of scale. The situation with economies of scope is similar: a company may find its average cost falling by adding a new product range, for example.

Also related to economies of scale/scope are **network effects**. If 95% of computer owners in the world are using Microsoft's operating system, then most companies and consumers would feel almost obliged to purchase Windows, as they would otherwise run into compatibility problems. The value of Microsoft's software is thus partially determined by the number of other people using it, and so a prospective entrant is put at a significant disadvantage. Accused of abusing its near-monopoly position, Microsoft is currently in litigation in a number of territories.

Next, **product proliferation** by the monopolist may prevent others from entering the industry. Rather than simply producing a regular version, Microsoft produces similar products aimed at slightly different target groups. For example, the additional releases of a student version, a professional version with databases, or a children's version with games would in fact lead to a situation where the potential entrant is faced with not just one competing product, but four. Potential profits decrease as the market is already well covered, and thus less scope exists for product differentiation.

Lastly, the existence of **barriers to exit** in an industry may prevent firms from entering. An exit barrier is a sunk cost that the entrant incurs upon deciding to produce in the given market that she is not able to recoup after discontinuation of production. Interestingly, barriers to exit act as an entry deterrent if they are incurred by either the incumbent or the entrant. If the incumbent faces large barriers to exit, this means that she might well produce in the short run despite making a loss. The potential entrant might find the move to enter too risky given the large sums of money lost upon discontinuation.

10.11 Chapter Summary

Assumptions of the Monopoly
- The monopoly can be regarded as the polar opposite of perfect competition in many ways.
- A monopoly is a market structure consisting of only one firm.
- The monopolist is a price setter rather than a price taker. Hence the monopolist faces a downward sloping demand curve.
- Monopolistic market structures exhibit significant entry barriers.
- We assume that consumers and producers to have perfect information.

Good Monopoly, Bad Monopoly?
- An industry in which a single firm can serve the market most efficiently is called a natural monopoly.
- An industry in which the monopolist is run by the government is known as a government monopoly.
- A firm serving the whole market within a specific region is known as a geographic monopolist.
- When a firm's position as the only producer of a product is protected by a patent (for some time), this firm is known as a patent-based monopolist.

Marginal Revenue Revisited
- Since the monopolist is facing a downward sloping demand curve, MR cannot be equal to price as is the case for the perfect competitor.
- Rather, MR being the derivative of TR with respect to Q is equal to the demand function, only with a slope twice as steep. The vertical intercepts of demand and MR curves are identical.
- TR is maximised if the firm sets a quantity at which MR is equal to zero. At this point, the area formed with the demand curve and the optimal price and quantity is as large as possible.

Profit Maximisation

- The monopolist maximises profit by producing a quantity at which MR is equal to MC.
- This can be shown graphically by noting the quantity at which MR and MC curves intersect. Using the demand curve, the corresponding quantity can be found. The difference between the ATC curve and the optimum price forms one side of the rectangle representing the firm's profit. The other side is the optimum quantity.

Shutdown Conditions

- The monopoly shuts down in the short run if the AVC curve lies above the demand curve at the optimal quantity.
- The monopoly shuts down in the long run if the LAC curve lies above the demand curve at the optimal quantity.

Marginal Revenue and Elasticity

- MR is positive for quantities corresponding to the elastic region of the demand curve ($|\eta| > 1$), it is negative where the demand curve is inelastic ($|\eta| < 1$), and equals zero where the demand curve is unit elastic ($|\eta| = 1$).
- MC always intersects MR in the elastic region of the demand curve.

Deadweight Loss to Society

- The eradication in surplus of a monopolistic pricing compared to a competitive pricing is known as deadweight loss to society.
- Comparing monopolistic pricing with competitive pricing, the same amount of consumer surplus and producer surplus vanishes. In addition, some amount of consumer surplus turns into producer surplus.
- The monopoly is regarded as an inefficient market structure due to the reduction in total surplus arising from its pricing and its inefficient means of production (in practice).

The Good Kind

- In industries where the lowest point of the LAC is reached for quantities close to the demand curve, a natural monopoly is likely to occur. In other words, such an industry can be served most efficiently by one firm.
- This lowest point of the LAC curve is known as the minimum efficient scale MES.
- When this point is reached for a quantity that is not sufficient to cover the entire demand, the industry is likely to be competitive.

- Where the MES occurs for very large quantities, the most efficient way of producing is if only one firm serves the entire market, as long as the monopoly is regulated.
- Having said that, even government-protected and regulated monopolies have a reputation for being inefficient, too expensive and out of touch with their consumers.

Price Discrimination

- Under first-degree price discrimination, the monopolist charges a different price to every consumer always equal to their respective maximum willingness to pay. This price discrimination is also known as perfect price discrimination, as consumer surplus is completely eradicated and the monopolist's profit is as high as it can be.
- Under second-degree price discrimination, the monopolist charges different prices for different quantities. In reality this often translates into bundle offers, whereby the average price decreases the larger the amount purchased is.
- Third-degree price discrimination is a case in which different prices are charged to different consumer groups. Examples of this are discounts for students or senior citizens.
- Under third-degree price discrimination firms must attempt to prevent arbitrage. This term refers to the act of the re-selling of the product from groups benefiting from advantaged pricing to others who do not.

Sustaining the Monopoly

- A monopolist may have absolute cost advantages over her competitors as she benefits from the learning curve. This means that the monopolist learns how to produce more efficiently, and this will let her MC decrease over time. Potential entrants do not have this learning experience.
- When the monopolist holds control over essential resources, this may also prevent others from entering the industry.
- As another way of deterring entry, the monopolist may hold marketing advantages over potential entrants. This may include preferential treatment with regards to advertising space and cost, as well as shelf space.
- The monopolist, unlike the potential entrant, benefits from economies of scale and scope. Not only does the monopolist enjoy falling average cost as output increases, but average cost also decreases as new product ranges are added to the existing product portfolio. In relation to economies of scale/scope, entry may also be prevented by the exis-

tence of network effects, which means that the value of the product increases as more people use it.

- Entry may also be deterred by means of product proliferation. This means that the firm, rather than producing only one product, markets a number of different but similar articles which prevent potential entrants from attacking a possible niche market.
- The existence of barriers to exit in an industry may also prevent others from entering. An exit barrier is a sunk cost that the entrant occurs upon deciding to produce in the given market.

The Profit-Maximising Condition

$$MR = MC \qquad (10.1)$$

Marginal Revenue and Price Elasticity of Demand

$$MR = p \cdot (1 - \frac{1}{|\eta|}) \qquad (10.23)$$

11. Game Theory

Introduction
Our goal in his chapter is to introduce game theory separately as a method, since we require these principles for Chapter 12. Game theory, or the theory of interactive decision making, deals with situations in which one player's actions affect the payoffs of others and vice versa. We will specifically cover the prisoner's dilemma game, coordination games, differentiation games and games of imperfect information. We will demonstrate how to display payoffs both in the normal form (payoff matrices) and the extensive form (game trees). We also apply game theory to a real world business example.

Required Knowledge
Beyond basic probability there are no specific skills that are required for successfully working through this chapter. Some basic terminology introduced in Chapter 1 is used here.

Key Terms
non-cooperative game, strategy, payoff, payoff matrix, normal form game, Nash equilibrium, dominated strategy, dominant strategy, equilibrium, symmetric game, asymmetric game, extensive form game, sequential games, backward induction, sub-game perfect equilibrium, prisoner's dilemma game, Pareto (sub-)optimality, infinite horizons game, coordination game, differentiation game, (non-)credible commitment, predatory pricing, imperfect information.

11.1 The Basic Tool Kit

Before we can start analysing games we need to be clear about the terminology. Firstly, what do we even mean by game theory? If you have seen the movie *A Beautiful Mind* you might remember that the story was about John Nash, winner of the Nobel Prize for his academic contribution to the study of what is known as **non-cooperative games**[1]. Put simply, a non-cooperative game is a situation in which two or more players have at least two decisions they can make with the objective to maximise their own gain by choosing whichever action gives them the highest utility. They do not care about the wellbeing of the other player – hence they do not "cooperate" with each other.

The decisions that players take in each game are known as **strategies**. As mentioned above, each player's welfare is dependent not only on their own strategy but also on the strategy of the other player. For example, if Toby plans to go to an electro-punk concert together with Dominik, his welfare will not only depend on who is playing at the concert but also on whether Dominik is going to show up or not. After all, going to a concert alone is only half the fun, right? What we have called welfare here is called **payoffs** in game theory, to make it applicable to both consumers and firms. For consumers you could think of a payoff as some level of utility expressed quantitatively, whereas for a firm this may be some monetary gain.

It is very important to point out early the possible danger of confusing payoffs with strategies. It is very tempting to say, for example: "the players choose a payoff of X". Making such a statement would, however, be false. One must always bear in mind that the only thing a player can choose is the *strategy and never the payoff* as the payoff depends on the other agent's strategy as well.

11.1.1 The Normal Form

Let us now be more specific about the concert example. Suppose that if Toby goes to a concert by himself his payoff will be 2, and if Dominik goes alone his payoff will also be 2. If both of them stay at home they both gain nothing, and finally if they go together they each receive a payoff of 5.

The situation is displayed in Table 11.1 as what is known as a **payoff matrix** or **normal form game**. The table illustrates both players' strategies (i.e. "go" or "stay at home") and their respective payoffs. The row player's payoffs are on the left and the column player's payoffs are on the right. So,

---

[1] The term "game" is used as this analysis can be applied to actual games such as cards or chess. However, the study of game theory finds application in many economic situations and even in other disciplines such as a politics.

for example, if Dominik goes to the concert and Toby stays at home, Dominik gains 2 and Toby gains nothing. This payoff pair is found in the bottom left box.

What is of interest to us now is to find out what will happen if the two agents were presented with this scenario in real life. More specifically we want to find out whether the game has an **equilibrium** — a natural resting point that nobody would want to deviate from. In order to find out what strategies players will want to choose, there is a simple but effective procedure that we can follow.

Table 11.1. A payoff matrix for a normal game

	T stays at home	T goes to the concert
D stays at home	0 / 0	0 / 2
D goes to the concert	2 / 0	5 / 5

Finding the Equilibrium

Think of yourself as the row player (D). What strategy will you want to choose? This (generally) depends on what the column player's choice is. Therefore, let us assume the column player has chosen to stay home. You can use your hand or a sheet of paper to cover the right column to simulate this scenario (if the column player stays at home, all payoffs on the right hand side of the payoff matrix become irrelevant). Now, what can you, the row player, do? You can either also stay at home or go to the concert by yourself. Staying home will give you a payoff of 0 while going to the concert will give a payoff of 2.

Clearly, 2 is better than 0, and given that we assumed that the column player chose to stay at home, we as the row player choose the strategy to go to the concert. We express this fact by drawing a circle around the 2 in the bottom left box in Table. 11.2 — a copy of Table 11.1. You will soon see why we are doing this. Now let us do the same thing again only this time assuming that the column player has chosen to go to the concert instead. Cover the left-hand column and determine what you as the row player would do. Again you have the choice to either stay at home which will give you a payoff of 0 or to go to the concert which will give you a payoff of 5. We circle the (left) 5 in the bottom right box, as going to the concert is again the preferred option.

Let us perform the same steps now assuming we are the column player. Let us firstly assume that the row player has chosen to stay at home in which case the column player can choose between a strategy yielding a payoff of 0 (also stay at home) or a strategy yielding a payoff of 2 (go to the concert by himself). Remember, it would be wrong to say that we choose between 0 and 2 as these are payoffs and not strategies.

Table 11.2. Solving for the Nash equilibrium, both player's best responses to each other are to go to the concert. For both players, going to the concert is a dominant strategy whereas not going is a dominated strategy

	T stays at home	T goes to the concert
D stays at home	0 ⁝ 0	0 ⁝ 2
D goes to the concert	2 ⁝ 0	5 ⁝ 5

Again, we will show our optimal choice given the other person's strategy, only this time we use *squares*. In this instance we will put a square around the 2 in the top right box (arising from the column player's optimal choice to go to the concert, assuming that the row player stays home), and another square around the (right-hand) 5 in the bottom right box (arising from the column player's optimal choice to go to the concert, assuming that the row player goes as well).

So, what was this exercise of circles and squares good for? By applying this technique we have sought to determine one player's strategy *in response* to the other player's strategy[2]. Therefore, the point at which circles and squares coincide signifies a pair of strategies for which each player's choices are the best responses to other player's best choice. Such a point is known as a **Nash equilibrium.**

---

[2] In this context it does not matter that the other player hasn't actually chosen anything. What is important to understand is that we find one player's best choice *assuming* the other agent has chosen a strategy. Whether or not the player really has chosen that strategy is irrelevant at this point.

> Nash equilibrium is a natural resting point of a game
> associated with a set of strategies which are
> best responses to each other so no player has an incentive to
> unilaterally deviate from their strategy.

Hence, a Nash equilibrium is a combination of strategies (two, in this case) for which neither player has an incentive to unilaterally deviate. In other words, no player will want to move away from his strategy by himself. Thus, it is clear why we call it an equilibrium: it is a natural resting point of the game. In Table 11.2 the Nash equilibrium is the strategy pair of "go" and "go".

Assumptions

We have reached our goal of finding out what will happen in a real-life situation. The first underlying assumption is that every participant has perfect information, i.e. they know of each other, the rules of the game and the payoffs of each strategy pair. The second assumption is that both players are rational, with the goal to maximise their gains. Unless otherwise stated, all of the games you will come across in this text are based on these assumptions.

Dominated and Dominant Strategies

Our analysis is not quite finished. You may have noticed even before we started talking about the game theoretic approach that it is always best for each player to go to concert. In other words, in this specific example, no matter what the other player does one is *always* better off going than not going.

For this reason, we call the strategies of both players of staying at home "dominated strategies". That is, they are strategies that will never be chosen by a rational agent. Graphically, what we have done in Table 11.2 was to put a line through both players' strategies of staying at home. The payoffs of the left-hand column and the top row are irrelevant, as they will never be played; they are eliminated from the game.

The dominated strategies bear their name from the fact that there is another strategy which is always better — the domin*ant* strategy of going to the concert. A dominant strategy is one which will always be played no matter what the strategy of the other person. In the above example, the dominant strategy for both players is to go to the concert.

Game Symmetry

Now we are almost done with the building blocks. The last thing we will discuss in this subsection is the topic of game symmetry. If players' payoffs are identical in every respect then the game is considered to be **symmetric**. If for whatever reason one player might gain more or less from going to the concert or staying at home than the other does, the game would be **asymmetric**. While the example of the concert game is symmetric, we will see asymmetric games later on.

11.1.2 The Extensive Form

Having shown games in the normal form, let us now analyse the extensive form. The main difference compared with normal form games is that there is some sequence with regard to the players' moves within the game. In other words, games are sequential rather than simultaneous. This is graphically presented in the game tree shown in Fig. 11.1.

Let us now look at the scenario from the previous sub-section again and assume that Dominik is able to move first and Toby moves second. Games of this type are analysed by **backward induction**. This means that we assume that the first player has already moved. Then the second player can choose his strategy. If Dominik has decided to go to the concert, Toby finds himself on the top node of the game tree where he can either choose to go (which will yield a payoff of 5 for both him and Dominik) or to stay at home (which will yield a payoff of 0 for him and 2 for Dominik). In this case, Toby chooses the former of the two strategies.

To highlight this decision graphically, we draw the top branch of the tree belonging to the strategy of going to the concert bold for both decision nodes. Toby's optimal strategy of going to the concert in either case is a **sub-game perfect equilibrium**. The concept means that a player is playing their optimal strategy when it is their turn, i.e. when they are at the decision node in a sub-game. Sub-game perfect equilibria show us strategies of players for all decision nodes even those which are never reached.

Since Dominik knows what strategy Toby will choose, he will maximise his gains and take this information into account when making his decision. In his mind, he can already eliminate the branches beyond the first decision node that are not bold, because Toby will never choose these. Therefore, in effect, Dominik can choose between going (yielding a payoff of

5/5[3]) or staying at home (yielding a payoff of 0/2), the former of which will maximise his gains. It so happens that this choice of strategy also maximises Toby's gains, but such an outcome may not always be observed.

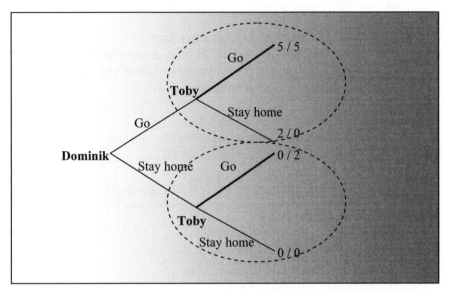

Fig. 11.1. A game in the extensive form with the two sub-games each emphasised by a dotted oval

Due to their simplicity and obvious solutions, the above games were not very interesting. The answer was that no matter what happens, it will always be best to go to the concert. After discussing specialised types of normal form games, we will return to another example of the extensive form with a more elaborate payoff structure. Our discussion thus far has mainly served the purpose of familiarising you with the basic concepts.

11.2 The Prisoner's Dilemma Game

The prisoner's dilemma game is perhaps the most well known non-cooperative game of all. It was first introduced by Flood & Dreshner (1950), although many associate it with John Nash who made vital contributions to this field of study. Let us explain the principle of the game:

---

[3] The player's payoff who moves first is shown on the left.

Suppose Sir Alan Sugar and Sir Richard Branson have been arrested for attempted collusion and are currently in prison until the trial commences. The Attorney General is looking for a fast conviction but has insignificant evidence at this point in time. He has therefore given both "prisoners" the following information:

"If you implicate your partner while he stays silent, he will serve a prison sentence of 10 years while you go free. If both of you implicate the other you will each serve a 2 year sentence. Finally if both of you stay silent you will each serve a six months sentence for minor charges."

Table 11.3. An example of a prisoner's dilemma game in which both players have an incentive to deviate from the "stay silent" strategy

	RB stays silent	RB implicates AS
AS stays silent	6 months / 6 months	10 years / No sentence
AS implicates RB	No sentence / 10 years	2 years / 2 years

Self-Interest Works Against the Players
Upon hearing this problem for the first time, it appears perfectly logical what should happen. "Of course, both of them will be silent." is what you might think to yourself. But put yourself in the shoes of one of the prisoners. You have just been given the above information and you are on your own in your prison cell. There is not an awful lot to keep yourself occupied with and you start pondering: "maybe I should implicate my partner? He has been quite a nuisance to me for several months anyway. Surely my 'partner in crime' is loyal and will remain silent, which means that I will go free, sparing myself a nasty six months in prison!
But hang on a second! Will my partner not be thinking exactly the same thing right now at this moment? May he be plotting against me? In fact, I guess he's been having this sly look on his face lately anyway! You know what? I'm now sure he is trying to betray me. He will implicate me!" All of a sudden, remaining silent carries a huge risk. 10 years in prison to be precise. How much trust and faith can you put in a person? Will my partner stay silent? Now, what will happen does not appear as clear cut anymore.

The problem is just as intricate when agents are allowed to exchange information. For that matter, they could be told the same thing at the same point in time while being in the same room together. It would not change a thing! Sir Richard may say to Sir Alan: "Let's both not say anything and everything will be fine!" Nonetheless, the thoughts in each one's head may still be present and push the agents towards implicating each other. The risk of ten years in prison is suspended over their heads as a metaphorical guillotine.

Prisoner's Dilemma Game in the Normal Form
Let us apply what we have learned earlier about the Nash equilibria. Table 11.4 is a copy of Table 11.3, only now solved for Nash equilibria using the square and circle technique introduced before. By now you should be able to find the equilibria yourself, but we will walk you through again for practice.

Suppose Sir Richard has decided to remain silent. Cover the right column. Sir Alan will choose to implicate Sir Richard as no sentence is better than 6 months. We put a circle around "No sentence". Now we assume Sir Richard implicates Sir Alan. We cover the left column. Sir Alan is now again best off to also implicate Sir Richard. We put a circle around "2 yrs". Implicating Sir Richard is therefore a dominant strategy for Sir Alan. Since the game is symmetric, the same reasoning works for Sir Richard and we arrive at one Nash equilibrium of a strategy pair of "implicate"–"implicate".

Table 11.4. In this prisoner's dilemma game, both players have a dominant strategy to implicate each other although it would be best if they could somehow alter their strategies so that they could achieve Pareto superior payoffs (indicated by the arrow)

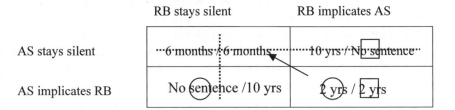

	RB stays silent	RB implicates AS
AS stays silent	···6·months·/·6·months···	····10·yrs·/·No·sentence··
AS implicates RB	No sentence /10 yrs	2 yrs / 2 yrs

Conclusion
As you can see, the game is as cruel as it is clever. The Attorney General, not having enough evidence (as that was our assumption), gave the two agents a game that will lead to a long conviction *even if both are innocent*.

Their own self-interest has led the agents to a situation which is clearly not as advantageous as the payoffs of the "silent"–"silent" strategy.

Pareto Optimality
The prisoner's dilemma game is very similar to what we have seen in Tables 11.1 and 11.2, with the marked difference that the Nash equilibrium here is not the best that the players can do. Therefore, the equilibrium is said to be Pareto **sub-optimal**.

Pareto optimality refers to a situation where both (or all, if there are more than two) players in a game cannot be made better off by a change in strategies without making at least one of the other players worse off by doing so. Pareto sub-optimality is the opposite: there *is* a way of making both or at least one of the players better off without making anyone else worse off. Specifically, 6 months each is Pareto superior to 2 years each.

> An outcome is Pareto optimal when a player's payoff cannot be increased from a deviation of the current situation without making any other agents worse off.

Game Theory vs. Neo-classical Theory
However, Pareto optimality will never be achieved under current assumptions because the agents' self-interest leads them to betray themselves, so to speak. This flies in the face of Smith's neo-classical economic theory which we are used to from microeconomic study these days: a reasoning that economic outcomes are always optimal as long as everybody pursues their self-interest. Of course, we are not suggesting that such principles are false. Quite the contrary: self-interest is indeed a prerequisite for economic growth. However, as we have just seen, in some instances self-interest inhibits agents from arriving at a Pareto optimal outcome, a situation in which more potential gains of the system are realised without making any of the players worse off.

Moving to the Pareto Optimal Strategy Pair
So, from this sub-optimal position, it would be the agents' goal to arrive at the Pareto optimal outcome. This fact is signified by the arrow in Table 11.4, which points from the Nash equilibrium to the Pareto optimal payoff pair. How to accomplish this falls within the study of strategy and man-

agement, and is therefore beyond the scope of this text. Which factors might be of relevance in arriving at a Pareto optimal outcome?

Firstly, **trust** is an important issue. If, say, you and one of your siblings were implicated in a similar fashion, would you really see your brother or sister locked up for 10 years while you go free? The years and years of knowing each have built a trust between you and your sibling and so cooperation is very likely to occur.

Moreover, the number of times a game is repeated would also be taken into account. In the extreme, there could be an **infinite horizon game** in which the game is played over and over again until "the end of time". In such a situation it is unlikely for players to deviate from the Pareto optimal strategies as they would punish themselves. Once trust is broken, it is difficult to get it back. Ideally, the players of a repeating game would make a pact whereby they both choose the strategies that yield a Pareto optimal payoff pair. Repeated games are analysed in more detail in Chapter 12.

Another way of forcing players to choose strategies yielding Pareto optimal payoffs is the drafting of contracts. One may indeed argue that this is the precise reason why contracts exist. Whenever a party has the incentive to unilaterally deviate, it may be a good idea to draft a contract which would specify some sort of sanction in order to reduce or eradicate the incentive of the other party to deviate from the preformed agreement. Too bad for Sir Alan and Sir Richard they didn't have a good lawyer present to write up a contract!

11.3 Coordination Games (Battle of the Sexes)

The battle of the sexes game is equally as famous as the prisoner's dilemma game. It derives its name from an original scenario along these lines: husband and wife have different tastes in music. While he likes to listen to Slayer, she likes Pavarotti. They have agreed to spend their Friday evening together at an artist's performance.

Table 11.5. An example of a coordination game in which players would like to choose the same strategies

	She goes to Slayer	She goes to Pavarotti
He goes to Slayer	10 / 8	2 / 2
He goes to Pavarotti	0 / 0	10 / 8

Table 11.5 shows us the players' payoffs. We can see that both of them value spending the evening together above seeing their favourite artist. Both receive some payoff from seeing their favourite performer by themselves (which is 2), but an even higher payoff (namely 8) if they settled for an artist that they don't like, so long as they are together with their partner. If they had to spend the evening apart and seeing a performance that they do not like, we assume they get a payoff equal to 0.

Solving the Game
So what are husband and wife to do in this game? Using the "circle-and-square-technique" from before, we get two Nash equilibria for strategies "Slayer"–"Slayer" and "Pavarotti"–"Pavarotti". If the players do not communicate, it is impossible to make sure that they will be satisfied. The wife, for example, could think to herself: "My husband has been really nice lately, I will grant him his wish and we will go with him to Slayer." But what if the husband has similar thoughts? Clearly, if he wants to forego some of his pleasure to make his wife happy by going to the Pavarotti concert while she shows up to Slayer, we arrive at the worst possible outcome for both. Something needs to be done.

One way to solve the battle of the sexes game is through commitment. The husband could call up the wife, for example, and say: "I will go to see Slayer today. If you want to come that would be great, but I will definitely go." If this were to happen, the wife, assuming she is self-interested and rational, will have no choice but to come along to the Slayer concert. Otherwise she would receive no payoff whatsoever. Of course, in real life, the husband might be wary of making such a bold announcement, as he might then have to deal with an angry spouse.

In any case, if agents are able to send credible signals about which strategy they are going to pursue, the battle of the sexes game can be played in an efficient way. This game is also called a coordination game because players will want to coordinate actions, i.e. *both want to pursue the same strategy*.

Games of this kind have a great degree of application in business environments, in particular with respect to strategic decisions by firms. These decisions include, for instance, if or how much to advertise, whether or not to price aggressively or how much to spend on research and development. These are applications of game theory that would be discussed in the academic fields of strategy and management.

11.4 Differentiation Games

Let us now discuss a different scenario. The two spouses went to see a musician they both like — James Blunt. Somehow they have managed to acquire VIP backstage passes with the chance to meet James. As the musician is a very shy person and absolutely cannot stand to have more than one guest in his dressing room at the same time, he can only see one of them, wife *or* husband. He is also very busy and does not have time to meet wife and husband one after another.

Payoffs
Consider Table 11.6 for the payoffs. We assume that if both enter, payoffs will be negative as James will get very angry and refuse to talk to them. The remaining payoffs are simple: if you enter, you receive a payoff of 10 from the pleasure of meeting the star, while you receive no such payoff if you stay outside. If both do not enter, their payoff will be zero each.

Table 11.6. An example in a differentiation game in which players would like to ensure that they do *not* choose the same strategy

	She enters	She doesn't enter
He enters	-2 / -2	10 / 0
He doesn't enter	0 / 10	0 / 0

This game is very similar to the one above, with the main difference that players will now want to avoid playing the *same* strategy. In fact, they will want to somehow agree to *differentiate* their strategies, i.e. they want to each play a different strategy to maximise their payoffs. This is why this is called a differentiation game.

Solving the Game

Again, one may come to an agreement if one person is able to commit to a certain action. If the wife says: "I will go inside for sure, no matter what you do" this might be an incentive for the husband not to try to enter. The fact that both would receive a negative payoff makes this a risky proposition, however. If the husband believes his wife is tough, he will definitely not want to enter the room!

11.5 A Business Application of an Extensive Form Game

Within the study of industrial organisation, game trees have a very useful application. We do not seek to go into much detail here, but for illustrative purposes let us consider one example of the principles that we have learned thus far.

The Assumptions

Consider a game in which we have an incumbent firm in the market, perhaps a monopolist, as well as another firm that is seeking to enter the market. The strategies of the potential entrant (whom we will assume to move first) are either to enter or not to enter the market. Suppose an entrant is attempting to move into the industry. The strategies of the incumbent would be to fight or not to fight this entry attempt. When we say "fighting entry", this may include aggressive advertising among other actions with the intent of driving the entrant out of the market[4].

Let us say that if the incumbent does fight the entrant, the incumbent will have a payoff of –2 and the entrant will have a payoff of 2. If the incumbent does not fight the entrant, both players gain a payoff of 4. Finally, in the case of non-entry, the incumbent's profits are as they were in the absence of the entrant whereas the entrant's profits are zero. These facts are shown in the game tree in Fig. 11.2.

---

[4] In reality, such actions are likely to be legally sanctioned.

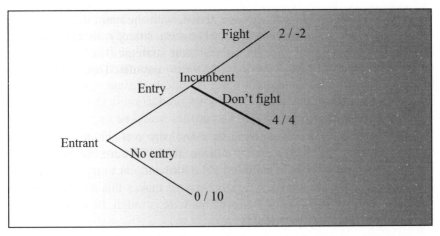

Fig. 11.2. This game of potential market entry in the extensive form shows a sub-game perfect equilibrium of the incumbent to not fight entry

Sub-Game Perfect Equilibrium

From the game tree we can see that the sub-game perfect equilibrium for the incumbent is not to fight the entry of the other firm. Fighting entry could entail price wars or large advertising expenditures, and so we assume that if the incumbent *is* fighting entry the firm will see its profits become negative, due to the associated efforts of attempting to drive the other firm out of the market. In the sub-game the incumbent will decide not to fight entry, as by refraining from doing so its profits will be 4 (instead of –2). Hence, the "don't fight" branch of the tree is thickly drawn.

A Different Scenario

Assume now that the payoffs of fighting were –2/–2 instead of 2/–2. In such a case, not only would the incumbent suffer losses from the entry of the other firm, but so would the entrant. In this regard this scenario is similar to the husband and wife example discussed earlier. The incumbent could pretend to be tough and say: "This is my market! If you enter I will fight you to the death." Such a statement could be labelled a **non-credible commitment,** since it is not in the incumbent's best interest to fight the entry if push comes to shove and the entrant actually enters. However, some firms may have an aggressive reputation of fighting any sort of entry by other firms into "their" market. In this context, potential entrants may in fact believe the commitment of the incumbent even if they have perfect knowledge; that is they know it would not be in the best interest of the incumbent to do so.

Repeated Games

Moreover, if we considered multiple time horizons, it could be the case that the entrant will also find the commitment credible. It is likely that the entrant possesses inferior financial capabilities compared with the incumbent, and the entrant may therefore not be able to sustain a price war very long. The incumbent may incur losses from production in the short run, but once the entrant has been muscled out profits would be back to what ever they were beforehand. If a game is described the same as in this section, unless otherwise stated, you should assume that future payoffs are already factored into the payoffs at the end of the nodes.

11.6 Imperfect Information

As mentioned in Section 11.1.1, the preceding examples all assumed that players have perfect information. Now, let us consider a game in which information is *im*perfect. Once again we will use the two spouses to help us illustrate the case. Fig. 11.3 is an extensive form game very similar to what we have seen early on in Fig. 11.1. The payoffs the players get are exactly the same as in the battle of the sexes game of Section 11.3.

So, Fig. 11.3 is nothing new. It is simply a different way of displaying the battle of the sexes game. Until now, when we used the extensive form it was understood that the player on the left was the first-mover, implying that there was some order in which the players moved.

However, if you remember the setup of the battle of the sexes game, there was no sequence in how the players moved. It is therefore a simultaneous move game. Now, when examining Fig. 11.3 you will have noticed that there is one main difference to the other extensive form games that we have looked at so far, and that is the dotted line connecting the decision nodes of the wife.

The dotted line has a special meaning that can be applied in varying circumstances. The line is a reference to the fact that there is imperfect information and that the player does not know which decision node she is on. The wife does not know her husband's decision prior to her own.

And why is this relevant for the battle of the sexes game? Because, although it *is* in effect a simultaneous move game, the implications for the players are actually the same *as if* it was a sequential game with imperfect information. Moving at the same time as the other player, is, in effect, the same as moving second without being able to observe what the prior move was.

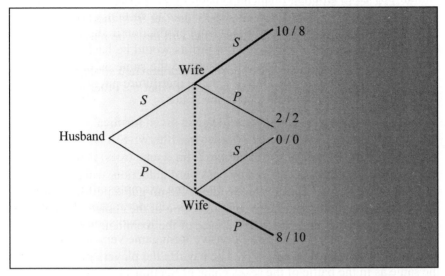

Fig. 11.3. A game in the extensive form with imperfect information. The wife does not know what strategy the husband has chosen (indicated by the dotted line between her decision nodes)

Therefore, *the extensive form with a dotted line connecting the relevant nodes* (this could be more than two) *can be used for simultaneous move games*. Showing the coordination game in a different form does not, however, help us find out what would happen in real life. The two sub-game perfect equilibria of the strategies Slayer and Pavarotti do not actually help the wife to make a decision. Remember, she doesn't know which node she is sitting on.

11.7 Chapter Summary

The Basic Toolkit

- Game theory deals with non-cooperative games. Such games are situations in which at least two players can choose from at least two courses of action. These actions are known as strategies.
- Every possible combination of strategies yields certain payoffs for each agent. Strategies must not be confused with payoffs.

- Simultaneous move games can be shown in payoff matrices otherwise known as normal form games.
- A Nash equilibrium is a natural resting point of a game associated with a set of strategies which are best responses to each other so no player has an incentive to unilaterally deviate from their strategy.
- A dominated strategy is a strategy that will never be played by a rational player.
- A dominant strategy is the opposite of a dominated strategy and is one that will always be played, no matter what the other player chooses.
- When two players' payoffs are identical given identical strategy pairs, such a game is known to be symmetric. Otherwise, it is asymmetric.
- For sequential games, the extensive form (game trees) is used.
- Sequential games are solved by backward induction, whereby the sub-game perfect equilibrium is found. A sub-game perfect equilibrium is the optimal strategy pair consisting of the choice of the first mover and the response to this choice of the second mover.

Prisoner's Dilemma Games
- In the prisoner's dilemma game, the players end up at a Pareto suboptimal outcome unless they can achieve co-operation through some mechanism.
- An outcome is Pareto optimal when a player's payoff cannot be increased from a deviation of the current status without making another agent worse off. The reverse situation would be labelled Pareto suboptimal.
- A prisoner's dilemma game can be solved through trust, repeated interaction (e.g. infinite horizons) or contracts.

Coordination Games
- The battle of the sexes game is also called a coordination game because there are two Nash equilibria but no dominant strategies.
- In order to solve this game, players need to coordinate their strategies (i.e. both should choose the same strategy), otherwise they run the risk of ending up in a Pareto sub-optimal situation.
- Coordination can be achieved through credible commitments.
- A non-credible commitment refers to a strategy that would leave the threatening player with a payoff inferior to what alternative strategies would have yielded.

Differentiation Games
- A differentiation game is the opposite of a coordination game, as players will want to choose strategies that are different from each other.
- Again such a game can be "solved" by the players making credible commitments.

Imperfect Information
- Games of imperfect information can be shown in the extensive form with a dotted line connecting the relevant decision nodes.
- The extensive form with the dotted line can also be used for any simultaneous move game because, by definition, there is no way for a player to observe the other player's strategy before choosing their own.

12. Oligopoly Competition

Introduction

In this chapter we will look at competition among few firms — so-called oligopolies. We examine three different types of oligopolistic competition: Bertrand, Cournot and Stackelberg. We compare the levels of price, quantity and profit of these types of competition with each other and also compare them to the outcomes under monopoly and perfect competition. Moreover, we examine collusion and discuss the circumstances under which it is sustainable.

Required Knowledge

Prior to working through this chapter, a good understanding of game theory (Chapter 11) is required. It is, moreover, advisable to understand Chapters 9 and 10 or alternatively 8. The concept of the discount factor introduced in Chapter 6 is also used here.

Key Terms

strategy, strategic variable, Bertrand competition, strategic complement, simultaneous move game, marginal cost (MC), reaction function, Pareto optimality, Nash equilibrium, Cournot competition, (inverse) demand function, strategic substitute, Stackelberg leadership, sequential game, first-mover advantage, second-mover advantage, collusion, cheating, discount factor.

12.1 Introducing the Oligopoly

In the preceding chapters we learnt about the monopoly and perfect competition. While these two market structures are to be found on either end of the competition spectrum, we now discuss the market structure of oligopoly which exhibits an intermediate degree of competition. The term "oligopoly" is derived from the Greek word for few sellers, and refers to a market structure exhibiting just that: *few* sellers.

The big difference compared with the market structures of perfect competition and monopoly is that, under oligopoly, firms behave strategically. Recall from Chapter 11 that there are many games in which the payoff to one player is not only determined by their own choice of strategy but is also dependent on the other player's strategy.

Under oligopoly, the situation is very similar. Setting a certain price or quantity, the oligopolistic firm must take into account the choice regarding this same **strategic variable** that the other firm(s) operating in the market makes. In our discussions, firms either set a price or a quantity and by doing so they choose a strategy. A firm's strategy could be, for example, to set a high price or to produce little.

A strategic variable is a decision variable by the firm.

Since the degree of competition in an oligopoly lies between the monopoly and perfect competition, one may expect profits of firms operating in an oligopolistic market structure to be somewhere between the profit levels derived in these two market structures. Whether this intuition holds true is determined by which one of the oligopolistic models discussed below (Bertrand, Cournot or Stackelberg) we look at.

General Assumptions

To begin with we mention the general assumptions present in the three models we introduce in this chapter. Firstly, under all models of oligopoly, there are at least two firms competing with each other. Moreover, as was the case in perfect competition and monopoly, all agents have perfect information. This means that firms have knowledge of each other's cost functions, and in the case of sequential games they know which path of action the leader has taken.

In addition, in all games that we look at in this chapter, products are homogenous. The implication of this assumption is that when one firm's price is ever so slightly lower than the other firm's price, the first firm will serve the entire market. The next assumption is that firms do not cooperate or collude with one another, and seek to maximise their own profit when choosing a strategy. This last assumption is relaxed in Section 12.5. Finally, firms' marginal costs are identical and constant.

12.2 Bertrand Competition

Bertrand competition[1] is a natural starting point in the discussion of the oligopoly because it is comparatively easily understood.

Bertrand Assumptions
Let us now discuss the assumptions specific to the Bertrand model, as shown in Table 12.1. Firstly, the strategic variable of the game is price. This kind of competition is intuitive and easily observable in real life. The second specific assumption of Bertrand competition is that firms move simultaneously. We have seen this in the preceding chapter where games were shown in the normal form (or alternatively shown by a game tree where the decision nodes are connected by a dotted line, indicating a quasi-simultaneous move due to lack of information).

Table 12.1. The specific assumptions of the competition model of Bertrand are that the strategic variable is price and that firms move simultaneously

	Bertrand	Cournot	Stackelberg
Strategic Variable	Price	Quantity	Price or Quantity
Move	Simultaneous	Simultaneous	Sequential

Outcome
What we are interested in knowing now is the level of profit that firms derive operating under Bertrand competition. From the preceding chapter we know that self-interested behaviour can result in Pareto sub-optimal outcomes. In fact, with Bertrand competition, the situation for the firms could not be any worse: They make no profits whatsoever and they set a price equal to marginal cost — just as we have observed under perfect competition.

But why should this be the case? Think about a scenario where you own a stand at a market place selling a rare type of fruit that only one other vendor is offering. Say that the cost of acquiring this fruit was £8.00 per kilo

---

[1] Named after French mathematician and economist Joseph Bertrand (1822–1900).

and you are now offering it at a retail price of £10.00. Having knowledge of your offering, and only having interest in his own gain, the owner of the other stall now has an incentive to undercut your price, even if it was only by a few pence. This would, at least in theory, result in him gaining 100% share of the market. Of course you see his cut in price and undercut even further due to your own self-interest.

Zero Profit — Even with Only Two Firms

This process will stop once both of you have reached a price equal to the marginal cost of £8.00. Therefore, the profit of selling the fruit is zero. This is quite startling if we think about it for a second. The finding within perfect competition was that if there is a *large number of firms* in the market, profits will be zero. It is now striking to see that the competition model of Bertrand predicts that this will happen even if there are only two firms in the market.

Bertrand (or price) competition under homogenous products leads to zero profits for firms.

Strategic Complement

At this point it is convenient to introduce the concept of strategic complements. A strategic variable is a strategic complement when a change in a strategic variable by one player prompts a change in the strategic variable of the other player in the same direction. So when one vendor lowers their price, the other wants to lower their price as well. Hence, the concept of strategic complements is closely linked to Bertrand competition. It is the opposite of strategic substitutes, which we discuss in connection with Cournot competition.

Introducing the Reaction Function

The behaviour of the two merchants at the fruit market that we described above can also be shown using a reaction function. Its graphical representation is given in Fig. 12.1. We recall that a function is a machine which is fed with the independent variable and gives us the dependent variable. Here the independent variable is the price of the other firm whereas the dependent variable is the price of the firm that we are analysing. The reaction function can be expressed both mathematically and graphically, although this section will only look at its graphical representation[2]. The meaning of the reaction function is intuitive. It tells us how one firm's strategy (i.e. its choice of price or quantity) *reacts* to the strategy of the other firm.

Continuous Undercutting

Let us have a look at the grey line labelled $p_1^*(p_2)$ in Fig. 12.1. This is firm 1's best response in its choice of price p_1^* given the price p_2 firm 2 sets. You will notice that the reaction curve is slightly below the dotted 45 degree line which means that as long as MC $< p_2 < p_M$, firm 1's price will be ever so slightly below firm 2's price, which has the effect of firm 1 capturing the entire market. Observing this, firm 2 also sets its price slightly below the other firm's price, and so we slide down the 45 degree line until we hit the point at which both reaction lines have kinks.

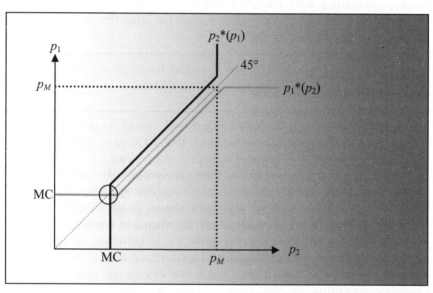

Fig. 12.1. A Bertrand reaction function. In response to the price of firm 2, firm 1 sets an optimal price $p_1^*(p_2)$ that is ever so slightly below the price of firm 2 p_2. The optimal price firm 2 sets in reaction to firm 1's choice of price is $p_2^*(p_1)$ and is also always just below the price of the other firm. This means that firms keep undercutting each other's price until they both price at marginal cost MC. This is where the Nash equilibrium occurs, indicated by the circle. The price will never exceed the monopoly pricing p_M as this maximises the firm's profit, and therefore the reaction lines are kinked at p_M

---

[2] When discussing Cournot competition, we will look at the mathematics as well.

This is where both firms price at marginal cost and receive zero profits. This is the Nash equilibrium in this game because the reaction lines intersect — in other words, firm 1 plays a best response to firm 2's strategy and vice versa, so neither of the firms has an incentive to deviate.

Monopoly Price

There is one aspect of Fig. 12.1 which we have not yet discussed. This is the monopoly price p_M. Graphically its significance is that both firms' reaction functions are kinked at that point. For example, firm 1 will never price above p_M, no matter what the other firm's price is. At the point at which $p_2 > p_M$, firm 1's price will be p_M.

In other words, as long as firm 2 prices above the monopoly price, firm 1 will not just slightly undercut firm 2's price (as was the case for prices between p_M and MC), but instead will simply set the monopoly price. This is reasonable because, irrespective of how high the other firm's price is, p_M is the price that maximises the firm's profit.

12.3 Cournot Competition

Let us now move on to Cournot competition[3], which is more interesting than Bertrand competition in one respect: under Cournot, firms *do* derive profits, which is what we observe in reality. As we can see in Table 12.2, the only change in the assumptions when compared with Bertrand is that under Cournot the firms now compete in quantity rather than price. Although the setting of a quantity may at first seem counter-intuitive, we recall from Chapter 10 that we treated the monopolist as a quantity setter. In theory, this might be all well and good, but does the choosing of quantity as the strategic variable make sense in real life?

Let us answer this question by looking at the oil industry[4]. There is a world market for oil, which means that demand for oil is determined by the combined willingness to pay of all potential buyers. At the same time, oil-producing countries decide how much to produce in a given time period. Therefore, the overall oil supply is the sum of all the production quantities

---

[3]Named after French mathematician and economist Antoine Cournot (1801–1877).

[4] The well-informed reader might say that the industry is a cartel and the quantity-setting model does not apply. Fair play to you, but let us assume for now that the oil-producing countries decide on their quantities independently.

by the oil-producing countries. The market price is then derived from the market clearing point where the supply demand curves meet. In other words, when producing at certain quantities, suppliers do not know what the eventual market price will be since they do not know what the other countries will produce. That is, they do not choose a price but instead choose a quantity, and let price result from market forces.

Table 12.2. The assumptions of the competition model of Cournot are that the strategic variable is quantity and that firms move simultaneously

	Bertrand	Cournot	Stackelberg
Strategic Variable	Price	Quantity	Price or Quantity
Move	Simultaneous	Simultaneous	Sequential

So, what are the levels of profit under Cournot? Suppose there are two firms in the market and we have a demand function of $Q = 5 - p$. Moreover, let the marginal cost of both firms MC_1 and MC_2 be equal to 2. The profit of firm 1 is then given by:

$$\Pi_1 = (p - MC_1) \cdot Q_1 \qquad (12.1)$$

Equation 12.1 says that the profit of firm 1, Π_1, is the difference between the market price p and the MC multiplied by the quantity Q_1 produced by the firm. As the market price is the same for both firms, we can drop the subscript for p. This has to be the case as we are dealing with homogenous products.

So where should we go from here? Since we know the demand function, we can simply rearrange and transform $Q = 5 - p$ into:

$$p = 5 - Q \qquad (12.2)$$

This is known as the inverse demand function. We must not forget that Q without a subscript refers to the quantity produced by the entire industry. As there are two firms, the quantity produced in the market is given by:

$$Q = Q_1 + Q_2 \qquad (12.3)$$

Coming back to our problem, we can refine Equation 12.1 by substituting Equation 12.2 for p:

$$\Pi_1 = (5 - Q - MC_1) \cdot Q_1 \qquad (12.4)$$

Next, we substitute Equation 12.3 for Q, which gives:

$$\Pi_1 = (5 - Q_1 - Q_2 - MC_1) \cdot Q_1 \qquad (12.5)$$

As a last step we incorporate the given information of $MC_1 = 2$ and multiply the equation out:

$$\Pi_1 = (5 - Q_1 - Q_2 - 2) \cdot Q_1 \tag{12.6}$$

$$\Pi_1 = 3Q_1 - Q_1{}^2 - Q_1 \cdot Q_2$$

Since firm 1 is a self-interested agent, it seeks to maximise its own profits. To do so it needs to take into account the strategy of firm 2, which is the quantity Q_2 firm 2 sets. We recall that to find the maximum of a function, we take its derivative with respect to the relevant variable. Therefore we take the derivative of Equation 12.6 with respect to Q_1 (and not Q_2), as we are interested in maximising firm 1's profit. This is:

$$\frac{\partial \Pi_1}{\partial Q_1} = 0 \tag{12.7}$$

$$3 - 2Q_1{}^* - Q_2 = 0$$

Rearranging and solving for Q_1 we get:

$$Q_1{}^* = \frac{3 - Q_2}{2} \tag{12.8}$$

Equation 12.8 is more significant than we might at first realise. It is the reaction function of firm 1 under Cournot competition and represents the first arithmetic expression in this chapter showing how one firm's strategy is impacted by that of the other firm. Putting it in simple terms, it is firm 1's recipe of what to do given firm 2's quantity decision.

Since the problem facing firm 2 is exactly the same as the problem facing firm 1, firm 2's reaction function will be the same as firm 1's. We can therefore take a shortcut by simply taking Equation 12.8 (the reaction function for firm 1) and replacing $Q_1{}^*$ with $Q_2{}^*$, and vice versa:

$$Q_2{}^* = \frac{3 - Q_1}{2} \tag{12.9}$$

The reaction functions that we have arrived at are interesting in their own right, but we have still not reached our goal of finding the firms' profits. How should we go about this? We have two equations in the firms' reaction functions and two unknowns in their strategic variables $Q_1{}^*$ and $Q_2{}^*$. Therefore, all we need to do is to plug one equation into the other at the equilibrium. At this point, we can write $Q_2{}^*$ instead of Q_2 in (Equation 12.8) since both quantities are equilibrium quantities. By doing so we will find the intersection of the two response functions, the Nash equilibrium. The order that we follow is not important. Let us therefore simply substitute Equation 12.9 for Q_2^* in Equation 12.8, which gives:

$$Q_1^* = \frac{3 - \dfrac{3 - Q_1^*}{2}}{2} \tag{12.10}$$

Solving for Q_1^* we get:

$$Q_1^* = 1 \tag{12.11}$$

When used in Equation 12.9, this yields the same quantity for firm 2. We can use these two bits of information in the profit function of firm 1 (Equation 12.5), and our task is accomplished:

$$\Pi_1 = (5 - 1 - 1 - 2) \cdot 2 = 1 \tag{12.12}$$

Since the problem of firm 2 is symmetric to that of firm 1, its profit will also be equal to 1.

Let us quickly recap what we have done: with the given information of a demand function and the marginal cost of the two firms, we differentiated one firm's profit function with respect to its quantity. This led us to the firms' reaction functions which when substituted into each other; this helped us find the quantity produced by both firms. These levels of quantity were then plugged back into the original profit function of each firm.

What is the relevance of all this? As you will recall, under Bertrand (which is a non-cooperative game) profits were zero. Cournot too, is a game in which firms do not co-operate, but here firms do derive profits.

> In Cournot competition with homogenous products, firms derive a positive level of profit.

Graphing the Reaction Function

As we have done earlier in the Bertrand case, we can also graph the firms' best responses to one another under Cournot. The marked difference is that now the strategic variable is quantity and not price. We also have an important advantage compared to the Bertrand case: we have the reaction function. Before analysing the graph let us therefore take a closer look at the example of Equation 12.8:

$$Q_1^* = \frac{3 - Q_2}{2} \tag{12.13}$$

By introducing a specific number for Q_2, we can see how one firm "reacts" to the output of the other. By "react" we mean that assuming one firm chooses a certain level of output, the other has some level of optimal output in response. Suppose firm 2's output was 3; using the above reaction function, firm 1 will choose an output of 0. We can see this by substituting 0 for Q_2 in Equation 12.13. By definition, Q_1^* is firm 1's optimal response in output level given firm 2's quantity.

Understanding the concept of how the reaction function works — how it helps us find one firm's best strategy in response to the other firm's strategy — is all we need to know to visualise the reaction function. The black line labelled $Q_1^*(Q_2)$ in Fig. 12.2 is that optimal response of firm 1 to firm 2's quantity.

Firm 1's reaction function $Q_1^*(Q_2)$ crosses the vertical axis at 3/2. By definition, any point on the vertical axis entails that Q_2 is equal to zero. In other words, if firm 2 sets a quantity equal to 0, firm 1 will set a quantity of 3/2. We can find this to be true by using Equation 12.13 and setting Q_2^* equal to 0. Since firm 2's problem is symmetric to firm 1 we can reuse Equation 12.9:

$$Q_2^* = \frac{3 - Q_1}{2} \tag{12.9}$$

Using the same logic as for firm 1, we can see that firm 2's reaction line $Q_2^*(Q_1)$ crosses the horizontal axis at 3/2. At this point, Q_1 is zero which means that firm 2 sets its quantity equal to 3/2 when firm 1 produces nothing.

The point at which the two reaction functions cross each other on the graph represents a quantity pair consisting of the two best responses to each other. Hence, no firm has an incentive to unilaterally deviate from its strategy. By definition, this is a Nash equilibrium. As shown in Equations 12.10 and 12.11, we find that both Q_1^* and Q_2^* are equal to 1 at the Nash equilibrium. This is indicated by the circle in Fig. 12.2.

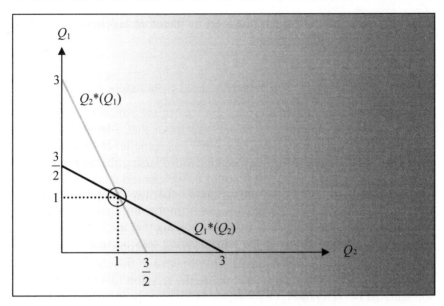

Fig. 12.2. The graph shows firm 2's best response in quantity to the quantity of firm 1, which is its reaction line $Q_2^*(Q_1)$. It also shows firm 1's best response in quantity to the quantity that firm 2 sets, which is its reaction line $Q_1^*(Q_2)$. The Nash equilibrium is found where both firms' reaction lines cross each other and where no firm has an incentive to unilaterally deviate from its strategy. This happens for $Q_1 = Q_2 = 1$

Strategic Substitute

As indicated earlier, the concept of strategic substitutes is linked to Cournot competition. A strategic variable is a strategic substitute if a change in the strategic variable by one player prompts an opposite change in the strategic variable of the other player. This can be observed by looking at the reaction lines in Fig. 12.2. When one firm increases its quantity, the other wants to decrease its quantity and vice versa.

12.4 Stackelberg Leadership

Let us now move to the last of the three competition models under oligopoly that we examine. Table 12.3 illustrates the specific assumptions of Stackelberg leadership. Firstly, the strategic variable can be quantity *or* price. The main difference compared with Cournot and Bertrand, however, is that Stackelberg is a type of game in which firms' decisions are sequential rather than simultaneous. Remember that in the previous chapter such scenarios were shown using game trees (without dotted lines connecting the second player's decision nodes).

Table 12.3. The assumptions of the competition model of Stackelberg are that the strategic variable is quantity or price and that firms move sequentially

	Bertrand	Cournot	Stackelberg
Strategic Variable	Price	Quantity	Quantity or Price
Move	Simultaneous	Simultaneous	Sequential

The sequential nature of Stackelberg entails that the firms' strategies are no longer symmetric. The leader (i.e. that firm moving first) will choose a quantity or price that is optimal to itself knowing that the follower (i.e. the firm moving second) will do the same, taking into account the leader's strategy.

Quantity as the Strategic Variable
Taking quantity as the strategic variable, let us now maximise the follower's profits using Equation 12.9, which we derived in the previous section. We assume that firm 1 moves first and replace Q_1^* with Q_L^* (L being used for "leader"), and Q_2^* with Q_F^* (F being used for "follower"). This gives:

$$Q_F^* = \frac{3 - Q_L}{2} \tag{12.14}$$

Now, rather than looking at the leader's *reaction function*, we determine the leader's *profit function*. It will soon become clear why we do this. This profit function is based on Equation 12.6 with a MC of 2. Again, Q_1 and Q_2 have to be replaced with Q_L and Q_F^*, respectively:

$$\Pi_L = (5 - Q_L - Q_F^* - 2) \cdot Q_L \tag{12.15}$$

Unfortunately, the similarities to Cournot end here. Rather than using a derivative with respect to the leader's quantity for any quantity by the follower, we have to perform a different operation beforehand due to the sequential nature of the game. We will now substitute the follower's problem into the leader's profit function to eliminate Q_F, so that we only have one variable left:

$$\Pi_L = (5 - Q_L - \frac{3 - Q_L}{2} - 2) \cdot Q_L \tag{12.16}$$

We can now take the derivative of the leading firm's profit function with respect to its quantity. This helps us find the quantity that will maximise the leader's profit:

$$\frac{\partial \Pi_L}{\partial Q_L} = 0 \qquad (12.17)$$

$$\frac{3}{2} - Q_L^* = 0$$

$$Q_L^* = \frac{3}{2}$$

We now find the follower's quantity by substituting the leader's quantity in the follower's reaction function:

$$Q_F^* = \frac{3 - \dfrac{3}{2}}{2} = \frac{3}{4} \qquad (12.18)$$

Now that we know what the industry output is, we can find the leader's profit by plugging the values that we have found for Q_L^* and Q_F^* in Equation 12.16:

$$\Pi_L = (5 - \frac{3}{2} - \frac{3}{4} - 2)\,\frac{3}{2} = \frac{9}{8} \qquad (12.19)$$

The follower's profit function is identical to the leader's problem (Equation 12.15) with the exception that the variable outside the bracket is Q_F^* rather than Q_L^*. We can therefore write:

$$\Pi_F = (5 - \frac{3}{4} - \frac{3}{2} - 2)\,\frac{3}{4} = \frac{9}{16} \qquad (12.20)$$

What we have seen in this example is that in a Stackelberg game with quantity as the strategic variable, there is a **first-mover advantage**. This means that the firm that is allowed to choose its quantity before the other can greatly increase its profits vis-à-vis the other firm, *and* the profits it would have derived in a simultaneous game. Using the same profit functions, in the simultaneous Cournot game, profits for each player were equal to 1, the follower's profit in the Stackelberg game is 9/16 (or 0.5625), and the leader's profit in the Stackelberg game is 9/8 (or 1.125).

Price Competition
As you know from the beginning of this section, price can also be chosen as the strategic variable in Stackelberg games. What will happen when this is the case? You are likely to know the answer already, albeit perhaps not explicitly. Any price that the leader picks (apart from a price equal to the marginal cost) will be undercut by the follower who then supplies the entire market. For this reason, when price is the strategic variable, a firm is said to possess a second-mover advantage in Stackelberg competition. However, when the leader sets a price equal to marginal cost, the **second-mover advantage** is not worth anything. Indeed, in reality, a leading firm which knows that it cannot derive a profit no matter what price is chosen may just as well set a price equal to marginal cost.

12.5 Collusion

In the Bertrand model, we have seen that although there were only two firms, the outcome was still perfectly competitive — the firms' profits were zero. Chapter 11 showed that when a game encompasses only one time period it may indeed be hard for firms to display the discipline to choose strategies leading to an outcome Pareto superior to that of perfect competition.

If the time horizon is infinite — or at least very long — firms may be able to fashion some sort of agreement, whether implicit or explicit, of how hard to compete. This enables individual and joint profits to rise compared with the non-cooperative situation. Let us look at a specific example to illustrate this point. Let the demand function be $Q = 70 - p$ and let marginal costs of both firms MC_1 and MC_2 be equal to 10.

If we perform the same steps as from Equation 12.1 through to Equation 12.12, we find that the Cournot profit is 400 for both firms. But could the firms do better than that? They can, but they must act jointly like a single monopolist. To find out what the firms' profits are, we will ignore the fact that they are two separate entities. The profit (for both firms) is therefore given by:

$$\Pi = (p - MC) \cdot Q \qquad (12.21)$$

$$\Pi = (70 - Q - 10) \cdot Q$$

Now we expand the equation and take the derivative of the profit function with respect to Q, thereby finding the optimal quantity Q^* for which profits are maximised:

$$\frac{d\Pi}{dQ} = 0 \qquad (12.22)$$

$$60 - 2Q^* = 0$$

$$Q^* = 30$$

Plugging Q^* back into the profit function (Equation 12.21), we find that industry profit is:

$$\Pi = (70 - 30 - 10) \cdot 30 \qquad (12.23)$$

$$\Pi = 900$$

Since industry profits are 900, each individual firm's profit equals 450. As we can see, by colluding with each other, each firm receives a payoff of 50 higher than under Cournot competition.

Cheating

Firms, however, may become greedy and yearn for even higher profits. But how could a firm receive profits even higher than (half a) monopoly? If one firm manages to unilaterally deviate from the collusive agreement, or to put it differently, to cheat, this firm may be able to increase its profits even further at the expense of the other firm. How does this work?

If one firm believes that the other is continuing to set a co-operative quantity, it can incorporate this information into its profit function and maximise its profits. The industry optimal quantity from co-operation is $Q^* = 30$, as we found out from Equation 12.22. Therefore, the deviating firm expects the other to set a quantity of 15 (i.e. half of 30), which the cheating firm takes as given. MC remains at 10. Therefore we write:

$$\Pi = (70 - Q_1 - 15 - 10) \cdot Q_1 \qquad (12.24)$$

Maximising profit in the usual fashion (i.e. taking the derivative with respect to Q_1) results in an optimal quantity that when substituted back into Equation 12.25 will ultimately yield a profit of $\Pi = 506.25$. Hence, the cheating firm has gained an additional profit of $506.25 - 450 = 56.25$ by cheating and not following the collusive agreement. Note that the collusion problem exhibits large similarities to a prisoner's dilemma. Taking that into account, we know that if it was a one-shot game, collusion would never be sustainable.

To Cheat or Not to Cheat — That Is the Question
Now the question arises of whether a firm should deviate from a collusive agreement and, if so, what the factors that influence such a decision are. As we have mentioned before, we assumed an infinite horizon game.

In general terms, cheating will be profitable if the one-time gain from doing so exceeds the long-term cost from that action. But what is the cost of cheating? Clearly, when one firm has displayed deviant behaviour, the other will no longer set a quantity that requires trust in the other firm. As this trust has been betrayed, further deviant behaviour can be expected and so the firm that was cheated on will set a Cournot quantity in subsequent periods. In other words, in our specific example, the cost to each firm resulting from the deviant behaviour of one of them is 450 (the collusive profit) minus 400 (the Cournot profit). This is 50.

If the game is infinite, and money tomorrow was worth exactly the same as today, we would not need to think a great deal about this problem and would indeed be able to say confidently that collusion will always be sustained as self-interested players would only hurt themselves. The one time gain of 56.25 would not justify the loss of 50 in every subsequent period.

Discount Factor
In reality, however, it is not likely that, say, a sum of money tomorrow would be valued as highly as that sum today. There are a number of reasons why this is the case, such as the opportunity cost of holding the cash. We can account for this by multiplying the future payoff by what is known as the discount factor. As introduced in Chapter 6, this is simply a number between 0 and 1 and is usually denoted as δ.

Let us now apply the discount factor to our example of cheating. Recall that cheating will be profitable as long as the gain from doing so exceeds the future cost of doing so. What we can now do is to state an inequality that must hold for cheating to be profitable:

$$56.25 > 50\delta + 50\delta^2 + \ldots \qquad (12.25)$$

The above inequality says that the one time gain from cheating (56.25) is larger than the sum of all future costs of doing so until the end of time. Each period the power of the discount factor rises by 1 as the opportunity cost etc. applies to every single time period. The logic behind this is identical to that of applying compounded interest. It is now necessary to restate the inequality because, in theory, it is infinitely long due to the infinite time horizons. Without showing the arithmetic steps (as this does not give us additional economic insight) we can display the above inequality in a more convenient way:

$$56.25 > \frac{\delta}{1-\delta} \cdot 50 \qquad (12.26)$$

We can now find the critical value for the discount factor for which one would be indifferent whether or not to cheat. To do so, we replace the inequality sign with an equality sign. By rearranging we find:

$$\delta \approx 0.529 \qquad (12.27)$$

Therefore, if the discount factor is *larger* than 0.529, it means that future payoffs are high enough for cheating not to be worthwhile and for collusion to be sustainable. When the discount factor is *smaller* than 0.529, future payoffs are valued relatively less highly than the present payoff and firms are inclined to cheat.

12.6 A Summary of Our Findings

In this section we tie together what we have learned in this chapter. In Table 12.4 we present our findings comparatively. How does the table work? The first row, for example, gives us firm quantity produced under each mode of competition[5]. The lowest output is observed under collusion (+), which makes sense as firms get together with the explicit (or implicit) goal of keeping prices high (or quantities low). Cournot gives higher quantities (+++) because firms now compete with each other to maximise their own profits.

Table 12.4. A comparison of the firms' output levels, prices and profits under Bertrand, Cournot and Stackelberg competition and collusion

	Bertrand	Cournot	Stackelberg Leader (Q)	Stackelberg Follower (Q)	Collusion
Individual Q	+++++	+++	++++	++	+
Industry Q	+++++	+++	++++	++++	+
Price	+	+++	++	++	++++
Individual Π	0	++	+++	+	++++
Industry Π	0	++	+	+	+++

[5] The plus signs serve a mere comparative function and can only be used to show a ranking for *each row*. We cannot, for example, say that individual profit under Stackelberg is the same as industry profit under Cournot simply because both are labelled "++".

Next we look at Stackelberg with quantity-setting distribution of market shares. While the leader produces more than in a symmetric Cournot game (++++), the follower produces less (++). Overall market quantities are higher under Stackelberg, as we can see in the second line. Finally, Bertrand competition yields the highest quantities because both firms produce half the competitive quantity and market prices are at marginal cost.

If we look at the individual profits[6], however, the ranking is a bit different. Under Bertrand the profits are zero. Cournot derives higher profits (+) whereas Stackelberg and collusion maximise industry profits where in fact the leader's profits are equal to collusive profits.

An open question is which model is the most realistic. All three have their merits and shortcomings. Bertrand competition seems to be most realistic, in that the strategic variable set by the firm is price. However, as real firms do make profits, the outcome under Cournot appears to be the most likely. Lastly, the predictions of the Stackelberg model are only applicable for sequential games. In conclusion, economists have to choose which of the oligopolistic competition models most closely maps the real-world situation that they are attempting to discuss. However, a pure scientist would argue that the applicability to real life is not the ambition of a model.

Remembering Which Is Which
One hint on the side: a good way to prevent you from confusing Bertrand and Cournot is to match the respective strategic variables to each type of competition. For Bertrand, the strategic variable is price, whereas for Cournot it is quantity. Simply match the sound of the words. p goes with "B" for Bertrand and "Q" goes with "Cou" for Cournot. For Stackelberg you could remember that it is a sequential game, where both words start with s.

12.7 Chapter Summary

Introducing the Oligopoly
- In contrast to market structures of monopoly and perfect competition, firms under oligopoly behave strategically. This means that when set-

---

[6] When we speak of individual quantity or individual profits, it is important to note that this will pertain to the leader if we are dealing with an asymmetric game.

ting their strategic variable, firms take into account the choice made by the other firm.

- A strategic variable is a decision variable by the firm.

Common Assumptions of Basic Bertrand, Cournot and Stackelberg Models

- There are at least two competing firms.
- All agents have perfect information.
- Products are homogenous.
- Firms do not cooperate with each other.
- Firms' marginal costs are constant and identical.

Bertrand Competition

- The specific assumptions of Bertrand are that the strategic variable is price and that players in the game move simultaneously.
- Under Bertrand competition, firms price at marginal cost and no firm derives any profit. This is very similar to what happens under perfect competition.
- A strategic variable is a strategic complement when a change in a strategic variable by one player prompts a change in the strategic variable of the other player in the same direction. This happens under Bertrand competition.

The Reaction Function

- Generally, a reaction function is either a formula showing the choice of one firm's strategic variable given the other firm's strategic variable, or it is the graphical representation thereof.
- The graphical representation of the reaction function under Bertrand competition shows us that the Nash equilibrium occurs where both firms' reaction lines cross each other. This happens where the price of both firms is equal to marginal cost.

Cournot Competition

- The principal assumptions of Cournot competition are that players move simultaneously and that the strategic variable is quantity.
- Since firms do not compete in price, they do derive a level of profit under Cournot which is in contrast to that under Bertrand.
- The profit under Cournot can be found by taking the derivative of the profit function (which we find by using the demand curve and the firm's marginal cost) with respect to its quantity.

- This gives us the firm's reaction function. The same can then be done for the other firm. By substituting one reaction function into the other, optimal quantities of both firms can be found.
- These quantities can then be used again in the original profit function to derive the level of profit achieved by firms.
- As was the case under Bertrand, where the reaction lines of both firms cross, a Nash equilibrium occurs.
- A strategic variable is a strategic substitute if a change in the strategic variable by one player prompts an opposite change in the strategic variable of the other player. This happens under Cournot competition.

Stackelberg Leadership
- Under Stackelberg competition, the strategic variable is either quantity or price.
- The main difference of Stackelberg to the other oligopoly models is that firms move sequentially rather than simultaneously.
- The sequential nature of Stackelberg entails that the firms' strategies are no longer symmetric. There is either a first-mover or second-mover advantage depending on whether quantity or price is the strategic variable, respectively.
- Finding quantities and profits of firms in a Stackelberg game using quantity as a strategic variable entails backward induction.
- We solve the follower's problem given the leader's quantity. By substituting Q_F^* with the follower's reaction function, there is only one variable left in the profit function. We can then take the derivative of this function with respect to that variable to find the level of output of the follower.
- This figure can then be used in the follower's reaction function to find his quantity. As a last step, profits can be calculated using these output levels.
- The leader's profit under Stackelberg exceeds the individual profit of firms under Cournot.

Collusion
- To show profits under collusion, we assume that the firms together act as one monopolist, and so all we need to do is to differentiate the profit function with respect to Q.
- We find that each firm's profit is higher than what it was under Cournot.
- A deviation from a collusive agreement is likely when the one-time gain of doing so exceeds the aggregated future cost of doing so. The

cost of cheating is the reduction in profit brought about by the "punishment" imposed by the firm that was cheated on. This punishment entails that the firm chooses a Cournot quantity.

- Mathematically, the cost from cheating is the sum of the future differences of collusive profit and Cournot profit each multiplied by the discount factor δ. For each additional time period that passes, the power of the discount factor rises by 1.

Glossary

Agent
An agent is an economic actor in the study of microeconomics and can either be a consumer, a firm or the government.

Aggregate Consumer Surplus
See Consumer Surplus, Aggregate

Aggregate Producer Surplus
See Producer Surplus, Aggregate

Arbitrage
Arbitrage refers to a situation in which consumers benefit from advantaged pricing by reselling a product to consumers who would have to pay higher prices if they bought directly from the firm. Under third degree price discrimination, firms must attempt to prevent arbitrage.

Asymmetric Game
An asymmetric game is a game in which the players' payoffs are not identical when they choose the same strategies. The opposite situation is a symmetric game.

Average Fixed Cost (AFC)
The AFC is the fixed cost FC divided by the number of units produced. It is inversely related to output. The process of decreasing AFC by an increase in output is known in business as "spreading overheads" or "fixed cost degression".

Average Product of Labour/Capital (AP_L/AP_K)
The average product of labour/capital is the total product divided by the number of units of labour/capital employed in the production process. It is a measure of the overall productivity of a factor of production. The vertical position of the average product curve is the gradient on the ray on the total product curve for that quantity of the input. The marginal product of la-

bour/capital curve cuts through the average product of labour/capital curve at the maximum of the latter.

Average Total Cost (ATC)
The ATC is the total cost TC divided by the number of units produced. It can also be expressed as the sum of the average variable cost AVC and average fixed cost AFC.

Average Variable Cost (AVC)
The AVC is the variable cost VC divided by the number of units produced.

Bad
A bad is anything from which a consumer derives disutility. An often cited example of a bad is pollution. The opposite of a bad is a good. In contrast to goods, bads may have a negative market price (such as garbage).

Battle of the Sexes Game
See Coordination Game

Bertrand Competition
Bertrand competition is an oligopolistic competition model under which at least two firms compete with each other, with prices as the strategic variable and simultaneous moves. In its simplest form, consumers and producers have perfect information, products are homogenous, firms do not cooperate and marginal cost is constant and identical. Firms under the simplest model of Bertrand competition price at marginal cost, so that no firm derives any profit. The other oligopolistic competition models analysed in this text are Cournot competition and Stackelberg leadership.

Budget Constraint
A budget constraint is the area in commodity space which is encompassed by the axes of the graph and the budget line. Any bundle lying within this triangle (including those lying on the line and the axes) is affordable. Any bundle lying to the north-east of the budget line is not affordable.

Budget Line
The budget line drawn in commodity space represents a collection of different consumption bundles. It can be drawn when the prices of the goods and the consumer's income are known. The intercept on each axis is the income divided by the price of the good on that axis. When connecting the intercepts, the resulting straight line is the budget line. The slope of this line is the negative of the price on the horizontal axis divided by the price

of the good on the vertical axis. The optimal consumption bundle is found where the budget line is tangent to the highest possible indifference curve. The budget line has its equivalent in the theory of the firm in the isocost line.

Capital (*K*)
Capital is a factor of production utilised by the firm in the production process. The price of capital is the rental rate r. Capital can be split up into real capital, which refers to inputs such as machine-hours, and money capital, which refers to financial assets. Other factors of production include labour, land.

Ceteris Paribus
The Latin term *ceteris paribus* meaning "other things being equal" is used in social scientific analysis to rule out the effect of all known and unknown independent variables other than the cited one(s) on a system. In this text, the term is not used because, unless otherwise stated, we assume that there is no effect of independent variables other than those specified.

Cobb–Douglas Production Function
The Cobb–Douglas production function is a production function where each factor of production has an exponent assigned to it and the sum of the exponents need not equal 1, which differs from the utility function. Total product is derived by the multiplication of the factors of production to the power of their exponents. Monotonic transformation must not be applied, as this would distort the output level.

Cobb–Douglas Utility Function
The Cobb–Douglas utility function is a utility function where each good has an exponent assigned to it and the sum of the exponents must always equal 1, which differs from the production function. Total utility is derived by the multiplication of the goods' quantities to the power of their exponents. Monotonic transformation can be applied to the utility function as the absolute level of utility has no meaning (the only important thing is the ordinal ranking of utility levels).

Commodity Space
The area encompassed by a graph with axes of quantities of two goods is known as commodity space. Every point in commodity space constitutes a consumption bundle. The equivalent of commodity space in the theory of the firm is factor-input space.

Complements
Complements are goods that are usually consumed together or used together in production processes. Perfect complements are goods which are only used together by consumers or firms at a rate that does not necessarily have to be 1:1. Indifference curves and isoquants for perfect complements are L-shaped. Substitutes are closely related complements.

Composite Good
The composite good is defined as the consumption of all goods other than X, where X is a single good used in the analysis.

Consumer
A consumer is an economic agent who has the goal of maximising utility. This can be done by finding the point of tangency between the indifference curve and the budget line.

Consumer Surplus
The consumer surplus is the monetary equivalent of the utility the consumer derives from taking part in an economic transaction minus that monetary equivalent of utility that she would have derived without engaging in the transaction. The equivalent of consumer surplus in the theory of the firm is producer surplus.

Consumer Surplus, Aggregate
Aggregate consumer surplus is the sum of all individual consumer surpluses in a market. On a traditional supply and demand graph, aggregated consumer surplus is the triangle encompassed by price and the demand curve up until the market clearing quantity. The equivalent of aggregate consumer surplus in the theory of the firm is aggregate producer surplus.

Consumption Bundle
A consumption bundle is a combination of quantities of goods. There is an infinite collection of different consumption bundles in commodity space.

Coordination Game
The battle of the sexes game is also called coordination game because there are two Nash equilibria but no dominant strategies. Hence, to solve this game, players need to coordinate their strategies (i.e. both should choose the same strategy), otherwise they run the risk of ending up in a Pareto suboptimal situation. Coordination can be achieved through credible commitments, hierarchy and history. Closely related to a coordination game is a differentiation game.

Cost–Benefit Analysis

Cost–benefit analysis is a way of approaching problems with the rationale that actions should be undertaken by agents if the cost (including implicit cost items such as opportunity cost) of doing so is lower than the benefit derived from the action.

Cournot Competition

Cournot competition is an oligopolistic competition model under which at least two firms compete with each other, with quantities as the strategic variable and simultaneous moves. In its simplest form, consumers and producers have perfect information, products are homogenous, firms do not cooperate and marginal cost is constant and identical. Firms under the simplest model of Cournot competition derive a positive level of profit. The other oligopolistic competition models analysed in this text are Bertrand competition and Stackelberg leadership.

Deadweight Loss to Society

The term deadweight loss to society refers to the loss of total surplus (i.e. combined surplus of consumers and producers) arising from monopolistic pricing compared to marginal cost pricing, as seen under perfect competition. It is part of the reason why monopoly is an inefficient market structure.

Degree of Homogeneity (*D*)

The degree of homogeneity D indicates if a production process displays decreasing, constant, or increasing returns to scale. When D is smaller, equal to, or larger than 1, decreasing, constant or increasing returns to scale respectively are present. When the sum of the exponents on capital and labour in the Cobb–Douglas function is smaller, equal to, or larger than 1, so is D. The degree of homogeneity thus lets us draw conclusions from the sum of the exponents on the input factors on the behaviour of the production process with respect to scale.

Demand

Demand is the willingness and the ability to purchase a good. The demand curve shows different quantities of a good that a consumer (or a group of consumers) is willing to buy for various prices. A change in demand is brought about by a change in any variable other than price. Demand must not be confused with quantity demanded.

Demand Function

A demand function is a term for the mathematical way of expressing the relationship between quantity demanded and price, or the graphical representation thereof. In practice, the inverse of the demand function is frequently used.

Demand, the Law of

The law of demand states that price and quantity demanded are inversely related. This "law" is violated by the theoretical curiosity of the Giffen good.

Derivative

A derivative is a measurement of the rate of change of an underlying function, if an independent variable exhibits an infinitesimal change. The derivative of a function $f(x)$ is taken with respect to the independent variable — here x — and expressed as $f'(x)$. Since the derivative is (most commonly) expressed as a function of the same variable as the underlying function, it allows us to show the rate of change of the first function for any value of the independent variable. Derivatives are invaluable for optimisation such as utility maximisation or cost minimisation.

Differentiation Game

In a differentiation game, there are two Nash equilibria but no dominant strategies, and players want to choose strategies that are different from each other. Such a game can be solved by the players making credible commitments. Closely related to a differentiation game is a coordination game.

Diseconomies of Scale

The term "diseconomies of scale" refers to a situation in a production process when average cost is rising as output increases. The opposite of diseconomies of scale are economies of scale.

Disutility

Disutility is the level of displeasure of the consumer resulting from the consumption of a bad (or the excessive consumption of a good). The opposite of disutility is utility.

Dominant Strategy

A dominant strategy is a strategy in the context of game theory that will always be played, irrespective of the strategies chosen by other players.

Dominated Strategy
A dominated strategy is a strategy in the context of game theory which will never be played by a rational player. It is the opposite of a dominant strategy.

Economics
The study of economics focuses on the efficient allocation of resources under conditions of scarcity. It is broadly divided into microeconomics and macroeconomics.

Economies of Scale
The term "economies of scale" refers to a situation in a production process where average cost is falling as output increases. Monopolies are often able to exploit economies of scale and thereby retain their dominant position. The opposite of economies of scale is diseconomies of scale. The concept of economies of scale is also related to economies of scope.

Economies of Scope
The term "economies of scope" refers to a situation where average cost is falling as a result of the addition of new activities/products to a production process. Monopolies are often able to exploit economies of scope and thereby retain their dominant position. Economies of scope are related to economies of scale.

Efficiency
In this text we discuss two sources of efficiency. One is the ability of firms to produce in a cost-efficient way; the other is the realisation of welfare-enhancing trades in a market. Perfect competition is an efficient market structure whereas the monopoly is an inefficient market structure.

Elasticity of Demand/Supply, Price
The price elasticity of demand/supply measures the responsiveness of the quantity demanded/supplied by agents in response to a change in price. Demand/supply is said to be elastic/inelastic when some change in price brings about a more/less than proportionate change in quantity demanded/supplied meaning that $|\eta|$ is larger/smaller than 1. When the change in quantity demanded/supplied is exactly equal to the change in price, demand/supply is unit(ary) elastic and $|\eta|$ equals 1.

Elasticity of Demand/Supply, Cross-Price
The cross-price elasticity of demand/supply measures the substitutability between two goods. It is defined as the change in the quantity demanded of good X as a result of a change in the price of good Y. The larger the cross-price elasticity of demand/supply, the closer the two goods in question are to being perfect substitutes.

Extensive Form
The extensive form depicts the strategic interactions of players using a game tree. It is usually employed for sequential games but can also be used for simultaneous-move games when decision nodes have to be connected via a dotted line. Another way of depicting games is via the normal form.

Factor of Production
A factor of production is an input with which the firm is able to produce output. Most commonly, the factors of production analysed in production processes are labour and capital.

Factor-Input Space
Factor-input space is the area on a graph encompassed by two axes depicting quantities of labour and capital. Every point in factor-input space constitutes some combination of labour and capital.

Firm
A firm is an economic agent with the goal to maximise profits. An optimal amount of output can be derived based on the market structure that the firm operates in. The desired level of output can be produced most efficiently by finding the lowest possible isocost line in factor-input space given an isoquant corresponding to the desired output level.

First-Mover Advantage
First-mover advantage refers to a situation in which a firm has an advantage vis-à-vis another player when allowed to choose its strategy prior to that player. In Stackelberg leadership models, a first-mover advantage arises in situations when quantity is the strategic variable. By definition, the concept only applies to sequential games. It is closely related to the second-mover advantage.

Fiscal Policy
This is a policy undertaken by the government regarding taxation and government spending. Fiscal policies can have profound effects on the overall economic performance of a country. Another important economic tool of

governments is monetary policy. John Maynard Keynes emphasised the importance of fiscal policy for sustaining economic success.

Fixed Cost (FC)

FC is the part of production cost that is entirely independent from the quantity produced. By definition, FC only arises in the short run. FC is distinct from variable cost VC.

Fixed Input

A fixed input is a factor of production, the quantity of which cannot be altered in the production process. Most commonly, the fixed input is capital in the short run. The cost arising from the fixed input is known as fixed cost. The fixed input is distinct from the variable input.

Free Trade

This is an economic policy without tools for suppressing trade such as tariffs or quotas. David Ricardo was an active proponent of free trade, and put forward the principle of comparative advantage. Free trade can be regarded as the opposite of protectionism.

Friedman, Milton

Friedman (1912–2006) is part of the Chicago school of thought that emphasises the importance of monetary policy while criticising Keynes's conclusion that the main cause of the Great Depression was misapplied fiscal policy in many countries. Friedman therefore drew economic thinking away from the perceived importance of fiscal policy towards monetary policy.

Function

A function is a mathematic concept showing the relationship between variables. It transforms an input (the independent variable) into an output (the dependent variable) via the use of an algorithm — a set of instructions. An example is $f(x) = 2x$. The graphical representation of a function may also be called a function.

Game Theory

Game theory is a way of analysing interdependent decision making. That is, an economic agent's actions affect other agents' payoffs and vice versa. Agents (or players) derive optimal strategies through analysis of the payoff structure in which combinations of strategies by different players are assigned payoffs.

Giffen Good

A Giffen good is a good that is so strongly inferior that the movement in quantity demanded prompted by a change in price moves in the same direction as the price change. This is brought about by the income effect overriding the substitution effect. It therefore violates the law of demand and so the Giffen good is a theoretical curiosity. The Giffen good is distinct from normal and inferior goods.

Good

A good is anything from which consumers derive utility upon consumption, or anything that is used by firms as a factor of production and which can be sold in a market for a price. In economics, the term "good" encompasses both goods and services. Goods demanded by firms are known as intermediate goods. The opposite of a good is a bad.

Hicks Decomposition

Named after Sir John Hicks (1904–1989), the Hicks decomposition is a way to graphically deconstruct the change in quantity demanded following a change in price into income and substitution effect. The Hicks decomposition requires three budget lines and two indifference curves.

Income Consumption Curve (ICC)

The income consumption curve is the connection of all optimal bundles (i.e. points of tangency between indifference curves and budget lines) at different income levels. It is also known as the income expansion path. The ICC is also sometimes referred to as the "income offer curve" or the "income expansion path".

Income Effect

The income effect is that change in quantity demanded of a good following a change in price of that good solely attributable to a change in real income. For a normal good, the income effect moves in the opposite direction as the change in price, whereas it moves in the same direction for an inferior good. The income effect is part of the entire price effect and is complemented by the substitution effect.

Income, Nominal

Nominal income is the amount of monetary units held by a consumer per time period. It is not affected by a change in the price of goods.

Income, Real
Real income is the purchasing power of a consumer's income, and is nominal income divided by a price index. It is therefore affected by a change in prices.

Indifference Curve
An indifference curve is a convex function in commodity space that represents an infinite collection of consumption bundles, all of which yield the same constant utility. The one indifference curve that is just tangent to the budget line yields the optimum consumption bundle at the point of tangency. The slope of the indifference curve is equal to the marginal rate of substitution. The equivalent of the indifference curve in the theory of the firm is the isoquant.

Indifference Map
The indifference map is defined as a sample of a consumer's preferences in the form of a collection of indifference curves in commodity space.

Inferior Good
An inferior good is a good for which quantity demanded decreases when income rises. It is distinct from normal and Giffen goods.

Intermediate Good
A good acquired by a firm for the process of production is known as an intermediate good.

Invisible Hand
See Price, Allocative and Rationing Function of

Isocost Line
The isocost line drawn in factor-input space represents a collection of different combinations of factors of production (i.e. labour and capital). It can be drawn when the prices of the factors of production are known. The intercepts on each axis are a specific cost level divided by the price of the input factor on that axis. When connecting the intercepts, the resulting straight line is the isocost line. The slope of this line is the negative of the price of the factor of production on the horizontal axis (usually labour) divided by the price of the factor of production on the vertical axis (usually capital). As the optimisation problem the firm is facing is cost minimisation rather than an output maximisation, there is no unique isocost line. The optimal combination of labour and capital is to be found where the

isoquant is tangent to the lowest possible isocost line. The equivalent of the isocost line in consumer theory is the budget line.

Isoquant

An isoquant is a convex function within factor-input space representing an infinite collection of combinations of factors of production, all of which yield the same constant output. The one isocost line that is just tangent to the isoquant yields the optimum combination of factor inputs at the point of tangency. The slope of the isoquant is the marginal rate of technical substitution. The equivalent of the isoquant in consumer theory is the indifference curve.

Isoquant Map

The isoquant map is defined as a sample of a firm's outputs in the form of a collection of isoquants in factor-input space.

Keynes, John Maynard

Keynes (1883–1946) is known as one of the founders of macroeconomic theory. In his 1936 publication *The General Theory of Employment, Interest and Money* Keynes emphasised the importance of government intervention to sustain economic well-being by means of monetary and fiscal policy, with his focus being on the latter. Prior to his time, government intervention was thought to be largely unimportant. Milton Friedman agreed with Keynes on the importance of monetary policy, but less so with the importance of fiscal policy.

Labour (L)

Labour is a factor of production utilised by the firm in a production process. The price of labour is the wage rate w. Other factors of production include capital, land and entrepreneurship.

Long Run

That shortest period of time it takes to vary all factors of production is known as the long run. By definition, all costs are variable in the long run. The long run is distinct from the short run.

Long-Run Average Cost (LAC)

The LAC is the long-run total cost divided by the number of units produced.

Long-Run Marginal Cost (LMC)
The LMC is the change in long-run total cost LTC brought about by a one-unit change in quantity produced. Alternatively, it can be defined as the change in LTC brought about by an infinitesimally small change in quantity, which means that LMC is the derivative of LTC with respect to quantity.

Long-Run Total Cost (LTC)
The LTC is the amount of labour employed times the wage rate plus the amount of capital employed times the rental rate.

Macroeconomics
Distinct from microeconomics, the study of macroeconomics discusses the behaviour of the economy as a whole. Rather than analysing the behaviour of consumers and individuals, macroeconomics takes a look at all consumers and all firms in a country and how they interact with each other.

Marginal Cost (MC)
The MC is the change in total cost TC or variable cost VC (as both changes are equal) brought about by a one-unit change in quantity produced. Alternatively, it can be defined as the change in TC brought about by an infinitesimally small change in quantity, meaning that MC is the derivative of TC (or alternatively VC) with respect to quantity.

Marginal Product of Labour/Capital (MP_L/MP_K)
The marginal product of labour/capital is the change in the total product (i.e. output) resulting from a one-unit change in the factor of production. Utilising calculus, the marginal product of labour/capital is the partial derivative of the total product function with respect to labour/capital. The marginal product of the labour/capital curve intercepts the average product of the labour/capital curve where the latter reaches its maximum.

Marginal Revenue (MR)
The MR is the change in total revenue brought about by a one-unit change in quantity produced. Alternatively, it can be defined as the change in revenue brought about by an infinitesimally small change in quantity, meaning that MR is the derivative of total revenue with respect to quantity.

Marginal Revenue Product of Labour/Capital (MRP_L/MRP_K)
The MRP_L/MRP_K is the marginal product of labour/capital multiplied by the marginal revenue of the good produced. The imperfect competitor employs an optimal amount of labour/capital, where the MRP_L/MRP_K is equal

to the wage/rental rate. The exception is when $VAP_L/VAP_K < w/r$, in which case no labour/capital would be employed in the production process. The concept of value marginal product applies to the perfect competitor as well, although the MRP_L/MRP_K may also be used.

Marginal Utility (MU)

The marginal utility is the change in total utility resulting from a one-unit change in quantity. Alternatively, the marginal utility can be defined as the partial derivative of the utility function with respect to the quantity consumed of one good.

Marginal Utility, Diminishing

The concept of diminishing marginal utility refers to the fact that the increase in total utility from an increase in the quantity consumed of a good becomes ever smaller as the quantity consumed increases.

Marginal Rate of Substitution (MRS)

The marginal rate of substitution is the rate at which the consumer is willing to give up one good in exchange for another while her utility stays constant. This is the slope of the indifference curve. The equivalent of this term in the theory of the firm is the marginal rate of technical substitution MRTS.

Marginal Rate of Technical Substitution (MRTS)

The marginal rate of technical substitution is the rate at which the firm is willing to give up one factor of production in exchange for another, while keeping output constant. This is the slope of the isoquant. The equivalent of this term in consumer theory is the marginal rate of substitution MRS.

Market

A market is a social arrangement in which buyers and sellers meet to take part in an economic exchange. This is distinct from the concept of industry, which only consists of firms.

Market Clearing Point

The market clearing point or equilibrium is the point at which supply and demand curves cross and where quantity demanded and quantity supplied are equal. At this point, the price and quantity are known as equilibrium price p^* and equilibrium quantity Q^*.

Market Structure
The term "market structure" refers to the characteristics of a market with regards to the degree of competition, the existence of barriers to entry/exit, and the influence of price on sellers. The market structures discussed in this text are perfect competition, monopoly and oligopoly.

Marx, Karl
The economic theories of Marx (1818–1883) are often associated with communism, under which public ownership is preferred to private owner-ship. Although such theories as put forth in the 1867 publication *Das Kapital* genuinely had the goal to end the alleged exploitation of the working class (proletariat) by the ruling class (bourgeoisie), Marx's economic theo-ries are today almost universally accepted as false. He is often cited as the ideological opposite of Adam Smith.

Mercantilism
This is an obsolete economic theory under which trade was regarded as a zero-sum game meaning that as one nation gains from it, the other loses out. Trade was regarded as advantageous only if one was able to trade on a surplus (i.e. exporting more than importing). The mercantilist system started to be undermined in the 18th century, and one important critic was David Ricardo, who offered an alternative rationale for trade with the the-ory of comparative advantage.

Microeconomics
The study of microeconomics, as distinct from macroeconomics, discusses the behaviour of consumers, firms and industries. The analyses focus on the optimal decision-making of rational agents given certain constraints.

Minimum Efficient Scale (MES)
The minimum efficient scale is the output at which the firm faces the low-est long-run average cost LAC. Where the LAC occurs for relatively low/high quantities, a competitive/monopolistic market structure is likely. Where average cost savings occur for large quantities, a regulated monop-oly may be the most desired market structure if its production efficiency can be assured.

Monetary Equivalent
The concept of monetary equivalent is used in consumer theory to quantify some level of utility in monetary terms.

Monetary Policy

This is a policy administered by the government or monetary authority with the aim to manage the money supply in a country. It is an important factor to regulate economic growth and keep inflation curtailed. Another important economic tool of the government is fiscal policy.

Monopoly

Monopoly is a market structure consisting of only one firm that supplies a unique product and has the power to pick a price rather than taking it as a given. Entry/exit barriers are significant and both producers and consumers have perfect information. The monopolist maximises profits where MC = MR holds true. Production quantity is lower than and price is higher than what would be the case under perfect competition. The monopoly shuts down in the short/long run if the AVC/LAC curve lies above the demand curve at the optimal quantity. From a static perspective, the monopoly is an inefficient market structure partially due to the deadweight loss to society arising from its pricing methods. Different types of monopoly include natural (see *Minimum Efficient Scale*), geographic, government (-controlled) and patent-based monopolies.

Nash Equilibrium

Named after John Nash (1928–), a Nash equilibrium is a natural resting point of a game associated with a set of strategies which are best responses to each other, so that no player has an incentive to unilaterally deviate from his strategy.

Network Effects

The term "network effects" refers to a situation in which the value of good depends on how many other users of the good exist. A frequently cited example is that of the telephone. Network effects may be a source for sustaining the dominant position of a monopolist.

Normal Form

The normal form is a method of depicting strategic interactions of players using a payoff matrix. It is used for simultaneous-move games. Another way of depicting games is via the extensive form.

Normal Good

A normal good is a good for which the quantity demanded increases when income rises. It is distinct from inferior and Giffen goods.

Opportunity Cost

An opportunity cost is an implicit cost of an action arising from a lost opportunity of engaging in an alternative action. It is taken into account in economic profit but not in accounting profit.

Pareto Optimality

An outcome is Pareto optimal when a player's payoff cannot be increased from a deviation of the current situation without making any other agents worse off. If at least one player can be made better off without reducing the welfare of any other agents, the situation is Pareto suboptimal.

Perfect Competition

Perfect competition is a market structure characterised by a large number of sellers, a homogenous product, no influence of firms on price through output (due to the perfectly elastic demand curve faced by each firm), free entry/exit and perfect information of both consumers and producers. The perfect competitor maximises profit where p = marginal cost holds true (where MC is rising). In the long run, perfectly competitive firms do not derive any (economic) profit. If price is strictly below AVC/LAC, the perfect competitor will shut down in the short/long run. Perfect competition is an efficient market structure.

Present Value, Net (P)

The net present value of money is used to show today's worth of some amount of money in the future. In order to calculate this, our capital growth function is simply solved for P. Present value calculations are frequently used for project evaluations.

Price, Allocative and Rationing Function of

The allocative function of price is the process whereby resources are directed towards production processes for which prices lie above cost and away from production processes for which prices lie below cost. The rationing function of price is the process by which existing supplies are directed towards those consumers who value them most highly. Both concepts are part of the principle of the invisible hand devised by Adam Smith.

Price Ceiling

A price ceiling is a maximum price in a market below the equilibrium price that is imposed by the government. The result of a price ceiling is excess demand.

Price Discrimination, First/Second/Third Degree

Price discrimination is the act of charging different prices to different groups of consumers. Since price setting power is required, price discrimination only applies to imperfectly competitive firms. First-degree price discrimination — or perfect price discrimination — entails that every consumer is charged exactly that price equal to their maximum willingness to pay. Under second-degree price discrimination the firm charges different unit-prices for different quantities. Third-degree price discrimination is a case in which different prices are charged to different consumer groups. Under price discrimination, firms must attempt to prevent arbitrage.

Price Elasticity of Demand/Supply

See Elasticity of Demand/Supply, Price

Price Floor

A price floor is a minimum price in a market above the equilibrium price imposed by the government. A price floor results in excess supply.

Producer Surplus

The producer surplus is that amount of money a firm gains from producing a profit-maximising output over the compensation that it would get from producing nothing. This is the sum of profit and fixed cost FC. On a graph with the axis of price and quantity, producer surplus can be shown graphically as a rectangle with sides/edges Q^* and $(p - AVC)$. The equivalent of producer surplus in consumer theory is consumer surplus.

Producer Surplus, Aggregate

Aggregate producer surplus is the sum of all individual producer surpluses in a market. On a traditional supply and demand graph, producer surplus can be shown as the triangle encompassed by price and the supply curve up to the market clearing quantity. The equivalent of aggregate producer surplus in consumer theory is aggregate consumer surplus.

Profit

The difference between total revenue and total cost is known as profit. Economic profit takes into account explicit costs (such as wages) and implicit costs (such as opportunity cost), whereas accounting profit only takes into account explicit costs. The profit curve can be derived by measuring the vertical distance between the revenue and the total cost curve. Profits are zero at the breakeven point.

Protectionism
This is an economic policy undertaken to suppress trade of certain goods using tools such as import tariffs and quotas. The rationale is to protect domestic industries that are threatened by international competition. While protectionism can be useful in certain circumstances, such as for the temporary protection of newly established industries, today most kinds of protectionism are criticised for stifling the economic growth of poorer countries. Protectionism can be regarded as the opposite of free trade.

Quantity Demanded/Supplied
The quantity demanded/supplied is a specific number of units demanded/supplied for some level of price of a good. A change in the quantity demanded/supplied can only be brought about by a change in the price of the good. The concept of quantity demanded/supplied must not be confused with demand/supply.

Question, Normative
A normative question is a kind of question that requires the application of a subjective norm to arrive at a question, such as "what economic policy should be applied?"

Question, Positive
A positive question is a kind of question regarding specific consequences of a change in a variable, such as "what happens to unemployment if the interest rate is increased?"

Reaction Function
A reaction function is either a formula showing the choice of one firm's strategic variable given the other firm's strategic variable, or it is the graphical representation thereof.

Reservation Price
The reservation price is the amount of money that one would have to be given in order to be indifferent between two activities.

Returns, Increasing/Constant/Diminishing
Increasing, constant and diminishing returns refer to situations in which an increase in the variable input (holding the other input fixed) results in an increasing, constant or diminishing increase in total product. In the latter case, a total decrease may also be possible. These concepts apply to the short run only. The law of diminishing returns states that all production functions will eventually exhibit smaller and smaller increases (and feasi-

bly decreases) in output when the variable input rises. Diminishing returns must not be confused with decreasing returns to scale.

Returns to Scale

Returns to scale refers to a situation in which both inputs are increased by the same proportion. By definition, therefore, it is a long-run concept. Situations in which some equal increase in both inputs results in a more than equal, equal, or less than equal increase in input are known as increasing, constant and decreasing returns to scale, respectively. Decreasing returns to scale must not be confused with diminishing returns. No matter whether a production function exhibits increasing, constant or decreasing returns to scale for specific quantities, it is still likely to exhibit diminishing returns when only one factor of production is increased.

Ricardo, David

Ricardo (1772–1823) was an advocate of free trade, pointing to the principle of comparative advantage that he introduced in his 1817 publication *Principles of the Political Economy and Taxation*. Comparative advantage says that every nation should produce what it is most efficient at producing (relative to other goods) and trade accordingly. This reasoning was an important advancement from the system of mercantilism.

Schumpeter, Joseph

Schumpeter (1883–1950) made important contributions to the study of overall economic performance via the concept of business cycles, each wave of which lasts for several years. Schumpeter is also well known for the principle of creative destruction, which he used to argue that the most desirable market structure is that of temporary monopoly rather than perfect competition. This idea was published in his 1942 work *Capitalism, Socialism and Democracy*.

Second-Mover Advantage

Second-mover advantage refers to a situation in which a firm has an advantage vis-à-vis another player when choosing its strategy after that player. In Stackelberg leadership models, a second-mover advantage arises when price is the strategic variable. By definition, the concept only applies to sequential games. It is closely related to the first-mover advantage.

Short Run

The longest period of time during which at least one factor of production is fixed is known as the short run. The short run is distinct from the long run.

Slutsky Decomposition
Named after Eugene Slutsky (1880–1948), the Slutsky decomposition is a way to graphically deconstruct the change in quantity demanded following a change in price into income and substitution effect. The Slutsky decomposition requires three budget lines and three indifference curves.

Smith, Adam
Smith (1723–1790) is often accredited with the title of "Father of Economics" as he was one of the first to recognise that self-interest is a prerequisite for economic success as he wrote in his 1776 publication *The Wealth of Nations*. Moreover, he is known for his laissez-faire approach to economics, which advocates as little government intervention as possible, the principles of the invisible hand and the division of labour.

Stackelberg Leadership
Stackelberg competition is an oligopolistic competition model under which at least two firms compete with each other, with prices or quantities as the strategic variable and sequential moves. In its simplest form, consumers and producers have perfect information, products are homogenous, firms do not cooperate and marginal cost is constant and identical. If quantity is the strategic variable there is a first-mover advantage, whereas if price is the strategic variable there is a second-mover advantage. The other oligopolistic competition models analysed in this text are Bertrand competition and Cournot competition.

Strategy
In the context of game theory, the actions taken by players are known as strategies.

Strategic Complement
A strategic variable is a strategic complement when a change in a strategic variable by one player prompts a change in the strategic variable of the other player in the same direction. This happens under Bertrand competition for prices.

Strategic Substitute
A strategic variable is a strategic substitute if a change in the strategic variable by one player prompts an opposite change in the strategic variable of the other player. This happens under Cournot competition for quantities.

Strategic Variable

A strategic variable is a decision variable by the firm. In this text the strategic variables that we discuss are price and quantity.

Sub-Game Perfect Equilibrium

The concept of "sub-game perfect equilibrium" means that a player is playing their optimal strategy when it is their turn, i.e. when they are at the decision node in a sub-game. Sub-game perfect equilibria show us strategies of players for all decision nodes, even those that are never reached.

Substitute

A substitute is a good that can be consumed or used as a factor of production in place of another good. Perfect substitutes are goods where consumers or firms are indifferent about which one to utilise (as long as there is no difference in price). Indifference curves and isoquants for perfect substitutes are straight lines. Complements are closely related to substitutes.

Substitution Effect

The substitution effect is that change in the quantity demanded of a good following a change in the price of that good which is solely attributable to a change in relative prices. The substitution effect always (i.e. for normal and inferior goods) moves in the opposite direction of the change in price. The substitution effect is part of the entire price effect and is complemented by the income effect.

Supply

Supply is the willingness and the ability to produce a good. The supply curve shows different quantities of a good that a firm (or an industry) is willing to sell for various prices. A change in supply is brought about by a change in any variable other than price. Supply must not be confused with quantity supplied.

Supply Function

A supply function is either a mathematical way of expressing the relationship between quantity supplied and price, or it is the graphical representation thereof. In practice, the inverse of the supply function is frequently used.

Symmetric Game

A symmetric game is a game in which the player's payoffs are identical when they choose the same strategies. The opposite situation is that of an asymmetric game.

Total Cost (TC)
The TC is the sum of fixed cost FC and variable cost VC. In the long run the TC is equal to the VC.

Total Product
The total product is another term for the output level the firm achieves. The term "total product curve" can be used when referring to the graphical representation of the production function. It can be drawn by putting output and a factor of production on two axes (while holding one factor of production fixed). The slope of the total product curve allows for inferences to be made about whether increasing, constant or decreasing returns are present.

Utility
Utility is some amount of pleasure that a consumer receives from the consumption of a good. The opposite of utility is disutility.

Value of Average Product of Labour/Capital (VAP_L/VAP_K)
The VAP_L/VAP_K is the average product of labour/capital multiplied by the price achieved for the good produced. If the VAP_L/VAP_K is smaller than w or r, respectively, hiring the first unit of the production factor is not reasonable as the firm would make a loss.

Value of Marginal Product of Labour/Capital (VMP_L/VMP_K)
The VMP_L/VMP_K is the marginal product of labour/capital multiplied by the price achieved for the good produced. The perfect competitor employs an optimal amount of labour/capital where the VMP_L/VMP_K is equal to w and r, respectively. The exception is when $VAP_L/VMP_K < w$ or r, in which case no labour/capital would be employed in the production process. The concept of marginal revenue product applies to the imperfect competitor.

Variable Cost (VC)
The VC in a process of production is dependent on the level of output. VC arises both in the short and the long run. Variable cost is distinct from fixed cost.

Variable Input
A variable input is a factor of production, the quantity of which can be altered in the production process. Most commonly the variable input is labour in the short run or any factor of production in the long run. The cost arising from the variable input is known as variable cost. The variable input is distinct from the fixed input.

Weighted Average Cost of Capital (WACC)

The WACC is the cost of capital weighted by source (such as debt and equity) and expressed as a percentage. While the interest rate can be used to arrive at the present value, using the WACC is an even more accurate way to measure this.

Index